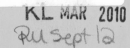

LABOR OF LOVE

THE STORY OF ONE MAN'S
EXTRAORDINARY PREGNANCY

THOMAS BEATIE

SEAL PRESS

Labor of Love
The Story of One Man's Extraordinary Pregnancy

Copyright © 2008 Thomas Beatie

Published by Seal Press
A Member of the Perseus Books Group
1700 Fourth Street
Berkeley, CA 94710

Library of Congress Cataloging-in-Publication Data
Beatie, Thomas.
  Labor of love : the story of one mans extraordinary pregnancy / by Thomas Beatie.
     p. cm.
  ISBN-13: 978-1-58005-287-0
  ISBN-10: 1-58005-287-8
  1. Beatie, Thomas. 2. Pregnancy--United States--Biography. 3. Female-to-male transsexuals--United States--Biography. I. Title.
  RG556.B43 2008
  362.198'20092--dc22
  [B]
                        2008031538

Cover design by Kate Basart
Interior design by Tabitha Lahr
Printed in the United States of America
Distributed by Publishers Group West

For Susan, my heart and purpose

CONTENTS

❖ ❖ ❖ ❖ ❖

Chapter 1

DEFINE NORMAL

I have been a daughter and a son, a sister and a brother, a boyfriend and a girlfriend, a beauty queen and a stepfather, a Girl Scout and a groom. But today I am just an ordinary human being in a whole lot of pain.

Today it is happening—it is finally happening. I am wearing an enormous, 4X white T-shirt, on inside out. The soothing, insistent sound of a heartbeat—around 140 of them each minute—is the only music in my otherwise quiet birthing room. My contractions are intensifying, and every couple of minutes I feel this surging pain that starts from inside my gut and radiates out. I remember trying to do a dismount from a chin-up bar when I was ten, and landing square on my back. That was the worst pain I ever felt, but this is way, way worse. Our midwife puts a cold washcloth on my forehead; my wife, Nancy, kisses me tenderly on my cheek.

It has been a long, hard, often surreal journey to get to this point, and now I have to summon one last big burst of energy for the final leg. "Gravity is your friend," says the midwife, urging me to walk around to try to speed things along. But the truth, I am finding, is that having a child is not in any way a passive act. You don't just show up and wait for the baby to arrive. You have to will the baby out of your body, and that means marshaling every last ounce of strength and resolve that you have.

Nancy puts her hand on my belly and feels our daughter thrashing around, and she tells me, "Don't worry, she'll be here soon." But the hours pass. I focus on odd little details to take my mind off the pain. Our midwife's left index finger is wrapped entirely in surgical tape; she cut it slicing whole grain bread that morning. This strikes me as neither a good nor a bad omen, just unlucky for her. I also notice she has a tiny diamond stud in her left nostril. You can barely make it out in the dimly lit room, but when she leans in to fix my blanket or move me from side to side, it sparkles. She's a wonderful woman, so calm and reassuring, and I like that she's obviously a bit of a hippie, too.

I am 100 percent effaced; I am also nearly fully dilated at nine centimeters. And still no baby. We got to the hospital in the early morning; it's nearly nighttime now. "Let us know when you feel the urge to push," says our midwife. "Not just pressure, but a real urge to push." Nancy starts watching out for what she calls my "pushy face," then asks if she can get her own epidural. That's Nancy: cracking jokes, making everyone feel at ease, and still remaining a tower of strength for me to lean on. That morning at home she sifted through a bowl of jelly beans and brought all the purple and orange ones—my favorites—to the hospital. She slips a couple of them to me—a simple, throwaway gesture between a husband and a wife—but it strikes me yet again, as it does every day, that I could never, ever have done this without her right by my side. Nancy gets up to straighten my sheets and touches my face with her hand. She says, "Your nose is really cold, like a puppy's."

A nurse gradually fills my IV with pitocin, which is supposed to increase contractions and speed along my labor. "Your uterus is really tired," the midwife tells me, and I think, *That makes two of us.* We're going on twelve hours now, but the nurse assures us, "That's the average length of labor for a first-time mother." Nancy gently corrects her by asking, "What about for a first-time father?"

A little earlier, our midwife brought over a red velvet sack filled with little slate tiles, each shaped like a heart and bearing a single word. "Pick one out and that will be your focus word," she says. Now I reach in, pull out a pink heart and show it to everyone. "Serenity!" says the midwife. But in fact, it's misspelled on the tile as "Sereinty." *How perfect,* I think—even my focus word is mixed-up, nonsensical, a deviation from what is known and expected. That has been the story of my entire pregnancy—no one has known quite what to make of it, or been able to truly understand what it means. To me, it couldn't be simpler. I am a person who is deeply in love and wants to have a child. But, just like my jumbled focus word, what I know it to mean and what the world reads it as are two very different things.

"Remember, Thomas, sereinty," Nancy tells me later. "Try to be sereine."

Things suddenly get serious; a doctor is hustled into the room. It is time for my baby to be born. "Let's get busy and push," the midwife says, and I push harder than I ever thought I could. The pain is searing, and I think I might pass out. But I keep pushing. I hold Nancy's hand tightly, and every once in a while I steal a look at my white, laminated hospital wristband. Just like my wife's hand, it's a source of strength for me. There's nothing all that unusual about it, unless you know my whole story. But a single thing on that band—a single, solitary letter—is, for me, a symbol of the most emotional and triumphant battle of my life. On the band, in simple type, it reads:

NAME	AGE	SEX
Thomas Beatie	34	M

Never before in history has someone delivering a child had the letter M typed on their wristband.

"Okay, here we go," says the doctor. "I can see her head."

Now it is time for me to meet my daughter.

❖ ❖ ❖ ❖ ❖

My name is Thomas Beatie, and I have a family. I have an amazing wife, Nancy, whom I love more than I thought possible, and a baby daughter who to us seems like an angel on earth. Sometimes at night I lie awake and think about how lucky I am to have the dream I dreamed so long finally come true. In my darker moments I've always feared that somehow I might lose what I have. But I know that we are a good and strong and loving family, and that we can withstand whatever the world throws at us. It has not been an easy trip for us to get here, and there are many, many people who would like to see us torn apart. But here we are, a mother and a father and a child—a family just the same.

This book is about many things, but above all it is about family. It is a subject I know something about. I have lived through the experience of an unhappy family, and the things I saw shaped me and led me to this moment in my life. I also know what it means to be part of a healthy family, to love someone unconditionally, to share all your hopes and fears with them, to make constant sacrifices for each other and to put each other's happiness above your own. I know the feeling of devoting yourself to making your family work—to prizing the intimacy of that bond above anything else in your life. I have some insight into this matter, if only because I have spent a great deal of time thinking about it, and because it means the world to me to have the family that I have. I hope that when you read this book, you will see something of your own family in my story, and that, if I have told it well, my story will make you take stock of the ones you love, and of how they love you in return.

Of course, the path I have taken to create my family is very different from yours. What Nancy and I have done is completely unprecedented. On the face of it, we do not look like an unusual couple at all. Yes, I am half-white and half-Asian, and Nancy looks Italian, but that alone would never earn us a second glance. It's also true that Nancy is twelve years older than I am, and sometimes we get asked if I am her son. But plenty of people in love come together at different ages. In many more ways we are just like any other married couple in our quiet community in central Oregon.

We take walks around the lake and hold hands, we work hard and try to save money, we were thrilled to buy our first home together, and we practically live in Costco. And then, like millions of happy couples, we decided to have a family. In these things we are no different from anyone else. Our dreams are white-picket dreams.

But it would be naive to think that we are not different. I am, as far as I can tell, the first fully legal male and husband to get pregnant and give birth to a child. In 1974 I was born female, and I lived the first twenty-four years of my life as a woman. But for as long as I can remember, and certainly before I fully knew what this meant, I wanted to live my life as a man. When I was young I was a tomboy: I dressed in boys' clothes, I did boy things, I resisted the trappings of girlhood—dolls, dresses, all of that. I identified with the male gender in every way. I never thought I was born in the wrong body, however, nor did I ever want to be anyone else. I was happy being me, because I knew who I was inside. I was never confused about my gender identity—I always knew, long before I could articulate it, that I was really male. If anything, I was sometimes confused about how to make the rest of the world understand my situation. But I never struggled with my identity, or fought it or tried to change the way I felt. It was just the simple fact of my existence: Outside I was female, but inside I was male.

And so for most of my life I dressed like a man, wore my hair like a man, and cultivated traits that most would consider manly. This was never a strategic decision or something I imposed on myself—it was always just the natural, organic way I preferred to be. Later, when I was an adult, I learned there were things I could do to make my body look more like a man's body. This does not mean that I was unhappy with my body the way it was. It means only that

I found a way to make the outside match up with the inside. I began taking doses of testosterone to build muscle mass, and I worked out strenuously to shape my body even more. The testosterone also gave me facial hair, and before long I looked completely and utterly masculine. I then went one step further, and had surgery to remove my breasts. Before the surgery I used to walk with a stoop to try to hide my breasts. But afterward I stood tall and straight, and I walked with a newfound purpose and confidence. I was finally the person I wanted to be, and believed I was all along.

As I said, making these changes did not mean that I was miserable or confused before I made them. They were instead convenient ways to strengthen my image of myself, and to make it easier for me to adapt in a world that defines gender strictly. There were two further steps I could have taken, and chose not to: surgically removing my female reproductive organs, and surgically constructing a penis. But I didn't feel that either step was necessary for me to feel any more like a man. The latter surgery, in particular, is a grisly, drastic, and difficult procedure, and most people who transition from female to male elect not to have it.

But there's another reason I kept my reproductive organs. The other driving impulse in my life, besides the certainty that I am male, has been the desire to create what I lacked in my childhood—a loving and nurturing family. Nancy, the woman I fell in love with—and married as soon as I was legally classified as a male after my surgery—had had a hysterectomy when she was younger, after having two children of her own, and could not carry another child. I had always wanted to have a biological child, so I kept my reproductive organs, figuring that I could have a surrogate use my eggs to conceive.

Yet when the time finally felt right for Nancy and me to have a baby, we thought long and hard about how to go about it, and the idea that we would use a surrogate mother started to make less sense. After all, I was fully capable of having a child myself. Getting pregnant had never been part of my plan, or even in keeping with how I lived my life as a man, but it was still biologically possible and thus an option we had to consider. After careful consideration—and after a lot of discussion about the hardship it might cause—we decided that no surrogate could ever care for her body or our child during the pregnancy as diligently and lovingly as I would. And besides, why would I ever pass along the privilege and responsibility of having my child to someone else, when I could, and should, carry the baby myself? I am not saying it was an easy decision—it was not. But in the end, the concerns we had about people not understanding or supporting our decision were not enough reason to farm out the pregnancy to a surrogate. Nancy and I decided that I would carry our child, and that she would breastfeed the baby. I would be the father, and Nancy would be the mother.

Once we reached this decision, I stopped taking testosterone. Nancy and I bought donor sperm from a cryogenic bank, and I got pregnant. It was an ordinary pregnancy in many ways, and in others it was not: While expecting, I appeared in *People* magazine, had carloads of paparazzi camp outside my home, fielded an offer from an artist who wanted to make a life-size marble statue of me, was besieged by tabloid reporters from countries around the world, and became, literally overnight, at once the most famous pregnant person on the planet, and the least understood. Nancy and I did not go public with my pregnancy for fame or money. We actually turned down offers worth hundreds of thousands of dollars to tell our story, and instead chose to be in *People* for free. We came forward because there was simply no way I could hide from the world—a pregnant man is, after all, pretty hard not to notice. We knew that people were starting to talk about us; we could see them whispering about us in grocery stores or at the gym. I could slink around and wear really baggy clothing, or I could stand up proudly and face the future head-on. Nancy and I chose to stand up. Yet neither of us was prepared for the media frenzy my pregnancy created, or for being seen less as human beings with feelings and dreams and more as symbols or inanimate cutouts on whom anyone could project their perceptions and prejudices. At one point I was the most searched-for person on the web, with nearly a million references on Google. The vast majority of items about me, I would discover, were negative.

At every step along the way I looked hard to find some precedent for what I was doing, to learn about anyone anywhere who could help me or give me advice. But there was no one. I wanted to look into the legal issues involving my pregnancy, but, again, I found nothing. And so I had to learn from my own mistakes, to rely on my own instincts, and to have faith in the sureness of my fight. It is one of the reasons I have written this book. I think my story is worth telling, for anyone facing long odds and daunting obstacles on the way to achieving the life they want.

I realize that what I am doing is strange and new, and that my situation confuses people. I know that sometimes when people are confused they get angry and lash out. Nancy and I have received dozens of death threats, been called monsters and freaks, and confronted a hatred so deep that it can wish our innocent daughter damned to hell. As much as we try to steel ourselves against the inevitable backlash our situation creates, we have been staggered by some of the comments directed at us.

But at the same time, we have received an outpouring of love and support far beyond what we hoped for in our wildest dreams. We have had neighbors rush to give us hugs and offer to help with yard work; strangers send us baby booties and expensive blankets; people from Fiji and Australia and China write us to wish us good luck. We have had a Christian pastor tell us he is rooting for us. Before our daughter was born we had a baby shower, and we hosted several couples with young children of their own. I had all but given up on ever having a baby shower; I figured it was just something that, sadly, I would have to do without. But my neighbors chose to rally around me, and their support surprised me and touched me profoundly. At the shower I watched all the little children run around, and realizing that they were a part of our world was one of the most emotional moments of our lives. To feel accepted, to be part of a community, is—especially for us—a very precious thing.

This book, therefore, will not try to change anyone's mind about us. We know that we will always get our share of good and bad reactions. All I can do with this book is tell my story, plain and simple. It is not for me to force anyone to approve of what I am doing, as if I could anyway. But I do believe that my family deserves a fair shot at happiness, same as anyone else's. I feel that we deserve respect, as well as equal treatment. These are things I have fought for, and will fight for until I die. In this I am no different from any father—I am passionate about my family, and determined to give them a life full of love and happiness.

In the fall of 2007, I went in for a checkup soon after a home pregnancy test told me I was expecting. I had an ultrasound and watched the monitor intently as a grainy image appeared. All I could see were two blurry, microscopic dots, indiscernible as human life but at six weeks all we have to go on—an embryo and a yolk sac, either healthy or not. At six weeks there is no allusion to a child, no wishful hints of a family chin, no names that suddenly seem right. No hopes or expectations, other than please, *please, let everything be okay.*

But then something happened on the monitor, a weird pulsing, some kind of flashing, and quickly the most awful thoughts took over. Was this a warning light? Was something wrong? For some reason, in this frantic moment, I focused on how the walls in the exam room were bare of any posters or framed pictures, save for a calendar with the image of a baby and the slogan "We believe the little things make all the difference." Was this what I would remember forever of this day of terrible news—some cheesy calendar? After all the people who rejected me because I transitioned to a man; after so many questioned my love for Nancy and believed we should not get married; after all the taunts and threats and even bottles hurled at us; after doctors turned us away and told us we made their staff uncomfortable; after psychiatrists rooted around for signs of deviance and mental illness; after relatives shunned us and hurt us in ways we could never have fathomed; after my own brother told me my baby would be a monster—after all of that, it had come down to this strangely blinking light on an ultrasound? To a barren womb in a barren room?

I held tight to Nancy's hand and asked the ultrasound technician about the light.

"That," the technician told me, "is your baby's heart."

This is the story of that little blinking light.

Chapter 2

PARADISE

I grew up in a castle. An old troll lived in our fruit garden, and alligators swam in our moat, and a beautiful blond princess in a pointed pink hat stood atop our tower, along its stone-block railing, waving to everyone below. Or at least that is how it all looked in a drawing I made for my parents when I was five. That drawing is not the very first thing I can remember precisely about my life. I have a fuzzy image of myself as a little girl, maybe two years old, with my long brown hair and my little quilt-patterned overalls, wading in the low surf of Kawaikui Beach Park and stepping on the thorny branch of a kiawe tree. The pain and the shock of it is still pretty clear, but I can't recall who picked me up or how much I cried. My first sharp memory comes later, when I was five, and it has to do with the drawing I made for my parents.

I remember, quite clearly, that this is how I perceived our home when I was young—as a fairytale fortress, impossibly big and magical, though in fact it was a 1970s-style, five thousand-square-foot, two-story house that my father designed and built himself on a bluff called Waialae Iki, an upper-middle-class residential area in Honolulu. I remember sprawling belly-down in the upstairs playroom, fists full of crayons, eager to imitate my father, an architect who fashioned great plans on the drawing board in his downstairs office. I remember the little scribbled circles of red and yellow meant to signify fruit, and I remember the jagged lines I used to create the top of the castle. I remember also the finishing touches I put on my little drawing—across the top, in scratchy letters that may have looked like birds, the inscription "To Mommy and Daddy. I Love You." And along the bottom, floating across the blue moat: "From Tracy."

One other thing: I remember the small figure I drew next to the princess, a smiling girl wearing an identical pink hat. The beautiful princess was my mother, Susan. The little princess was me.

A child's drawing is not complete, however, until it is held up by small clutching hands or displayed on the laps of mothers and fathers and praised as brilliant and beautiful and purchased with a pat or a hug. And so I ran down our hallway that day, my drawing flapping in my hand, searching for my parents to show them what I made. What happened next is something I will never forget. I heard a sound I knew to be my father's voice, but distorted. It was a loud, ugly, jarring yell, a ragged, sawtooth blade of a noise that even today evokes fear and dread as I recall it. I heard this sound as it shattered the silence of our echoey home, and I froze in my tracks and grabbed the railing that ran along the hallway. Slowly, I began to work my way toward the sound, down the flight of stairs carpeted in Cookie Monster blue, past the empty family room and into my father's office, where I finally saw them. Many times as a child I would stand behind the aquarium that rested between the office and the living room wall and watch my parents through it, enjoying how they looked like a shadow-puppet show with Silver Dollars and Bala sharks flying incongruously over their heads. I can't be sure that I watched my parents through the tank on that long-ago day, but the memory of it has absorbed the blurry aquarium view just the same, and that is how I remember seeing them screaming at each other.

And then this—an eruption. I am in the open doorway, unnoticed, when my father snaps. His hands crash down on the drawing board, splitting a plastic ruler into slivers. A wooden cup of pencils explodes in the air. His office chair jolts backward and topples as he springs to his feet. The whole thing is as fierce and sudden as thunder. And then it is I who is screaming, and I run away as fast as I can. And when I reach my room I realize my drawing is still in my hand, and that, during my father's burst of fury, I have crumpled it in my fist.

It was the first time I truly saw the violence that lived inside my father—a turbulence that came to torment my mother and me. His punishing rages were awful, destructive, and, as much as anything else, defined our family life. My father, with his broad shoulders and his round biceps and his jet black hair and the green jade ring he always wore, large as a Spanish olive, and the thick fold of hundred-dollar bills he always kept in his wallet, and the strong clean smell of aftershave that went with him everywhere, and the dark, glazed, glaring eyes that never smiled even when he did. My father was a larger-than-life figure to me, at first an all-powerful king, a builder of castles, and then a sort of monster, menacing and impossible to defeat—sort of like the troll beneath the bridge. "I will put the mean daddy in the dungeon," I once told my mother, as she explained to me yet again how my father had not meant to scream at her, and how he loved us and would never hurt us. But before long my image of my father was set—he was unpredictable, dangerous, a villain.

Conversely, my mother was the hero of my story, fair and good and beautiful. She was born in Minnesota, and her blond hair and pale skin contrasted with the features of Hawaiian women, and with those of my half-Filipino, half-Korean father. It was easy to see her as a force of light, and my father as an agent of darkness. And once I learned of his capacity to harm us, that's exactly how I saw them. My mother was everything I wanted to be—kind and loving and graceful, dignified and soft-spoken, a picture of elegance and in every way the opposite of my brutish father. My mother was a magnet to me; I had absolute freedom to touch her, to grab hold of her arm or her leg, to climb all over her and play with her hair and feel, when she hugged me, entirely embraced. I cannot remember, to this day, a single time my father hugged me. I have seen fraying photos of him holding me right after I was born, but the only time I remember having any contact with him at all was when I leaned against him once in the water of our backyard pool. He also liked to lie on the carpet and have me walk back and forth on his back while he watched TV. I knew that it helped him relax, so for years I was happy to do it, but now I find it sad that nearly all of the physical contact we shared was between his back and my feet.

These stark differences between my mother and father— her softness and vulnerability, his savagery—created a schism that destroyed our family. Looking back, I feel it was inevitable that we would not survive the ill-fated pairing of my parents, and that their marriage would end in tragedy, as it eventually did. All families, I now realize, are made up of different fabric. Some are tough like leather, and some flimsy like cotton. Some families are woven through with enough love and tolerance to accommodate any trauma, any sin. Some have the toughness of muscle and sinew. But others are made of weaker stuff. These families can take only so much wear and tear before they come apart at the seams. My parents were both strong, determined people; my father made it out of the slums of Kalihi and my mother worked hard to earn her master's. But as a family they were not nearly as strong, and I think I know why—because they were, from the start, a flawed, doomed pair.

Before it was all over, my father had crushed my mother's spirit, driven her to an awful loneliness, drawn blood from her delicate face, and left her weak and defeated. One day when I was twelve, I came home from school and looked around our empty home for my mother, who should have been there to greet me. When she did not come home that night, my father finally told me that she was sick, and that police had found her wandering around Waikiki Beach, and that she would be away for a while, to get better. I believed him, at least at first. But soon I would learn the truth. Soon I would understand that what had actually happened was far, far worse. Soon I would know the consequences of the rupture in our family.

❖ ❖ ❖ ❖ ❖

The American revolutionary Patrick Henry was my great-great-great-great-great-grandfather, and Benjamin Harrison, twenty-third President of the United States, was my mother's mother's father's mother's father's brother. My great (times five) grandfather, William Henry Harrison, was also a U.S. president and, despite the efforts of doctors treating him with castor oil and Virginia snakeweed, died of pneumonia and jaundice after thirty-one days in office. Yet another ancestor, also named Ben Harrison, signed the Declaration of Independence, right below Thomas Jefferson.

My blood is the blood of America, and the roots of my family run deep in American soil. Yet I grew up feeling like a foreigner, in the middle of an ocean, more than two thousand miles from the mainland. It was my mother, Susan Nickels Beatie, who first made the long, long trip to Hawaii, yanking our genealogical charts halfway around the world.

In many ways, I am who I am because of my mother's vulnerability to the lush allure of the islands. She had a deeply romantic view of Hawaii, and its mystique seduced her and held sway over her long after her harsh life should have set her free. All of those famous Americans are on my mother's side; her great-grandfather John Beatie owned plantations and kept slaves before making his way from Virginia to San Francisco in a stagecoach. Though the Great Depression wiped out most of the Beatie family fortune, John's grandson John William Beatie might well have struck it rich by marrying an heiress named Jeanette Nickels—had her wealthy family not cut her off for marrying him. Instead, my grandparents lived in humble homes, and their first daughter—my mother—grew up in a perfectly modest way in the mostly frigid climate of Minneapolis, Minnesota.

It was anything but an idyllic childhood. When Susan was only nine years old, her mother died. My mother later told me that cancer took my grandmother, but a family friend believes it was suicide. With Susan's mother gone, her father became an impossible alcoholic; things got so bad that my mother's younger sister, Tyler, was sent to live with two kind elderly sisters, Virginia and Posey, who had a home next door. My mother and her sister never lived together again, and for the rest of their lives they were a little like strangers. I guess you could say they both survived the swift and sad disintegration of their family. But survival is always partial; it takes a piece of you as its price. I don't think either sister was ever the same after losing their mother, and one of the most precious things they had to give up was any chance of a meaningful bond between them.

Still, my lovely mother was extremely popular in high school; she had a lot of friends, got good grades, went out with handsome boys. After my grandfather moved what was left of his family to Georgia, my mother enrolled at Georgia State University and started chasing a career in academics. She was primarily interested in education, believing she was best suited for work that was somehow child-centric. I see her interest in education as an interest in family. She was trying to find a way to make children stronger.

She was set to pursue a master's degree in special education, but first she took a fateful vacation. She and a friend traveled to Hawaii, and soon my mother was hopelessly in its thrall. Perhaps it was the warm weather; she was, after all, used to achingly cold winters. Perhaps it was the foamy white crescents of perfect beaches. Perhaps she fell asleep one night to the sound of the murmuring surf, or took an evening stroll in a fragrant kukui grove, or liked the way her painted toenails looked through the flawless waters of the sea. Whatever it was, my mother fell in love. One day she and her friend took scuba lessons from some locals. Two men were in the class with them. My mother agreed to go on a date with one of them, named Bobby, while her friend dated the other, a fellow named Abraham. After their first night out, they decided to swap. And so my unlikely parents came together.

Hawaii is the only land my father has ever known. His father arrived there from the Philippines in an immigrant wave in the 1920s, looking for work in the sugarcane or pineapple fields. Family lore has it that my grandfather, Florencio, had to flee his native country because he killed a man. I have no reason to doubt this theory. In Hawaii he met a Korean woman named Ake, who had been a mail-order bride for her first husband and bore him eight children before he died. Ake met Florencio when he walked into the bar where she worked as a hostess. Again, family lore includes speculation that she was actually a prostitute. My father would never say this was true, but I can certainly believe it.

I was told that my grandparents didn't get married until many years after my father was born. Their first son, James, was struck by a car and killed when he was three; my father came along soon after as a replacement. He arrived on Abraham Lincoln's birthday, hence his name. His father found work pulling seaweed, or limu, out of the ocean and selling it to people who pickled it and sold it as a delicacy. Florencio made a good living and stored wads of cash in hiding places in his home. Sometimes rats would eat away at his savings, but that never made him want to move it to a bank. He did, however, buy a small, four-unit apartment complex in Kalihi, and that's where my father grew up.

I heard many stories about how strong my grandfather was. How he could do inhuman things, like crack open a macadamia nut with his teeth and eat chicken heads. My father described him as a kind of superman, with powerful arms and massive hands. I know he used those arms and hands to beat his son. Many years later, my father would tell me I was lucky to merely be spanked or hit with a stick. His own father, he would say, broke bones.

My father says he remembers seeing the Japanese planes buzzing low overhead in 1941, and hearing the bombs dropping in the distance. Perhaps that is why he joined the Air Force and learned to fly planes. He was married for about a year and had a boy, Barry, but the breakup was bitter and my father had to fight for the right to even visit his son. My father had golden brown skin and jet black hair, and sideburns like Elvis, and muscular arms like his father, and when my mother saw him shirtless on the beach and took scuba lessons with him, and swapped dates with her friend, and fell in love with him, she was surely falling in love with what he represented—the magical islands of Hawaii itself. In her eyes, he was the whole package: dashing, exotic, *exciting*. My father can be a charming man, and he no doubt worked that charm on any number of pretty white women from the mainland, but my mother was especially seduced by it, and she was the one who did not go away.

I get angry when I hear my father tell his version of the courtship. He says that he did not want to date my mother, that he was tired of seeing American women, and that he agreed to go out with her only because his friend Bobby—intent on dating my mother's friend—insisted. My father says he pushed my mother away, and that she kept coming at him, and that he finally gave in.

The truth is, he would have been crazy not to pursue my mother. She was smart and beautiful, with a dazzling smile and an ability to make anyone who met her feel she was their friend. He was, in fact, enormously lucky to have been in the right place at the right time—in her path as she desperately tried to escape her past. The beauty of this newfound paradise lured her, and she chose to start over in a place as different as any she knew. It was not that my father cast a spell over her; it was that he was part of the spell the islands cast. They lived as boyfriend and girlfriend in my grandfather's apartment complex, and in 1969 they got married in a simple beach wedding. My mother wore a Hawaiian-style leaf lei, and my father wore a white cummerbund.

I come along not too far into this story. After my mother finished up her master's degree in special education at the University of Hawaii, she went to work at an elementary school and supported my father while he studied architecture. I'm not sure where he got the money, but once my father had his degree he bought some land on a high hill on Waialae Iki, a mostly undeveloped ridge between Kahala, the ritzy home of Diamondhead and million-dollar mansions, and Hawaii Kai, where most of Hawaii's white population lived. My father owned a little less than an acre on that hill, but when he decided to build a house there—the first residence in the area—he took a huge step forward in his life. He bought raw materials, contracted a small crew, and pitched in to build an enormous 1970s-style home, with large open rooms and smaller, elegant quarters and, of course, sweeping views of the island from one end to the other. It was unlike any other home in Hawaii, I later learned. There is no question that my father had some talent as a designer of homes—he built many houses and buildings in

Hawaii and developed a reputation as a gifted architect—and no better example of it than the five thousand-square-foot home he built for himself—the home I came to think of as our castle.

❖ ❖ ❖ ❖ ❖

I arrived in the new house not much later than they did. My mother has told me she couldn't keep food down while she was pregnant with me; I like to think it was because she was so excited for me to come out. My birth was unremarkable, except for the scare it gave my father. When he first saw my feet, he was shocked because he thought my toes were fingers; maybe he thought I was born with four hands.

I was a firecracker right from the start: stubborn, willful, confident. I walked and talked way ahead of schedule, and from a very early age I had a lot of opinions, particularly about things that affected me. When I was little more than an infant and my mother tried to wipe food off my face, I'd push away her hands and say, "No, tongue will lick."

I remember that I always thought my mother was special. I didn't really have anyone to compare her with, but I had the sense, even then, that she was a rarity. I think her appearance may be part of the reason. For one thing, she looked so different from me. She had a slender face and an elegant jawline, and soft, straight, shiny blond hair that fell past her shoulders, and eyes that changed color from green to swirls of brown and blue, depending on her mood.

After a street artist drew her portrait, she always complained about her "Bob Hope ski-jump nose," but really it was perfectly even and the tip of it wiggled just a little when she spoke. She was, to me, as beautiful as a woman could possibly be. And there I was, with short dark hair and a round face like my father's, and skin several shades darker than my mother's, and a stick figure I could never imagine would ever be like my mother's curvy physique. We were, in fact, opposites, and I am sure I idealized her and came to see her as everything I could only hope to be.

But it was about more than just her looks. She had a remarkable aura, too, a mix of patience and compassion. She was a special-education teacher at Pearl Harbor Kai Elementary, which meant she took on the toughest cases and served, at once, as teacher, psychologist, law enforcer, and, quite often, diaper changer. I remember that she met constantly with her students' families, that she helped coordinate the local Special Olympics, and that she was often late for dinner because she was involved with some or other school matter—and all for around $12,000 a year. I couldn't quite understand how she could possibly have the patience or energy to do all that, but I remember that she did it without complaining and with memorable grace. This quality, which I have come across in precious few other people in my life, is indeed what made my mother so uncommon. I recognized it early on and I yearned to be just like her, in appearance and in the way she lived.

We had our special little rituals. I can still feel her lightly brushing the hair from my face as I drift off to sleep or wake up from a night's slumber, and I can still smell the faint aroma of the hand lotion she used. I recall clearly the warmth of her body as she let me press against it. I remember mornings with her in the yard outside our home, with the mild Kona winds swirling leaves around our feet, and her olive green and mustard yellow robe trailing in the breeze. I remember riding in her sparkling, apple green 1968 convertible as she drove me to school in the mornings, and nestling in the carpeted passenger's legroom compartment, which I considered my private cubbyhole. I remember looking up to see my mother's golden hair swirling in the wind.

I remember, too, the moment when my mother shared her happiest news with me. It was the day after I had seen my father erupt at her, and smash his fists on his drafting table, the day after he introduced me to the very concept of violence and aggression. She, of course, knew that I was upset by what I had seen, and she came to wake me the following morning and took me to school in her car. I burrowed beneath the glove compartment and tied my braids under my chin like a bonnet, and looked up to see my mother motioning to the passenger seat. I took her hand and came up and sat next to her. "I want you to know that your father and I love you very much," she told me. "What you saw yesterday was just your mother and father disagreeing. Your father had a hard day, that's all. It's nothing to be worried about."

There was something distant in her voice, as if she didn't believe what she was telling me. "Daddy loves us very much and would never want to harm either of us in any way," she said. "You know this, don't you?" I tried to protest. I was opinionated. I thought I knew better. I knew what I had seen. "Tracy, listen to me," my mother said firmly. "Things are going to be just fine." It must have been apparent I didn't believe her, because she kept going. "There is something else I want to tell you," she said. "It's something that I hope you'll enjoy because Mommy is very happy about it."

"Do you have a surprise?" I asked.

"I do, baby," my mother said. "We're going to have a little visitor."

I was five years old and didn't understand. How? From where? Why? My mother patted her belly. "From inside Mommy," she said. "Mommy's going to have a baby."

I don't know why, but as soon as I understood that my mother was going to have another child, just as she had had me, I knew that she was going to have a boy. I told her so, right in the car. "I don't know about that," she said. "We'll see." But I persisted. Looking back, it was not a guess or a wish—it was a certainty. I bet my mother a lollipop ring that she would have a boy, and I was prepared to break open my Miss Piggy bank to buy one if I lost, but I knew that I would not have to. Maybe I am romanticizing our relationship, all these years later, and merely imagining that I was so sure about the sex of her child—that somehow I intuited it. But I don't think so. We were connected in some immeasurable way, and we still are to this day. I even told my mother that I wanted my brother to be named John. She was shocked to hear this because her father's name was John, something I did not know at the time. My mother kissed my forehead that morning and wished me a good day at school, and as she left me with Mrs. Door at the red front gate, I watched her drive away. I waved until she was out of sight, then told everyone I was getting a brother.

I watched my mother go through the pregnancy, and I marveled at the changes to her body. I couldn't believe there was a little baby in her belly, but there it was, so big and round, and I couldn't keep my hands off it. I'd laugh when my mother balanced a bowl of ice cream on her stomach, and I yelled when she took my hand and let me feel the baby's elbow poking against her skin.

And then it happened: One day, my mother walked into the house carrying a little bundle of something. My brother, Anthony, was a much larger baby than I had been, and my mother had to be cut open. Yet he was, compared with me, completely docile, an easy baby. I loved having a little brother—he was like a living doll I could play with. I helped my mother give him baths, change his diaper, dress him up.

When he grew big enough for us to play together, boy, did we have fun. Well, at least I did. My brother still talks about mean things I did to him, but I only remember us grabbing our boogie boards and running down to the beach together, and surfing and snorkeling and basically living in the water. When my father built a pool, Anthony and I would take eight or nine boogie boards and stack them up and I'd have him sit on top of them, as if he were on a floating palace, until a board shifted and they all came tumbling down. Some days, I'd take a hand truck from the garage and stack the boogie boards on it, and put a couple of pillows on top, so Anthony could sit there and I could push him around like it was a rickshaw. We went all over the neighborhood like that, I pushing him on the hand truck, and he loved the ride. We built a pretty stable platform, so he never once fell. He tried to push me once or twice, but I was too big and he was too small.

Another time, I went out with a huge beach umbrella after watching *Mary Poppins*. I wanted to see if I, too, could float in the air while holding an open umbrella. I climbed up a cinderblock wall that was about five feet high; sure enough, Anthony was right there below me. I jumped a couple of times, and I may have even believed the umbrella slowed me down by a fraction of a second before I landed. Either way, I was thoroughly amused, and so I urged Anthony to try it, too. He climbed up diligently, grabbed the umbrella tightly, and, with something like blind faith in his older sister, jumped off. He landed on his butt and screamed to the heavens.

I can't claim to have always been a perfect little sibling. We had a small boat that we kept tied up on the dock behind our home. There was a murky little swell of water surrounding our cul-de-sac, full of jellyfish and other crawly things. The boat, too, was a mess; it was so old the bottom had a giant hole in it, so you could see straight through to the water just an inch or two below the broken floor of the boat. One time, I told Anthony that the hole was fixed, and he jumped right into the boat and crashed through into the murk. He disappeared for a few seconds, then emerged flailing and, once again, screaming. Eventually he scampered up onto the dock, dripping seaweed. He never forgave me for that one, but I still have to smile when I think of him splashing around.

To this day, my brother remembers much of our childhood as my being intentionally malicious, but the truth is that I had to share my mother's attention with him, while he gobbled up all of my father's attention. No one ever said that my father would have preferred a son when I was born, but he clearly couldn't have been happier once he finally got one. Little Anthony was the pride of his life. I knew immediately, even as a five-year-old, that my father adored having a son, in a way that he had never enjoyed having me. He would take Anthony with him on trips and on adventures, something he rarely, if ever, did with me. He would take him to air shows and boat races. He took Anthony with him to watch planes take off from the airport, and he told him, "Son, one day you'll be flying those planes." I don't know which one of those things was more devastating for me to miss—the time alone with my father, or his encouragement. I would have killed for either one. I don't think I resented my brother all that much back in those days, though; we were, after all, just a couple of kids trying to figure out what life was all about. And I did still have my mother's affection to console me. I am happy that my brother got to spend so much time with our father, but I am sad that there was no time left for me—and that my father made no effort at all to disguise this inequality of favor.

It's not surprising, then, that my father became a kind of one-dimensional figure for me. He was powerful, yes, a provider, but he was by nature dark and depriving, too. From the time I witnessed that first fight, I saw things that only bolstered this early impression of him. My brother may have seen him as loving and supportive, but to me he was capable of great destruction, someone to protect myself against.

When I was young we had a funny little dog named Koko. He was a miniature dachshund, and I loved him like crazy. I hugged him all the time and played games with him, and laughed when he walked along a thin little ledge that ran along a hallway, and had to walk backward to return because he was too long to turn around. He was a friend to me, a silly, happy, loyal friend. One day he joined my parents and me in the downstairs living room. My father had this habit of spreading a newspaper on the floor, then getting on all fours to read it. Somehow that helped with his back pain. On this day, young Koko ran right for the newspaper and peed on it. Initially I laughed, but my father took his dress shoe and hurled it at the dog. It hit him in the head, and he went into convulsions. I didn't see the shoe hit Koko, but I heard it and I turned around in time to see him shaking. My mother took Koko to the vet, but he never came home. My parents never explained to me what happened to Koko, and soon my mother bought me another dog to replace him. But I knew that my father had killed my dog. Like a lot of the violence in our home, we didn't talk about it. We just endured it, sealed it away, moved on.

Chapter 3

MY FATHER'S WAY

*O*kay, *deep breath, here you go. Just do it. Just pick up the phone.*
Call him. Get it over with, once and for all.

"Dad? It's me. Happy birthday."

It is easy to remember my father's birthday because he was born on Lincoln's birthday, but my father's turning sixty-nine was only partly the reason for my call on February 12, 2007. I had something I needed to tell him, and I was pretty sure I knew how he would take it.

But first, some idle chitchat. My father tells me about a knee surgery he's about to have. He had found a top surgeon, the best knee guy in Hawaii, and this doctor had squeezed him into a cancellation, so my father wouldn't have to wait the customary year and a half for his operation. He's also excited that this new type of surgery will cut his rehab time from a year to just two months. All the medical talk is a lucky break for me; it allows me to segue right into what I want to tell him.

"So, Dad, good news. Nancy and I are finally getting medical insurance."

"Good," my father answers. "Finally."

"Well, Nancy already has hers, but mine is still being approved," I explained. "Mine's a little trickier. You know, because I am a legal male but I still have all my reproductive organs."

A deep, brooding silence begins to build on the other end of the call.

"Most typical plans don't cover certain procedures for a man, but we've got an arrangement with the insurance company and it looks like we'll be able to get all the coverage we need."

I wait for a response, but there is none. *Come on, just do it. Blurt it out.*

"And, Dad, I have something to tell you."

"What is it?"

Come on, come on. You're dying to know what he will say, and maybe he'll even surprise you. After all, if there's a single person in the entire world who *ought* to be thrilled by what I'm about to say, it is my father.

"Dad, as soon as I get my full medical coverage, Nancy and I are going to have a baby."

Silence.

"Actually, I'll be the one having the baby."

Dead silence.

What can I do but go on? "We've already had my ovaries and hormone levels checked out by a fertility specialist, and they're as good as gold. We have a donor all picked out. He's tall and good-looking and intelligent. It could be a matter of weeks before I'm pregnant."

I hear my father draw a breath. "Wow," he finally says. "That's neato."

And that is all either of us has to say. We mumble goodbyes and the call is over, just a minute or two after it began. One of the most important phone calls a child can make to a parent, and for me it passes in less time than it would take to order a sandwich. There is no "Congratulations!" No "Do you have a name picked out?" Just silence and "neato." I'd allowed myself to hope he'd react differently—a little, anyway. But in the end, I am not all that surprised; this is what I have come to expect from my father. Even the survival of his lineage, the passing on of his genes to a new generation, is not enough for him to be able to set aside his deep disgust for me. Still, it hurts—I can't deny that. His silence today is just another way he has found to cause me pain.

❖ ❖ ❖ ❖ ❖

My father was the disciplinarian of the family, and yelling and hitting were the ways he kept his children in line. But my father's spankings were not at all about discipline. Many, many people were spanked as youngsters, or hit with switches, or whacked with belts. Such harsh treatment is an accepted part of many cultures, and parents everywhere who were raised by stern hands go on to physically punish their children in turn. I am certainly not unique in that I got spanked, and spanked often, by my father. But I am convinced now that my father's punishments were more than controlled, purposeful attempts to alter my behavior or teach me responsibility. My father's spankings were outlets for his rage. I can still picture him, holding tight to my thin wrist with one hand and using the other to pepper my bottom with swift, open-handed swings. I can see his contorted face, and I can feel his consuming anger. My father was not in control of himself during those outbursts. Something would snap inside him; he would give in to his indignation, his temper would flare to boiling, and he would spank me until his fury was good and spent. My father's spankings taught me only one thing: to be afraid of him.

In fact, I honestly feared that one day my father would actually kill me. To this day, I have dreams in which he tracks me down and comes at me, and attacks me with a knife or a stick. In these dreams I try my best to get away, but for some reason I can't move. My feet get stuck or I fall down, and then my father is on me and I wake up with a deep, deep sense of relief that I am not really dead.

When I was around eight years old, my parents asked if I would prefer a second floor to be built on our house, or, instead, a backyard pool. Surely they knew what my answer would be, and almost as surely they had already decided what they wanted to build. Even so, I was thrilled to be able to conjure up a pool just by saying I wanted one and then, just a few months later, have it in the back yard. It was this wonderful peanut-shaped pool, with an attached, water-level, blue-tiled Jacuzzi, a white fiberglass twisty slide, and a stubby, ice-blue diving board. It was truly a child's dream, and I spent countless hours in and around the pool I had magically caused to appear. I spent so much time out back that the sun bleached the tips of my dark hair; I would flip the hair over my head so that only the blond parts showed, and I would turn to my mother and say, "See, I look just like you!" I loved it when my mother swam with me in the pool, though she didn't do it very often. Sometimes on summer weekends she would tie her hair up in a bun and do a few laps. I used to make fun of the way she swam, with these strange, robotic arm movements and her head whipping from side to side as she desperately tried to keep her hair from getting wet. I would jump at her, shrieking with glee, trying to land big splashy cannonballs next to her.

On even rarer occasions, my father would get in the pool with Anthony and me. He would never say anything—he'd just whip off his shirt and dive straight into the deep end. Whenever he did this, Anthony and I would dive in after him and chase him around the pool. He never let us catch him; instead, he'd swim to the bottom of the pool, slinking across it like an alligator, then swim up behind us and grab our legs, pretending to bite them like they were giant chicken bones. It was playful, yes, but there was something terrorizing about this little ritual between us and our father. The sense of menacing that he produced was thrilling, in a way, but the fear we felt when he came up behind us was real. To this day, I have an irrational fear of unknown things living in the depths of any body of water I happen to enter, regardless of its size or how safe the water looks on the surface.

There was another thing my father did in the pool that freaked us out. He had an uncanny ability to stand in the shallow end, waist deep, then walk methodically on the floor of the pool all the way to the deep end. Once the water came over his head, he didn't begin to bob on the surface, as anyone else would. Instead, he somehow managed to keep his feet on the floor and walk along the bottom of the pool. It was as if he were walking on dry land. He had so little fat on his body, and his bones were so dense, that he had no buoyancy at all. It thrilled Anthony and me to see this—we'd run into the house and grab a wooden cup of spare change, and sprinkle dimes and nickels into the pool, watching them zigzag all the way down to where our father was, standing and waiting. Somehow he'd stay down there for long, long minutes before finally coming up for air with the coins we'd thrown in cupped in his fists.

Because of feats like this, and because my father spanked me so hard, I began to fear him as I might fear an animal in the jungle. He seemed feral, inhuman, somehow. I remember walking by the living room one day and seeing my father on the floor, reading a newspaper. He had no shirt on, and the color and texture of his smooth, darkly tanned skin instantly made me think of a moray eel that had scared me during a trip to Oahu's popular southeastern beach, Hanauma Bay. I was wading out in the crystal-clear water some thirty feet from shore when I saw what looked like a long dark sock beneath the surface. But this sock seemed to be growing longer and floating right at me. I peered down to see it more closely, and I noticed that it had a face, with two wide eyes and pieces of flesh hanging off its head, and a set of sharp, jagged teeth. Just as I realized it wasn't a sock, it lunged toward me in the water and bit down on the sand just inches from my foot. I screamed and frantically splashed away from it. My mother laughed at first because she thought I was just goofing around, but the slinky moray eel, with its tapering hues of deep purple and its nightmarish teeth, made a deep impression on me. It had scared me in some primal way I couldn't fully comprehend.

And that was the image that came to mind as I watched my father get up from the floor, his stiff black hair skewed and parted in the back from sleeping on it, his dark, leathery skin stretching across his broad back, the tendons in his elbows and triceps rippling as he adjusted his weight. Whatever it was that scared me about that moray eel lived inside my father, mostly dormant but always ready to stretch to its fullness and harm me in some way.

My father hit me about three times a week. Most of these were hand spankings, though sometimes he used what he called "the stick." It wasn't really a stick, it was a rigid piece of plastic, with raised ridges along the sides, like a length of racetrack for Hot Wheels cars. These ridges would leave marks on my body when he was done. Sometimes the stick would break in two, and my father would keep both halves, so he'd have two sticks to hit me with. He kept them all over the house, so one would always be near. These beatings sometimes drew blood and always left bruises, but I still dreaded them far less than the hand spankings. My father had fat, thick worker's hands, with fingers that felt like they had iron in them. I swear I could feel the bones in his hands, especially when he aimed for my thighs.

Of course, I was powerless to stop these beatings, though at night I dreamed long and hard that one day I might not be. In the second grade we were given an assignment to draw a picture that illustrated our answers to the question "What would it look like if you had magical powers?" Most of my classmates drew things like a store full of candy, or a room full of presents. My drawing showed me clinging to the ceiling of our home, naked except for a shirt, with my legs and butt colored red from getting hit. Beneath me, my father flailed at me with a stick. On the drawing, I wrote, "I wish I had magic to make myself fly through the air. And the thing I most like about magic is I could run away from my father when he comes to spank me."

My teacher did not call Child Protective Services when she saw my drawing. Instead, she returned it with the praise "Good idea!"

❖ ❖ ❖ ❖ ❖

One day when I was ten, I sank to the bottom of the pool and stayed there, just as my father liked to do. It was hard for me; I had to wave my arms around desperately, but somehow I managed to stay down there. Through eight feet of water I could see the refracted figure of my father. I knew he was barking at me to come up, but I couldn't hear anything. It was peaceful at the bottom of the pool, and it felt safe. He couldn't get to me down here, or at least it would take him a while. It was as if I had discovered some kind of temporary forcefield. When I was young I had a thing for superheroes. I liked to invent new characters with amazing powers and awesome names and draw them with their fluttering capes and their bulky chests. I envied my made-up heroes their strength and confidence, but mostly I envied their ability to fly—the very ability I gave myself in the drawing about my most-wished-for power. What a thing it would be, to zoom off into the sky and leave a cloud of dust in your wake, and the slack jaws and stunned faces of your enemies. But kids can't fly. They can't even run that fast, at least not compared with adults. And so I did what was in my power to do—I sank.

Kids can also hold their breath, and so I did that, too, for a minute or so, before breaking the surface to get air. There was my father, ranting, waving his fists. I swallowed the sky and swam back down, away from him. How long could I stay there in my safe, soundless spot? Forever was the plan.

My older half-brother, Barry, was over that day and we'd been horsing around in the back yard, tossing a football, being silly, having fun. We didn't get to see a lot of Barry; he lived on his own and he came around only a few times a year. He was like an invisible member of our family. He was short and had a thick build, and he liked to talk a lot, like my father. But in family photos he is always the one in the back or off to the side. I liked him, though, and I was happy to see him.

That day he'd grabbed a little Nerf football that was floating in the Jacuzzi and tossed it underhand to me. I loved that football; it was painted gold and black and it fit right in my little hand, unlike regulation-size footballs. I tossed it back to him and we got a little game of catch going, gradually moving farther and farther apart. Finally, I got on the diving board as he ran toward the house, and he urged me to throw the ball as far as I could. Well, I did just that, and what a beautiful spiral it was. It sailed through the sky and headed right toward Barry, who jumped high to catch it. But it flew over his hands and hit a bottom-louvered jalousie in the family room of our house. The sound of shattering glass echoed through the house, through the yard, through the entire valley. It was, in my memory, a thundering noise, as if the house itself had let out a painful shriek.

Sure enough, my father came running out and took a long look at the devastation. This was no ordinary crime, you see. My father was a builder, and he had renovated this house, and I had damaged something he'd built. Knocking over a lamp or gouging a hole in a wall—these were offenses that drove my father crazy. Really, I was a well-mannered kid: I didn't play with balls indoors, I didn't jump on the furniture. But sometimes I would break things—that's what kids do. My father loved orchids, and he liked to have them in vases around the house. Once, I was thoughtlessly swinging a plastic toy sword and I cut the head right off one of his prized orchids. I can remember the severed flower floating to the ground and rolling to a stop by the sofa, dead for sure. I got a really good spanking for that one. And now I had destroyed an entire *window!*

"What the hell . . . " my father stammered, surveying the shards of glass. Neither Barry nor I moved a muscle. Suddenly, my father looked right at me and I froze.

"Dad, it was an accident," Barry said. But my father kept on coming. He came at me like a lion approaches its prey, slowly, deliberately, sure of its power. "Tracy, you get over here right now!" he yelled. And that's when I jumped, delaying the inevitable. I knew the longer I stayed underwater—the longer I kept my father waiting—the worse the whipping would be. If he had to jump in and drag me out, I'd get the beating of my life, especially given the nature of my offense. But I stayed down there as long as I could, until eventually I had to surrender, and I floated up to the shallow end.

I had barely put my foot on the bottom stair before my father yanked me out of the pool by the neck of my T-shirt. He kept me raised above the ground and gave me two quick, stinging shots to the back of my left thigh and my butt. As soon as he let go of me, I ran into the house, crying, and curled up into a ball beneath my desk. I shivered as I waited for what I knew was coming, and within seconds my bedroom door flung open and my desk—all of it—was lifted from over me. And then I felt the sharp lashing of the stick. My father's wrath in these moments was at least as terrifying as the pain. There was something about the way he came at me, so forcefully, so relentlessly. He was an unstoppable force, and he never quit until he had left me good and bruised and wailing with tears.

Most of the time, I didn't do anything all that bad to earn my beating. A lot of the time, I didn't do anything at all. We had this saying in our house: "If Anthony cries, Tracy cries." My father would say it with a wag of his finger, and the meaning was clear: If he saw my little brother crying for any reason, he'd assume it was I who'd made him cry, and I'd soon be in tears, too. Once, I had my friend Maria over, and she snuck off into my brother's room, and soon I heard him bawling. She must have done something to irritate him—take a toy away, tease him. She ran back into my room and locked the door. That was a huge mistake. As soon as my father heard Anthony crying, he ran to my room and rattled the door. Finding it locked, he flew into a rage, and he pounded on the door and finally kicked a hole right through it, and then it merely gave way and came off its hinges. And then he was inside, and he grabbed me by the arm and lifted me off the floor, and right in front of my cowering friend he beat me with the stick as I dangled helplessly in midair.

The biggest flaw of "If Anthony cries, Tracy cries" was that it gave my little brother a whole lot of power over me, especially as he got older. Not surprisingly, he learned how to use it pretty quickly. All he had to do was cry some crocodile tears, and he could get me punished whenever he pleased. He knew very well he was my father's clear favorite. Now he had an infallible weapon to not only get me punished, but also wring some extra sympathy out of our father. And so little Anthony became a masterful fake crier. When he wanted my last stick of gum, he'd threaten to bawl if I didn't hand it over. Other times, he'd get mad at me for some reason and fake cry just to get back at me. I'd beg like crazy for him to be quiet, but Anthony didn't have much sympathy—and as soon as my father showed up, there was no pleading my case.

For much of my childhood, I didn't personalize the beatings I got. I had already written off my father as a malicious force, and I figured that I was just unlucky to always be in the path of his wrath. My father was never the nurturer: He didn't cook my meals or buy my clothes or put me to bed, or any of that. What he did was spank me, and I accepted that. But along the way I began to realize he never beat Anthony the way he hit me. That he could muster such anger and emotion for my beatings, while sparing Anthony any such abuse, was a pretty good indication that he did not care for us equally. There must have been something about me that offended him and made it easy for him to brutalize me. It wouldn't be until years later that I'd really get it: It was my sexuality. He simply did not know how to handle a daughter who was not feminine, who was not the little girl he'd imagined he'd have.

But even back then I understood that something about my manner displeased him deeply. I had a lot of chores that I performed around the house for money. I would do the dishes, clean the windows, wash the cars, fold clothes, whatever I could do to earn an extra quarter or two. Helping with the laundry earned me 25 cents. Same for unloading the dishwasher. Hosing down the family car was good for $2. Cleaning the smaller windows cost my parents 15 cents; the larger ones were a quarter. Vacuuming the house got me 50 cents, a pretty good haul. I remember passing the vacuum one day while my father sat nearby and watched. He didn't say anything at first—he just stared and stared, seemingly amazed by something. Finally he got up and came over and yelled at me. He didn't like the way I was vacuuming. I was standing in one spot and pushing the vacuum away from my body, then drawing it back. He yelled that I should be walking and pushing, walking and pushing, covering more ground. "Walk five steps forward, then five back," he told me, and so I did, but he still wasn't happy. He believed I wasn't truly devoting myself to the task, that I was simply going through the motions. He said I was pampered and lazy, and that I felt I was above such dirty work. Really, I was just a skinny little girl trying to push a big old vacuum. But my father absolutely hated my body language, and saw it as evidence that I believed I was better or more important than I was. He spanked me right then and there, with the noisy vacuum still gulping.

❖ ❖ ❖ ❖ ❖

The spankings did not define my childhood, certainly not in the way that they now define my memory of it. Back then, they were just part of the deal, something to be endured. In fact, my father's absence was far more of a factor in my upbringing than his presence. I didn't know it back then, but my father cheated on my mother regularly, and there were long stretches when he simply wasn't home. She didn't tell Anthony and me why our father wasn't around, and frankly, I didn't much care. I came to understand that sometimes my father would be in the house with us, and other times he'd be somewhere else. Sometimes he'd be gone for a few days, sometimes several weeks. I just accepted that this was so.

I did, however, much prefer the times when he wasn't around. These stretches were like a vacation for all of us, and everything in the house felt different when he wasn't there. It was as if we all had more air to breathe, and thus came to life more fully. For one thing, we didn't have to worry about his moods. When he was home, his mood was the central dynamic that governed our lives. If he had a bad day at work, my mother knew to stay away from him, and a heavy gloom would drift from room to room in the house that night. It took me the longest time to learn to read my father's moods, as my mother had learned so crucially to do. I insisted on running up to him when he arrived and badgering him with questions: "Can we go to the beach this weekend?" or "Can we get a turtle?" He would shrug wordlessly or cast me away with a wave, but I came back, undaunted, day after day. Finally, my mother would intercept me before I got to him and find out what was on my mind, and usually she would say, "Honey, don't ask him that right now." And that's how I learned that my father was moody, and that his bad moods were something we had to tiptoe around.

When he wasn't there, everyone's mood was always good. We suddenly became an American family, not a Hawaiian family. My mother was from the mainland, and she grew up on meat and potatoes, but when she married my father she got a stack of recipes from his mother and learned how to cook his favorites dishes. We ate a lot of Korean and Hawaiian fare—there was always a big pot of steaming white rice going in the kitchen. My father loved kim chee, a pickled-cabbage concoction, and my mother served that to him a lot; she also cooked up a lot of his favorite delicacies from scratch. Once in a while my mother would sneak some asparagus or artichokes onto our dinner plates, but my father didn't approve of any mainland dishes, so we rarely ate the kinds of meals most kids in the United States are used to. But when my father was away, my mother would break out the good stuff: pizza and burgers and macaroni and cheese. Gosh, we loved those special nights, when we got to eat good, greasy food. It became yet another reason not to miss my father, and to dread his inevitable return.

Nights, too, felt endlessly more magical without my father in them. My mother was the one who tucked me into bed every night from the time I was born until I was twelve; my father never once performed this precious little ritual, not even when he was around. But on his exile nights my mother's spirit was lighter, more buoyant, and our time together in those moments before sleep was somehow sweeter and happier. When bedtime rolled around, my mother and Anthony and I would form a crazy conga line, with my mom's hands on my shoulders and mine on Anthony's, and we'd march from the family room down the hall to our bedroom, all of us walking funny, kicking our feet, loosey-goosey. Once we were in bed, we'd pull her down with us, and she'd sit beside us and tell us stories, and finally she would hug us tight and say, "I love you" and goodnight. On these carefree nights I would demand more hugs, or longer hugs, or I simply wouldn't release my mom when she tried to get up. I didn't want her to leave.

There was one other enormous benefit to my father's absences, but only now do I realize that it was the main reason for the relief I felt. It was not that he couldn't spank me when he wasn't there. As I said, I hated my spankings, but I accepted them as part of my life. No, it was that when he wasn't there, he could not do something else.

He could not hurt my mother.

❖ ❖ ❖ ❖ ❖

We had a black and tan striped tomcat, Tigger, who liked killing doves and finches and leaving them for us as prizes on our front mat. I loved Tigger—he was a fine cat—but I hated his killing habit. It upset me to find the carcass of some poor little bird on our stoop, its guts ripped out and its feathers bloodied. Once, I caught Tigger running around with a tiny bird in his mouth. I chased him and yelled at him and got him to drop it, and I felt elation at having pulled off such an amazing rescue. I knelt beside the injured thing and had Anthony bring me some water from the kitchen. Before he got back I saw that Tigger's teeth had left a hole in the bird's slender neck. I could see blades of grass right through it. Still, I took the water and poured it in the bird's beak, thinking I might save it. The water poured out through the hole, and I knew that the bird was dead. My brother and I came up with a posthumous name for it—Champion—and we buried it in the back yard.

I added Champion to my nightly prayer list, and I mourned him for many weeks. Finding dead birds is part of the ritual of childhood, and some kids aren't the least bit troubled by coming across one. But for me, it was traumatic. As a child I fell in love with birds, and I love them to this day. I identify with them and feel a special kinship with them, and some of the time I even envy them. Years later, as an adult, I had some revelations about my fascination with birds. For one thing, bird experts can tell a bird's gender from its plumage or the color of its beak, but most people can't tell if a bird is male or female. Perhaps subconsciously this was one of the reasons—as I crept up on my own gender-identification issues—that I felt great love and affection for birds. Consciously, though, what dazzled me about them most was their ability to fly—just like my invented superheroes. This was the most magical power imaginable, and only birds possessed it! I covered the walls of my room with pictures of exotic birds, and naturally I begged my parents to bring some home for me.

By the time I was nine, I had a small air force worth of parakeets. My father, the builder, hammered together an aviary out in the back yard to house them. It was made of wood and mesh wire, maybe eight feet tall and five feet wide, with wood perches running from one side to the other. This may have been the single nicest thing my father ever did for me. I moved all five or six of my parakeets into the aviary, and sat inside with them as they fluttered about. There was Spike, my green parakeet, and Sky, who was light blue, and countless others. I loved them all, and I took their care and feeding very seriously. The problem, though, was that I needed to drag the garden hose into the aviary to clean off their droppings. It was a thick old hose, and I was a thin little girl, and the door to the aviary had no springs. The first time I dragged the hose in there, the door stayed open and Spike and Sky flew out. It happened so fast. I dropped the hose and ran out and saw them flittering away. They stayed near each other, uncertain in their flight, but in seconds they disappeared behind the house. I was shocked, devastated, crushed. I couldn't tell my father about it because I was sure he would have blamed me for my stupidity. I knew it was my fault, and I felt terrible. My only consolation was imagining that Spike and Sky were happier now, with the whole wide world as their playground.

Keeping parakeets in the aviary outside was well and good, but I also needed to have a bird near me in my bedroom. The chosen bird was my favorite of all—a peach-faced lovebird whom I named, inventively, Peaches. She had rosy cheeks and light green wings, and a little light blue patch of feathers underneath. She was small, with a short stubby tail, and even though her wings weren't clipped she never flew anywhere. Instead, she loved hanging out with humans. I'd put her on my shoulder and walk around the house with her. She'd stay there for hours, happy as could be.

I adored Peaches. I liked building her little toys made out of wood chips and glue, and once I built her a little house made out of chopsticks and Saran wrap. I put her toys inside and then I put her in there, too. She didn't like it much, and walked right out. I tried again: same result. I guess she was fine with the small plastic-bottomed cage that I kept right next to my bed. At night I covered her cage with a small blanket, and together we would drift off into sweet, silent sleep.

I had owned Peaches for about two years when the worst thing happened. Sometimes I would walk through the house and Peaches would follow right behind me, taking miniscule steps but more or less keeping up. On this day, Anthony was throwing a tantrum, as he often did. This time he was screaming about some blanket that he wanted, a Superman blanket, and he was running from place to place trying to find it. Suddenly, he tore out of the bedroom, flung open the hallway closet door and furiously slammed it shut. The door swept Peaches up and crushed her neck.

I ran back to her and saw that she was convulsing. Her neck was twisted, and there was blood on her feathers. I remember that she was alive for a while, a few seconds at least. Her wings twitched and her tiny eyes blinked. But I knew right away that I would not be able to fix her. I knelt beside her, and I let my long hair drape around her, like a curtain, and I wept for her as she died right there in the hall. I heard Anthony run away crying; I'm sure he knew he was in trouble and wanted to get to my mother first. I wanted to chase after him and punch him and cause him terrible pain, but I also wanted to stay with Peaches. My anger won out, though, and I ran after Anthony and cornered him in the kitchen. But before I could get to him my mother stepped between us, and she talked me down and explained to me that Anthony hadn't done it on purpose. I knew that this was true, but I also knew that my brother was thoughtless and reckless. He never cared for the birds Tigger killed, and he didn't care about Peaches. I came to realize how spoiled Anthony had become as a result of my father's favoritism. He never apologized for killing Peaches, as some children might have, and he went on his way that night as if nothing had happened. I found a shoebox and lined it with tissues and put Peaches inside, and the next day I buried her in the back yard. I marked her grave with two or three white rocks and a little wood cross, but those lasted only a week or so before Tigger or Anthony or some other creature ran roughshod over them.

I prayed for Peaches every night—for Peaches and Champion. It strikes me now that there was yet another reason I may have loved birds so much. Despite their ability to fly, they are exceedingly fragile things. They weigh mere ounces, and their feet are nothing but twigs. Unlike dogs and cats, who are tougher beasts, able to fend for themselves, birds are wispy, ephemeral. I loved them for this, for their fragility, and for their dependence on me.

Back when I lost Peaches, though, I was learning a painful lesson: What is fragile does not always survive. Spike and Sky found an open door and flew away, into a world beyond ours. They were, it turns out, the lucky ones. For in our world there were always hazards and dangers, crashing doors and bloodthirsty cats, and other traps from which the weak and unlucky could not be sprung.

❖ ❖ ❖ ❖ ❖

The police came to our house a handful of times on domestic-dispute calls when I was growing up. Anthony and I would be shuttled off to another room, but we'd creep back out to get a look at the officers with their black guns and thick belts and crackling radios. I'd hear my mother crying as she told her side of the story. By the time I was eleven, I had seen my father hit my mother. I had also come upon fist-size holes in the wall after fights. I came to know how it would unfold: My parents would argue about something, and my mother would say something to trigger my father's rage, and then he would pounce.

One of the worst hits she ever took was partially my fault. This was during one of those stretches when my father was living somewhere else. I was old enough by then to realize that my parents were having problems, but I didn't know exactly why he wasn't home—whether he had been kicked out or was living with another woman. One night, my mother gathered Anthony and me and said we were going to spend the night somewhere else. I was excited until I found out we would be staying in the home of some other man. He was in every way the opposite of my father: Caucasian and tall, with shaggy blond hair down to his shoulders. He was lanky and muscled, and he smelled of body odor. I later learned he was a carpenter, and that he was working on some Tudor-style home in Kahala. This house was completely unfurnished, and Anthony and I slept on the living room floor while my mother stayed in the bedroom with him. I didn't ask my mother about it, and on our way home the next day she told me, "Don't mention this to your father."

But when we got home my father was there, and the first thing he asked me was "Where have you been?" In that moment I knew I was caught between my parents, and that only a lie would spare my mother a beating. But I also knew my father would surely be able to tell I was lying, which would mean a beating for us both. I tried not to say anything to him at all, but he demanded an answer. I was terrified that he would strike me, and I didn't know what to do. In a whisper of a voice, I told him the truth.

My father went berserk. He started yelling at my mother in the dining room, getting close to her and backing her into a wall.

She managed to slip away and run around the dining room table, but he chased her like a hungry dog. I watched as my father grabbed at chairs and pulled them down in his effort to get at her. I was scared to death. Finally, he caught her by the arm, held her in place, and swung his closed fist at her. He hit her hard, right on the mouth. It was a horrible noise. My mother fell back and let out a little scream, and then covered her mouth, more out of shock than anything else. When she pulled her hand away, I could see blood on her lips. My father stood there, breathing hard, and then started yelling at her again. She scurried away and called the police, and when they got there they looked at my father's hand and saw that his knuckles were bleeding. He had the audacity to laugh about it, and to tell the police that my mother had hit him in the hand with her teeth. He never properly treated that cut, so it became infected and his hand swelled up to twice its size. He blamed my mother for that, too.

My father had always had a temper, right from the start, and he had often terrorized my mother in the past. But somehow this time felt different. It was as if my mother, having being chased and captured and punched in the mouth in front of her children, like some kind of animal cornered by hunters, had had the spirit knocked right out of her. There was no fight left in her after that. Maybe the plan formed in her head that very night. Maybe it took her a few more days. But that punch was, for my family, the beginning of the end.

Chapter 4

THE NOTE

When I was five, we moved to a new home and my father built a koi pond in the front yard. The pond was a magical and sometimes frightening place, teeming with beauty and mystery and life. My father built it in the shape of a figure eight, and lined it with rocks set in cement. He fashioned a huge gazebo around and over the pond, and he added a waterfall on one end of it. And then, when he was finished building, came the koi.

We didn't have two or three or even a dozen koi in the pond. We had *hundreds* of them. Japanese koi are enchanting creatures; they have wonderfully bright and shimmering colors, and back then they seemed to me like living ornaments. My father stocked the pond with goshiki koi, which were mostly black but accented with red and blue; with asagi, which had red and blue scales; with white-skinned kohaku; with the amazing hikari-moyomono, rich with color splayed on their shiny, metallic surfaces. He also had a few large, prized kin gin rin, majestically streaked with fluorescent gold and silver. I know now that he must have spent thousands and thousands of dollars amassing so many expensive koi; the big ones alone surely cost him $1,000 each. But it was his hobby, and every now and then he would add more koi to the pond. Before long it was so crowded with fish, you could barely see through them to the bottom.

I was drawn to these magical fish, but the pond was also a very intense environment to be around. Because there were so many koi, the water was always dark and filthy, and my father added a bunch of plecostomus, or algae suckers, to the mix. These algae suckers were as nasty and ugly as the koi were pretty. They were dark black fish that clung to the side of the pond, and once in a while when my father stuck his hand in the water, an algae sucker would attach itself to his arm, and my brother and I would shriek at the sight of it. We called them yuks, because they were so yucky, and they kept us from wanting to stick our own hands in the pond.

Still, we enjoyed feeding the koi, though this, too, was intense. We'd grab handfuls of fish pellets and spray them in the water, and the desperate koi would madly attack the food. Dozens of them would swarm the spot and thrash against each other and even flip into the air; the aggressive ones would get more than their share of pellets, while the meek ones wound up with nothing but bruised scales. Koi will eventually recognize the voice of the person who feeds them, and will jump and dance when they hear it, in antici-pation of their meal. Some koi can even be taught to eat out of a human's hands. But we had a dense, swarming universe of koi, and dinnertime for them was a real event, a massive, splashy commotion. I liked feeding them, but at the same time I was always scared to death of falling in and getting sucked into the frenzy.

Years later, I thought about getting some koi of my own in Oregon, where I now live, but owning and caring for them is an expensive and delicate proposition. The very things that make koi so magical—their delicate grace, their preening brightness, their fondness for swimming near the surface to trawl for food and show off their colors—also make them especially vulnerable. If a koi pond is not properly constructed—if it isn't shaded by trees to block the view of hawks, or built deep enough to discourage herons or badgers from wading in, or surrounded by a fence or a stone border to prevent raccoons or even cats from taking a swipe—any one of these crafty predators can clean out your koi pond in a hurry. As a child I learned that I could not always protect what was near and dear to me; that no matter how beautiful and elegant something may be, there are always predators waiting and willing to destroy it.

❖ ❖ ❖ ❖ ❖

Our new house was much smaller than the home my father had built for us just before I was born. It was a simple, one-level ranch-style house in Hawaii Kai in East Honolulu. My father busted out a wall and made sliding glass doors for all three bedrooms, and he decorated the place with furniture he salvaged from a naval base where he did some work. I remember we had a couple of standard-issue military chairs in the house. I decorated my bed-room with banners my mother gave me from her high school and college. I liked them because they were colorful, and because they belonged to her.

Nearly all of my memories of my mother, good and bad, take place in that house. If I close my eyes I can still see her there, moving around the kitchen or the living room in her '70s-style polyester dresses, or in the pink and light blue terry-cloth jumpers she liked to wear. I can see her getting ready to go out for an evening and pinning a brooch on her lapel, maybe the dragon one or the lizard one, or my favorite, the butterfly. Mostly, I can see her smiling. My mother had a dazzling smile, and she was generous with it. Her smile could instantly wash away any sadness; it was comforting and conspiratorial, a suggestion that no matter what was wrong, you had her and she had you and everything would be okay. Few things in my life have ever made me feel as good as my mother's smile, or even the memory of it. I have a handful of black-and-white photos of my mother from when she was four years old; in them, she is bundled in thick winter clothing and fuzzy hand muffs—a tiny child braced against the brutal Minnesota winter. But in all of them she is smiling, and it is the same smile I came to know. To this day I can't even think of that smile without smiling myself. Recently I received a letter from my godfather's daughter, which said, "When you smile in thought when you think no one is watching you, you remind me a lot of your mother." Few letters have ever touched my heart quite like that one.

Even the worst of my father's beatings could not rob my mother of her smile for long. It was always there when I needed it, and because of that I was able to retain a certain amount of innocence during my childhood. I knew that things were bad in our household, and I endured beatings from my father, too, but I was also able to shuffle all the bad stuff into a distant compartment in my brain—to remain, in a way, blissfully ignorant of what was really going on. That, I now realize, was one of my mother's greatest gifts to me—with her powerfully soothing smile, she was able to shield me from reality and allow me to be a child for as long as possible. It was, I think, a heroic feat, and as good a measure of her humanity and compassion as any I know.

But there'd come a time when my mother's smile disappeared. It was striking, too, because it happened not long after one of the happiest times of our lives. In the summer of 1986, I finished the sixth grade, my last stop before junior high school. As a reward, my mother took Anthony and me to California for a remarkable vacation. We left my father behind in Hawaii, which by itself was enough to ensure a fantastic time. The three of us did one fun thing after another for three solid weeks. I remember riding a merry-go-round and seeing the fog-shrouded Golden Gate Bridge in the distance on every spin. I remember eating at Fisherman's Wharf, and I remember staying in a cabin on the Russian River. We took a long drive from San Francisco to Disneyland and Knott's Berry Farm in Southern California, and I remember the three of us on all sorts of rides. It was a giddy blur of activity, and easily the best time of my twelve-year-old life.

I also met my Aunt Tyler for the first time on that trip. We were in Golden Gate Park when I noticed my mother talking to a woman with shoulder-length red hair and a face that looked uncannily like my mother's. Anthony and I were called over from where we were playing and introduced to my mother's sister. I was shocked. My mother had mentioned her sister only once or twice in the past, and never in enough detail to make her take root in my mind as an actual person. It never truly occurred to me that I had another family member living in some far-off city. By the way they spoke to each other, it was clear why my mother rarely mentioned her sister. They stood in that park and talked for just a few minutes, and looked like they could have been two strangers who bore a vague resemblance. I am sure they hugged goodbye, but I don't remember their doing it. They did not act at all like two sisters who hadn't seen each other in years. Whatever emotional bond might have existed between them had long been severed by then. They were not friends, if they had ever been—they were barely even sisters anymore.

After that strange encounter, we resumed our fairytale vacation, and toward the end of the trip my mother took us to meet an old friend of hers, Steve Waterfall. I liked Steve for a lot of reasons, not the least of which was his whimsical last name. We also met Steve's identical twin brother, Tom. The exactness of their faces was weird and thrilling to me. Unlike Tom, Steve wore thick-rimmed glasses, which made him look like one of my idols, Clark Kent. Don't get me wrong, I loved Superman, too, but shy, bumbling Clark was even more of a hero to me, perhaps because he was easier to identify with. And here was Steve, who, like Clark, was a little goofy. He seemed unsure of how to act around Anthony and me, but he did his best to show us a good time. He took us camping at the base of Lake Tahoe, and we all fished for trout by day and roasted marshmallows over a fire at night. The wonderfully easy time we spent by the lake, and the vivid smells of campfires and pine trees, are sweet and satisfying memories I cherish deeply.

But the biggest reason I liked Steve was that he seemed so fond of my mother. It was amazing to see him smile at her, touch her arm and hug her for no reason, and treat her with respect and affection. I had only ever seen my father frown and yell at her, or brush her off with a wave of his hand, or mock and insult her. I can't say that I ever saw my father act tenderly toward his wife. And yet here was Steve, treating my mother as if she were some kind of princess. And she, too, seemed different around him: looser, happier, more carefree. My mother later told me that she and Steve had dated for a time before she met my father. But even before I learned this, I began secretly hoping that Steve Waterfall would run away with all of us so we could start a new family in California, away from my father. He didn't, of course; he merely kissed my mother goodbye after our fishing trip was over, then disappeared from our lives. As much as I hoped and prayed and fantasized, Clark Kent did not turn into Superman.

And then the vacation was over, and we were back in Hawaii. A new school year was about to begin, and my mother, like she did every year, started getting ready for another semester of teaching. While moving boxes in her classroom, my mother somehow hurt her shoulder and had to go see a doctor. I never learned the details of this injury; I was told about it only later, as an explanation of what would ensue. My mother's doctors gave her a shot of penicillin, and immediately she became gravely ill. She spent the next several weeks in bed, fatigued and depressed. It turns out that she was allergic to penicillin; apparently it said so right on her chart. Even so, her doctor continued giving her shots, and she got even sicker. One morning, my father informed us that my mother had gone away to get better.

Waking to discover that my mother was gone was horrifying. Without her at home, there was no home at all; it was just an empty, spooky place. I demanded that we go see her, and my father had no choice but to take Anthony and me to the hospital where she was recovering. When we got there, it was clear that it wasn't an ordinary hospital. My father had checked her into a mental institution.

The first time we all went to see her in the psych ward of the Castle Medical Center, my mother was standing right in front of the elevator when its doors opened on the third floor. She knew we were coming, because she had been sitting by her window for hours, waiting for us to arrive. I learned that she would sit in the same spot by that window all day, every day, waiting to catch a glimpse of us heading in to see her. I didn't really understand what was going on, but the shock of having to leave my mother alone in this strange, sterile place, and getting to see her only for short visits every now and then, was shattering.

It remains inconceivable to me that my father would have committed my mother to a mental institution. Apparently the only solution he could come up with in the face of her deep depression was to turn her over to doctors—getting rid of her, in effect. Never mind how it affected Anthony and me to not have our mother around; even bedridden and despondent, she was far more nurturing than he could ever be.

Caring for her in her depressed state was something that my father was simply incapable of doing. In his world, women existed to serve and care for the men, not the other way around. Let someone else fix her, he figured. I have never been able to forgive my father for having arrived at that decision. How can you abandon someone you love in their direst hour of need? How can you not want to be there for every one of their darkest moments? How can you simply toss someone away like that, just so you don't have to deal with their problem? Sometimes, I force myself to see my father's side of things—clearly, he did not understand what was happening to my mother, and it may have scared him, or perhaps just annoyed him. Maybe he even thought he was doing the best thing for her. But no matter how I try to see it, he still left my mother to sit and stare out a window for days on end, all alone and doped out on god knows what, desperate to spot the children she loved so she could squeeze a hug out of them before they were whisked away. I can't help but see this as an act of unfathomable cruelty and cowardice on his part.

❖ ❖ ❖ ❖ ❖

My mother was gone for more than two months, and when she came home it was as if the sun had come out after an endless winter. I felt immensely relieved to see her there again, and all my fears slipped away. Something awful had happened, something terrifying, but now my mother was back with me and all was right with the world. That fall, I switched over to the private Mid-Pacific Institute for the seventh grade, and I was excited to be starting somewhere new.

And yet my mother had not really gotten better at all. She returned to teaching, but she didn't seem to have the same enthusiasm that she'd had for it before. Two days before Thanksgiving, she was still in bed when it came time for me to leave for school. By then I was old enough to take a bus by myself, but I still cherished the few morning moments I got to spend with my mother before I left. On this day, I found her in bed, and in no hurry to get up. I ran in to tell her about a big math test I had that day, and about how much I had studied for it, and to hear her wish me good luck and tell me how smart I was. But she didn't answer me; she just lay in bed, sluggish, sullen, distant. Her eyes were tired, with dark bags beneath them, and her skin was pale and wan. None of the spirit and vitality that I knew to be my mother was evident that morning. It felt chillingly as if someone else were in that bed. I did everything I could to perk her up; I told her that I loved her and I hugged her tightly, I made funny faces, and I asked her again to wish me luck. I was scared because she couldn't even muster a single word. She just stared off vacantly. But I kept trying nonetheless, grabbing her, *being* with her, until finally she turned to face me. In a soft, far-away voice, she spoke.

"Good luck on your test, Tracy," she whispered. "I love you."

Somehow, she managed a smile.

All morning at school I felt an urgent need to speak to my mother again. I forced myself to focus on my math test and I aced it, but then all I wanted to do was tell my mother how well I had done. At lunchtime I called her from a school pay phone, but no one picked up. During my afternoon classes I fought off a sickening sense of dread. Finally, when the last bell rang, I sprinted the quarter mile to the bus stop, then ran the last few blocks home with my book bag bouncing on my back. My heart was racing so fast, it felt like someone kicking my chest.

I pushed open the front door and went looking for her. I ran to her bedroom but it was empty, sheets strewn on the unmade bed. I called out to her and dashed into the kitchen, but it was empty, too. *Without my mother, there is no home, it's just an empty place.* I ran outside and wanted to yell her name at the top of my lungs, but I knew my voice would echo through the valley, and that seemed too desperate a thing to do. So I ran back inside and went into my father's office, and on his desk I saw a folded piece of paper. I picked it up and read the words, but I couldn't understand what they meant. Separately, they were words I knew, but strung together they made no sense. I picked up the phone and called my father at work.

"What is it?" he said.

"Mom's not here. I found a note on your desk."

He was quiet for a long moment, and then asked me to read the note. When I did, his voice cracked in a way I had never heard before. He said, "Oh no."

I can't remember the exact wording of the note my mother left, only that it was short, just a few words.

It said something like, "I can't do this anymore."

❖ ❖ ❖ ❖ ❖

When my father came home a few hours later, he told Anthony and me that police had found my mother wandering around Waikiki Beach. He said that she was fine, and that she would come home the next day. I cried nonstop for an hour, mostly out of relief, but also because I was still scared and confused. I remember little Anthony hearing the news and watching my face for a reaction. When I burst into tears, he did too.

The next morning, Anthony and I got ready for school, same as always. But before we could leave, my father stopped us in the hallway. I was stunned to see his face—his eyes were red and filled with tears. I had never seen him cry before in my life.

"Your mother isn't coming home anymore," he told us. Neither of us knew what he meant or what he was trying to say.

"She jumped from the thirty-second floor of the apartment building up the street. She is not coming home."

My instinct was to reach out and hold on to Anthony. He measured my reaction again, and picked up on my panic. A seizing, sickening wave of realization washed over me and nearly knocked me off my feet. I held Anthony tightly and let the tears come. I gasped for breath between long, droning wails, and I felt weak in a way I had never felt before. I was filled with a deep, exhausting revulsion, with shock and fear and confusion, and my body heaved and shuddered. It was the day before Thanksgiving in 1986. I was twelve years old and my mother was gone.

I cannot write these words, even today, without feeling sick. What does it mean to lose a parent at such a young age—to have the only source of love and affection in your life taken away in an instant? It shreds you to the core, caves in your chest and hollows out your heart, and tears up every bone and sinew in your body. It leaves you spent and wasted. It produces a pain that cannot be relieved, a grief that cannot be consoled. The person I was, so defined and sustained by my mother's love, died on that day, too.

I have been someone different ever since. I have a wound that will never heal, not if I live for a million years. Today, I feel an infinite sorrow when I think of how I lost my mother. Back then I stopped thinking or feeling at all. I just shut down.

I don't remember much about my mother's funeral. I suppose I have willfully blocked it out, or perhaps I cried too much that day to take notice of what went on. I believe there were a lot of people there, though I can't recall who. I remember sitting at the front of the chapel, just a few feet from a glossy wooden casket. A framed photo of my mother—her latest school picture, I think—sat atop the closed casket. Earlier that same year, my grandfather had died, and at his wake he was laid out in an open casket. I had passed by it and looked at his face; his skin was gray and leathery, and he looked like a giant doll. But he also looked like he could open his eyes at any moment, and I stared at the strange stillness of his body until it freaked me out and I scurried away. Seeing my first dead person was terrifying, but my mother's closed casket was far, far worse. There was nothing to see, except for a photo of her smiling face. What exactly was I looking at? Was my mother in there? I'm pretty sure my father didn't say any words; he left that to Barry, his oldest son. I remember crying loudly, and if I root around deep enough I can almost summon the image of my father crying, too.

Life changed drastically without my mother around. There was no one to cook for us anymore, so my father stuffed the freezer with TV dinners. Much of the time he wasn't even home, so Anthony and I often fed and cared for ourselves. Sometimes my father would take Anthony with him, and the two of them would sleep somewhere else, leaving me alone. That's when I began the practice of writing my thoughts in journals. I would get myself up at 4:00 AM, finish my homework, then fill notebook after notebook with letters to my mother, plans for the future, feelings about life, everything. I was no longer the carefree little tomboy who spoke and acted without a filter. In a very real way, I almost completely withdrew from life into my journals. For most of the next two years, I shut down my exterior persona and more or less went through the motions of my life, connecting with no one, sharing nothing, existing but not living. I stopped eating, or at least I ate so little that I grew alarmingly frail. Naturally, my father had no idea how to handle my depression. I could sense his frustration, but I didn't care. I was in a very deep, protective funk, designed to minimize my interaction with the world. My already strained relationship with my father was now barely any relationship at all.

One day, he told me that I needed to see a doctor. He was worried about my health, and about how much weight I was losing. He put me in the car and drove me to a Kaiser Permanente clinic about twenty miles away from our home. I remember wondering why we needed to drive so far away when there were doctors much closer to where we lived.

At the clinic, a nurse had me slip on a thin hospital gown, and a doctor came in to give me a physical checkup. His first move was to try to stick a thermometer up my butt, but I pulled away and refused to let him do it. Very quickly, the doctor grew irritated and left the room. I saw a chance to escape, so I changed back into my clothes and snuck out of the room. I didn't see my father anywhere, so I ran down a hallway and out the front door. I sat next to my father's car in the parking lot and waited for him to show up.

Suddenly, four men in white coats came running toward the car. It was a frightening sight, and it froze me to my spot. The men grabbed me by my arms and legs and carried me, kicking and screaming, back into the clinic. They strapped me to a gurney, and one of them told me, "Now you won't be hurting yourself anymore." I had no idea what he meant by this: How had I been hurting myself? I looked around for my father but still couldn't see him. Then two different men wheeled the gurney out of the clinic and into a waiting ambulance. They drove me several miles to another building, which I soon learned was an adolescent mental hospital.

My father was doing to me exactly what he had done to my mother. He didn't know how to handle the very understandable grief and depression I felt over my mother's suicide, so he simply dumped me off on someone else. I spent my first day at the mental hospital by myself in a padded room. I was shot with a couple of needles, and pretty soon I was in a daze. The next two days were filled with meetings with psychiatrists, more needle shots, and endless small white cups holding pills. I was thirteen years old, and the youngest patient in the hospital.

On the fourth day, they let me go. I am sure my father would have preferred that I stay longer, but I later learned that it was costing him $1,500 a day to keep me there, so perhaps that's why I got to leave. I have no idea what the doctors discovered about me, or if they told my father that I was an ordinary child going through an intense period of mourning. Maybe they agreed with him that I was somehow a danger to myself. But I didn't think then, nor do I think now, that there was anything wrong with me besides a seriously broken heart. My mother's suicide forced my father to try to be a real parent and not just a disciplinarian, and he had no idea how to do it.

❖ ❖ ❖ ❖ ❖

Many times in my adulthood, I have thought about how my mother's death must have affected my father, and if he was going through a dreadful, untenable ordeal of his own. But, once again, I cannot muster much sympathy for him. I know that maybe I should be able to, but I can't. If he loved her or cared about her at all, he would have honored her while she was alive and tried to honor her memory after she was gone. But I don't believe he was ever emotionally capable of truly loving or caring about my mother. Am I being harsh in holding his emotional shortcomings against him? Perhaps. But I simply cannot feel any other way about him. He let us all down, over and over, especially in the moments when we could have used him most.

But just as I hold my father responsible for so much of what happened to our family, I have often wondered how my mother could have abandoned us, too. For years after she died, I struggled with that question—knowing what life would be like for Anthony and me with only our father to raise us, how could she have done what she did? My deepest fear was that she had killed herself to escape all of us, including me, and not just to escape my father. How could I be sure that she had not? And it bothered me more than I can say that I never got to tell her about how I aced that math test. She knew I was taking it—didn't she care? Had I not told her that I loved her enough? Did she feel unloved, even by me? Did I not do enough to try to rouse her from her deep depression, to brighten her days and make life better for her? Even that morning,

I had a sort of intuition about her death; I sensed something was terribly wrong, yet I went to school anyway, as if it were just an ordinary day. Why didn't I heed my gut feeling and stay with her? For years I was haunted by my paltry effort to cheer her up that morning. Too little, too late—and the consequence of coming up short was to be a lifetime of shame and guilt.

On top of all that, I had to fight off a pointless and painful feeling that my mother was not really dead. After all, I had never seen her body; I had no real proof whatsoever that she had passed. She was simply there one morning and gone that afternoon. It turns out that my father never saw my mother's remains, either. He could not bring himself to go to the hospital to identify her body, so he sent Barry to do it instead. When I learned this, I was even more disappointed in my father. How could he have sent his son to do this ghastly thing, just to spare himself the pain? It was a few months after my mother's death before my father finally shared a single detail about what had happened. Until then, I knew nothing about the circumstances of her suicide, beyond her having made her way into a vacant thirty-second-floor apartment (she worked part-time as a realtor) and hurling herself off its balcony. But then my father, for some bizarre reason, chose to pull me aside one day and tell me that when they found my mother's body on the walk-way below, the impact had pushed her hips straight up through her shoulders. It was, and is, a horrifying image, and I still cannot believe that my father described it to me. He must have known that it would give me horrible nightmares, that I would never be able to shake the image from my mind. Sharing that detail was a cruel, sadistic thing to do. It was so grotesque, so unthinkable, that for me it did not count as proof that she was actually dead. It simply confused and tormented me even more. For years I would picture my mother's crumpled body on the ground, and then in the same day imagine that she was alive somewhere, walking around and waiting for me to find her.

Writing about these feelings, and asking my mother questions in the countless journals I kept, helped me to break free of some of the guilt and confusion I felt. Initially all I felt was sadness and loss, but over the years I also felt betrayed by what my mother had done. My journaling helped me work through all of that, to the point that now I mainly feel just sympathy and heartbreak—sympathy for her because of the utter hopelessness she must have been feeling. She was physically ill and mentally drained, battered not only by the carelessness of her doctors, but, more devastatingly, by her years in a destructive, abusive marriage. For all the love, kindness, and generosity that my mother put forth in the world, she received precious little in return. It kills me inside to think of how the island paradise that so enchanted her when she first moved to Hawaii became a loveless and desolate place from which she must have felt there was no escape.

I finally assured myself that my brother and I were not responsible for what happened. But believing this did not make her suicide easier to accept. All it did was make it a little more comprehensible. The rock-bottom truth, I realize now, is that I will never really know how much of a part her illness played in her suicide. Nor will I ever know for sure how much my father is responsible for her death. It's been my lifelong struggle to find a way to live with this uncertainty, and to prevent it from haunting me any longer.

The best way to do this, I have found, is to focus on what was good and beautiful and pure about my mother when she was alive. To celebrate her intellect and her elegance and her gentle nature by emulating them in my life—by consciously choosing my own destiny every day. Part of me has always feared that nature would pull me toward my father's terrible traits—the selfishness, the cruelty, the deliberate shunning of emotion. My brother Barry and I have discussed this over the years; we have both felt an internal pull toward my father's personality, and sometimes we have found ourselves mimicking some or other obnoxious part of his behavior. It is like a primal seed, yearning to be fed and sprouting despite our best efforts to tamp it down. But we do not have to succumb to it, not if we don't want to. Whatever foul residue of my father dwells inside my being must share space with the powerful, nourishing legacy my mother left. I can choose to live my life the way she lived hers, and I make this choice every single day. I choose to live with love and with kindness. I choose to celebrate my mother through my words and actions. I choose to keep her alive inside me, shining brightly, forever with a smile.

And still, I miss her terribly, more and more as the years roll on. I feel excruciating sadness when I think of what my life would be like if she were still alive—especially now that I am a parent myself. I often find myself wishing I could ask her for advice, or simply share with her some of the beautiful pleasures of having been pregnant and having a baby. That I can't seems horribly, tragically unfair. I long to touch my mother again, like I used to when I was young—when I would crawl all over her body and cling to her every limb like a baby monkey. This longing is so deep that it inhabits my dreams. For years I have dreamt that I see my mother from afar in a crowd. I see a blond woman, dressed like my mother used to dress, and she's walking briskly away from me, so I run as fast as I can to catch up to her. Sometimes I cannot reach her, and the dream ends this way. Sometimes I reach her and spin her around, but it turns out to be some other blond woman, not my mother. Every once in a while I dream that I catch her, and that she is my mother; in some of those dreams she is robotic, as remote as the day she died; in others, she is so happy that I have finally found her, and she hugs me as hard as she can, until I wake up.

Since she died I have gone to visit her grave several times, sometimes out of a sense of obligation, sometimes because I hope it will make me feel close to her. She is buried in my father's family plot in a cemetery in Honolulu. It is a lovely place, surrounded by trees, calm and peaceful. During the day, it gets really hot but it's still the best time to visit, since the mosquitoes attack when the sun goes down. I can sit near the grave and just enjoy the solitude. Best of all, her burial place is very near a koi pond, much like the magical pond we had in front of our home. The koi are happy there, and their gold and silver scales reflect the sun and create a kind of light show. It is hard for me to see a koi now and not think of my mother. Their beauty, their fragility, the sense of wonder they create—I think of these things as I sit beside my mother's grave. For a final resting place, it is indeed a beautiful spot. I want so much to think that my mother is there, that she has finally found the peace that eluded her during her life.

But try as I might it just doesn't feel to me like she is there.

For years after she died, I held onto her favorite pea-green and mustard-yellow robe. I wore it all the time because it still smelled of her, or at least I imagined that it did. *Here is my mother,* I thought, *in this robe.* But I wore it so often that eventually whatever smell it might have held disappeared. I also saved the last bottle of perfume she ever owned. I would lift the metal cap and smell the fragrance that used to be hers. *Here*, I thought, *here is my mother, in this bottle*. But eventually the small amount of perfume that was left inside the bottle evaporated, and the cold metal cap no longer carried her smell, and with that there was nothing left of my mother at all.

Chapter 5

LITTLE BROWN BOY

I was ten when I discovered a hard truth about myself. I learned that I could make people hate me just by being me.

One of my schoolmates, Natasha, an African American girl with long black hair and a slight overbite, was the one who delivered the lesson, as cruelly as if she had done it out of malice and not, as was the case, because she felt confused. Natasha was new to our school, but like most girls at Hahaione Elementary, she wore fluorescent skirts and jelly shoes and shiny bangles and bracelets on her skinny wrists; she traveled in buzzing packs of other giggling girlie-girls; she was graceless in the manner of most adolescents, but also assured and forward in a way I could only dream of being. I don't recall her ever making fun of me, like a lot of the other girls did, or ridiculing my brother's old hand-me-downs—ragged construction T-shirts and polyester running shorts. I remember her ignoring me, which back then was kind of a blessing.

I cut my hair short that year. It was never all that long to begin with; I'd always insisted on getting it cut before it crept past my collar. But this time I cut it myself, with blunt construction-paper scissors. It wasn't a premeditated thing, or out of any flash of frustration. It was just, I guess, an intuitive response, like picking at a scab or biting on a jagged fingernail. I didn't really form the thought *You need to have short hair.* I just cut it one day until I could see my ears. It didn't occur to me that I looked a lot more like a boy with short hair, though clearly I did. I have strong features and a square jaw, and without the softening of long hair, the last defense of my biological gender was lost.

Apparently, this was when Natasha developed an old-fashioned crush on me. It was hardly some big, sweeping romance, even by grade-school standards. I don't think she ever actually spoke to me directly, outside of a group. But I do remember her looking at me across the schoolyard and smiling before looking away. And I heard from other classmates that she liked me. The thrilling stuff of a youthful crush—attraction without desperation, desire unspoiled by action. A simple bit of innocence, but even this was doomed to end wretchedly.

It was only a matter of time before someone told Natasha that I was not a boy, as she believed. It was just as inevitable that they would break the news to her in a way that maximized her embarrassment. "You like another girl!" they told her. "The boy you love is really a girl!" Natasha, to her credit, did not believe them. She would find out for herself, and not brush off her feelings for me based only on the mocking chatter of classmates. I was in the hallway outside math class when she marched right up to me and stared hard at my face.

"Is it true that you're a girl?" she asked point-blank.

I was caught off guard, and I looked down at my feet before answering. "Yes" was all I said. I could see her face turn red in an instant. I could tell that she was angry and hurt.

"Why did you try to fool me?" she asked. I hadn't, of course. All I had done was cut my hair and smile back at her. But I didn't defend myself. I didn't say anything.

"Why would you do that to me?" Natasha asked. And then she was gone, down the hallway, back to her pack. These were the only words we ever shared with each other.

Her embarrassment, though, stung me badly, and I felt instantly responsible for it. I had always known that I was different from other children. I spent most of my time by myself, scooping up crabs at the marina, while other kids were out playing and laughing together. My own questions and isolation were, mercifully, just my own, and I could handle them. But now I had made someone else angry and upset. I had embarrassed someone and opened her up to ridicule. I had caused her to feel confused and estranged from her friends and from the world she understood. And she had, in turn, lashed out at me, blamed me, caused me pain. This was the moment I realized there was a social problem with who I was— that whatever turmoil I was facing would also, invariably, involve those who crossed into and out of my life. Imagine learning at such a young age that your very appearance—your very identity—is enough to trigger such confusion and animosity. Imagine knowing that people will hate you for no reason other than you are who you are. In that brief confrontation with Natasha, the protective wall I'd been building around myself came crashing down. Even if I kept to myself, I was vulnerable to attack. I would no longer have to deal solely with my own expression and identity. I was now responsible for all the hurt and harshness my presence on this planet produced. This was the first awkward overture of my life's central theme.

Little Tracy can make you hate her without even trying.

❖ ❖ ❖ ❖ ❖

I almost never got mad at my mother, but one day she made an offhand comment that got me so angry, I nearly screamed. She remarked that the bridge of my nose was nothing like hers— that it was flat, like my father's. She said it in front of a friend of hers, and afterward they laughed at how little I actually resembled my mother. They weren't being mean; they couldn't possibly have known how damaging that comment was for me. But I was so upset I started crying, and I stormed off in a fit, feeling betrayed.

Naturally, it was horrible for me to have validation that I looked more like my father than my mother. My mother was the most beautiful woman I had ever seen, and to be told I looked nothing like her was to be told I wasn't pretty. My mother was an absolute paradigm of beauty for me: the blond hair, the hourglass figure, the radiant smile. I honestly believed she was worthy of being crowned Miss America, and it frustrated me when she laughed off my suggestions that she enter the pageant. How distressing, then, when people would see us together and remark that I didn't look anything like her. Some people even said I couldn't possibly be her daughter. On top of that, to be told I looked like my father suggested I had more of him in me somehow, more of a connection to him and less of one to her. So when my mother, too, confirmed my physical similarity to my father, I was shattered. I wanted to be thought of as beautiful, just like her. Instead, her beauty became an unattainable and taunting reminder of my own insecurities.

As I got older, a part of me was deeply afraid that I would *end up* looking like my mother. As a child, I may have wished that people found me pretty, or that they felt I was in every way just like my wonderful mother, but the truth is that physically I struggled to imagine what it would feel like to look as feminine and beautiful as my mother looked. I knew that at least physically, we were opposites. We didn't have the same hair color—hers was fair and flaxen, mine brown like koa—or the same eye color, or even the same skin color. She had a real woman's body: small waist, shapely hips, long torso, curves everywhere. I had a short torso and long legs; I looked like a plank of wood.

Even as I went through puberty, not much changed. No hips, negligible breasts. It was around this time that the idea that I might eventually look like my mother began to scare me. Sometimes I would get a glimpse of her naked body as she changed or went swimming, and the contrast between her voluptuousness and my stick figure was so stark that part of me grew terrified of my body changing so drastically into something that looked like hers. I envisioned my hips suddenly expanding outward in one fell swoop, bones creaking and skin stretching and all. I thought about my breasts suddenly ballooning, and my butt finally popping into existence. Was I really going to grow and change into that? I wondered. Much as I wanted to look like her, these were not changes I welcomed. They were too drastic, and I feared they'd turn me into a whole new person altogether.

So which was it? Did I want to be beautiful like my mother, or didn't I? The honest answer is—both. I was just a kid, after all, sorting through a lot of different emotions and feelings. And I was confronting a tricky dichotomy in my life (long before I ever knew what a dichotomy was). My parents were not only physically dissimilar, but also polar opposites in behavior. Given my mother's kind, gentle, and loving disposition and my father's emotionless, brutish character, it was a given that I wished more than anything to be like my mother. However, it wasn't lost on me that in many ways I was much more like my father. It was as if I were being pulled between two opposing forces, and my genetics were dooming me to end up in my father's camp. What's more, while I wanted to emulate my mother's grace and elegance, I was actually much more comfortable emulating my father's manly behavior. All kids try on their parents' personalities for size, copying their mannerisms until they settle into a pattern all their own, blended from the two. But in my case, many more of my father's masculine traits—some of which I despised—were a part of who I was from an early age.

Part of me wanted to be more like my feminine mother, while I preferred to act like my masculine father. I wanted to be beautiful like her, but became comfortable with a body that looked like his. It's probably why I gave myself the short haircut that so confused and angered my classmate Natasha. It wasn't a conscious choice I was making between two genders—it was just the way I was wired. I was born female, given the middle name Lehuanani, which means "beautiful lehua flower." I was anatomically suited to live my life as a woman. Certainly, this would have been the least complicated choice I could have made. Had I embraced my female identity, I surely would not have faced a lifetime of ostracism and obstacles, nor incurred the wrath of strangers and family alike. But no one can say they are living an authentic life if they are not true to who they fundamentally are. Gradually, I found a sort of harmony between these two forces in my life, and that enabled me to be happy in my own skin. It was not a short or easy process to find this balance; it has taken me nothing less than a lifetime.

❖ ❖ ❖ ❖ ❖

I did not consciously choose to become the Pregnant Man because of who my parents were—as if I might try to actualize some bizarre, self-created hybrid of my mother and father. Nothing could be further from the truth. Who I am today is who I always was, from the very beginning. My parents were huge influences on me, same as anyone's parents, but they did not shape my sexuality. They shaped only my perception of it, and of what it means to be a man and a woman. Had I merely wished to emulate my mother and shrink away from my father, why wouldn't I have stayed a woman, and done everything I could to be beautiful, just as she was? Conversely, had I merely wished to avoid evolving into a thuggish man like my father, why on earth would I have transitioned into a male at all? I simply had to discover who I was deep down, and somehow become that person. That, in a nutshell, is what we all have to do. I just had an extra little challenge thrown in: I was born a woman, but I always felt more comfortable living like a man.

Even as a little girl, I was known as the Little Brown Boy. That's what all the other kids would call me teasingly. My skin wasn't really brown; I was fair at birth. But because I spent so much time in the sun, I was deeply bronzed, like my father. I was also usually the tallest student in my classes, girl or boy. On top of that, I wore my older brother's drab hand-me-downs, not the frilly, feminine stuff other girls liked to wear. All of that together made most people instinctively think of me as a boy.

And I didn't do anything to discourage that perception, either. Because I didn't bond with girls or boys, I spent a lot of time by myself, fishing, building fortresses, and engaging in other "boy" activities. I liked playing with Hot Wheels race cars and building Lego spaceships, and, of course, I had my invented superheroes to keep me company. I also loved sports and was really good at track. In elementary school I set a standing-long-jump record that remained unbroken for a decade.

The truth is, I had exactly the body I needed for my life. It was a good, lean, blocky body, tough and durable. I was no stranger to skinned knees, scraped elbows, stubbed toes, even broken arms. I was constantly hurling myself into the air and crashing to the ground. I'd fly off bicycles, or trip over rocks, or smash my foot into the asphalt while trying to kick a ball. I was the very definition of a tomboy. One time I rode my bicycle through a neighbor's yard and straight into a rock pile; I broke my right arm and had to wear a cast for weeks. Two days after they finally took off the cast, I broke my arm again when another student grabbed my legs while I was hanging off a jungle gym and swung me so hard I sailed through the air before hitting the ground. I was always dirty or sweaty or bloody or all of those things. I was, to put it mildly, not dainty.

I also had instincts that many would say were masculine. Because of my height and my appearance, I got picked on a lot, but rather than slink away in tears, I usually fought back. I have a vague memory of being in the fourth grade and chasing a boy around the desks, angry as heck. I don't remember if I caught him or not, but I remember the feeling of having no other option but to go after him. Another time, a boy hit me in the arm, perhaps just to tease me, but I punched him right in the face. I have no idea where the instinct came from, but it was there. I remember the boy's face registered absolute shock for a few seconds, before he started wailing. I was sent off to the principal's office, my knuckles bleeding from the impact of his teeth.

Another time, in the sixth grade, I think, the class was playing dodgeball when a boy caught me off guard and, out of turn, heaved the big red ball right at my face. All the other kids laughed at me, and it stung so badly that I felt myself starting to cry. I am sure I did cry, but I didn't *just* cry. I also went right at the boy and tackled him to the ground. We rumbled around in the grass for a while, probably to a draw, before the teachers pulled us apart.

I was simply unafraid of getting into fights, and part of the reason was that I knew I would never get a worse beating than the ones I got at home. My father's spankings toughened me up—hardly a silver lining, but they did. Being spanked so often also gave me a pretty good sense of my vulnerability, and of what I needed to do to protect myself. Maybe I couldn't fight off my father, but I sure as hell wasn't going to let some boy at school get in any free shots.

I started taking karate when I was in the third grade. It was Shotokon-style karate, which is fairly robotic and not the best self-defense method in the world, but I got to practice punching and kicking on a heavy bag, and I learned basic blocks and moves. More important, I developed self-confidence, and pretty soon any fear of confrontation I might have had was gone forever. Even back then, I noticed that my muscles were getting bigger, and that karate was changing my body. I liked these changes, and I really liked feeling strong and powerful. Karate would remain a major part of my life, and to this day I credit it with helping me become the person I was meant to be.

Needless to say, in the years following my mother's death, much of that self-esteem I'd built up through karate disappeared. My two-year depression that let me ghostly thin also had the effect of making me insecure about the way I looked. Today, when I look at photos of myself in those days, I simply can't believe how frail I was. During those two years, I was neither feminine nor masculine in my behavior. I was a complete social outcast who had no sense of myself at all, and who avoided human contact as much as possible.

The irony is that during that dark period, I had plenty of male admirers. In ninth grade, I had just one friend, Katie, the only girl who didn't move to another table when I sat down next to her in the cafeteria. We ate lunch together pretty much every day, and I didn't pay any attention to the boys in our class. But then one day a boy named Byron came up and asked me if I would be his girlfriend. I was surprised but also immediately flattered; I knew what it meant to have a boy be interested in you, and I welcomed the attention. I said yes right away, and just like that we were a couple. He was kind of cute—tall, scraggly blond hair, athletic body—and we "dated" for about two weeks, though I didn't have the slightest idea what dating even entailed. I was just happy to have someone who thought I was pretty.

At one point during our short-lived relationship, we packed some juice and fruit and had a little picnic on a blanket down by the marina. Halfway through it, Byron leaned over and kissed me. I felt something hard in his shorts and I asked him what it was. Byron got red in the face and said he didn't want to talk about it. Immediately, he got up and left. I didn't feel anything when we kissed, other than a sense of relief that someone was accepting me. Kissing a boy seemed like a ritual of adolescence, and to be kissed meant to be part of the group, to have something in common with other kids—sort of like owning the hot pair of designer jeans everyone is wearing. But beyond that, my first kiss was not exactly an occasion for fireworks. I liked my arrangement with Byron, and we passed notes back and forth in class: "I really like you, let's meet later," or "I'm glad you are my girlfriend." One day I decided to send him a note that read, "Do you still love me?" with a box for yes and another for no. I watched him check a box and send the note back, but when I read it I was shocked; he'd checked no. I confronted him, after class and asked him why he didn't love me anymore.

"Because my friend Ryan says you're ugly," he replied. "He said you're an Asian girl, and Asian girls are ugly. He said I should be dating a white girl."

I scrambled to defend myself, and told him he shouldn't listen to his friend because his friend was a jerk. But very quickly the pain I felt turned into anger. The next day I came into class and poured a small carton of milk over Byron's head. I got sent to the principal's office, but I didn't care. I had been rejected, and nothing could make me feel worse than being rejected. My father had rejected me, and in a way my mother had, too, and now a boyfriend who I thought loved me had kicked me to the curb. My first kiss with Byron was not a big event in my life, but his rejection of me surely was.

Being told I was ugly played into one of my oldest anxieties, and the insecurity I felt led me to do something drastic. It was something that had been building for a while. In the months after my mother died, my father began urging me to sign up with a local modeling agency; he figured that might snap me out of my tomboy ways and finally turn me into a woman. After Byron rejected me, I agreed to my father's plan. He took me to an agency in Honolulu, and they helped me put together a portfolio full of posed head and body shots. They also taught me etiquette and grooming skills, and how to apply makeup. I couldn't stand any of these rituals of womanhood. I hated wearing makeup, and I especially didn't like prancing around in women's clothing. I felt embarrassed to look at myself in the mirror when I was dressed that way, and I was convinced anyone could tell that I was essentially pretending to be female. Instead, people told me I was pretty—that I looked like a cross between Brooke Shields and Tia Carrera. I didn't like the way I looked as a model, but I did enjoy the attention, and so I went along with one of my father's more desperate ideas.

I allowed him to enter me in the 1989 Miss Teen Hawaii USA pageant.

❖ ❖ ❖ ❖ ❖

There I am, on a grainy, badly framed videotape of the event, all of fourteen years old and wearing an absurd Christmas outfit—a little red skirt and silly white boots. I am on the stage of a cavernous hall that used to be a pineapple cannery, and I am dancing to a rock version of "Joy to the World." On my face is plastered a smile as fake as a Christmas tree in Honolulu.

"Good evening, my name is Tracy!" I tell the crowd. Our hosts for the evening, an actress who has done some work on *The Young and the Restless* and a local news anchor with a leering mustache, give speeches about the rules and stages of competition while I rush backstage to change into my horrible black and yellow one-piece Body Glove bathing suit—the only women's bathing suit I have ever owned. The judges, we are all told, are "looking for proportion and tone of the body, as well as poise and grace." I have never really thought about any of those four things, so I have no idea how I'll measure up.

There are more indignities to come on this balmy December evening. A middle-aged man in a rented tuxedo escorts me down the two big bleacher steps on the back of the stage, and then to the front, where I pose in my dark navy velour and chiffon dress and my high-heeled pumps and my pinned-up hair for the evening-gown portion of the show. I wonder why I didn't wear my long, highlighted hair down, rather than bunching it up in a big knot. A handful of us are named finalists in the event, and I am the first one picked.

And then it is time for the question that will decide the winner. News Anchor Man approaches me and tells me to "speak right up because Mr. Microphone is not very sensitive." Later that night, other contestants will be asked, "What's your favorite sport?" and, "Tell us about being a cheerleader." One blond girl, who looks ten years older than me gets this question: "What is it about dancing that excites you?" The music "makes you move," she replies. "It's a release from reality." I will not be asked about sports or dancing.

"You are a direct descendent of two U.S. presidents, Benjamin Harrison and William Henry Harrison," says News Anchor Man. "Have they influenced your life?"

I know the answer to this question is yes. I know I should say something like, "They make me proud to be an American," or, "They have given me a reason to be interested in history." But I am fourteen, wearing chiffon, and unable to stop smiling. So I say, "They haven't really influenced my life because it was so far back." News Anchor Man moves on to the cheerleader.

My father was in the audience that day, and I can only imagine how he felt when he heard my uninspired answer, or when, not much later, I lost the title of Miss Teen Hawaii USA to a seventeen-year-old girl who had been flown in from the mainland just for the contest. But I know exactly how I felt to be there. I hated every single moment of the competition. As I stood on that stage and modeled women's wear and smiled so hard that my jaw hurt for days afterward, I knew full well that I was a fraud. I lacked the one basic requirement to be in the pageant—I was not really a Miss.

And yet I also wanted desperately to win. Winning would have made my father proud of me. I was so starved for affection and praise that I was willing to bury the person I was and play a character who was alien to me. Watching that grainy tape today would make me shudder with embarrassment, maybe even horror, but the truth is that I wouldn't even recognize that skinny girl in the puffy dress. I feel no connection to her whatsoever. It would be as if I were watching someone else's home movies. She is not me, and I am not her. If anything, I feel sad for her.

That was my one and only beauty pageant, thankfully, and after that I went back to being a reluctant girlfriend. My next beau was a millionaire's son named Jason. His parents owned an expensive house not far from where I lived, and I wound up there one day as a guest of his sister, a classmate of mine named Melanie. I quickly realized their parents weren't around that afternoon; we had the house to ourselves. There were only a handful of us there, and music was playing, and one boy was mixing drinks. It was not an atmosphere I was used to, and I got a little nervous. Suddenly Jason was standing really close to me; he struck up a conversation. He was holding a drink in his hand, and he looked a little wobbly on his feet. He said that he really liked me and he started kissing me, and I was too shy and nervous to tell him to stop. Finally, he asked me if I would be his girlfriend. Once again, his kissing meant nothing to me. I was fourteen years old, and I had never experienced any sort of sexual awakening. But I did like the feeling of having a boyfriend, and so I said yes. But I dumped Jason after two weeks when I saw him pull a baggie full of weed out of his pocket. I was afraid of drugs, and I didn't want anything to do with anyone who used them.

More boyfriends followed. There was Rocky, who was half-Vietnamese and half-white; I found him appealing because, at last, I found someone who sort of looked like me. Rocky seemed angry all the time, and he didn't make me feel very safe. He liked going into the woods and hurling knives and ninja stars at trees. He crawled through the window of my bedroom one night, and we got into my bed and kissed. For some reason, the kissing made him even angrier, and he crawled back out through the window, and that was that. I couldn't imagine what it was about kissing that could rile him up that way; for me, it was the same as shaking hands. There was no emotional or sexual component to it at all, just as being someone's girlfriend felt the same as being his friend.

Finally, there was Mark, my last high school boyfriend. He had been our paper boy for years, and that made dating him feel kind of weird. But he was also tall and blond and handsome, and all the girls were crazy about him. I no longer fantasized about looking like my mother, or felt afraid that I'd ever be as voluptuous as she was, but I did begin thinking that I would like to have a child who looked like her. Here, suddenly, was the perfect father. Mark was madly in love with me, and when he went away to military school he wrote me long love letters professing his undying devotion. He said he wanted to marry me so we would never be apart. But I felt like we were already spending too much time together as it was. He liked to have me over to his house and just sit and stare into my eyes for hours. He'd say he never wanted me to leave, but I was usually cold or hungry or had to pee, so all I wanted to do was get up and go. He'd say, "Don't you feel the way I do? Don't you feel those butterflies?" I didn't, and I felt bad about that. I wanted to like him, and I even thought about what it would be like to get married right after college and have babies and buy a house—all the things a girl is supposed to dream about. But I just didn't feel anything for him. There was no connection whatsoever; my heart didn't skip a single beat.

In the end, my breakup with Mark was ugly. I heard a rumor from a friend that Mark had raped someone's sister, and though I had no way of knowing whether it was true, I became petrified of him and I refused to see him again, but I never told him why. He was devastated. Eventually, he went into basic training for the army, but he kept sending me long love letters for months. His letters were so desperate, so sad, and I felt terrible about not telling him why I'd broken it off. But in part it was because his love for me was too intense, and it became uncomfortable to be around him. I couldn't understand why he liked me so much. I still had no clue about sexual attraction, so his grand professions of love just seemed strange and scary.

I was nearly finished with high school by then, but emotionally I was still a shy little girl. I was no longer dressing like a boy, but neither was I dolling myself up. Mainly I wore vaguely feminine outfits, like denim shorts with little white tops. I was still a long way from settling into a comfortable identity. But the beginning of my awakening was not all that far off. It would happen half a world away from Hawaii, in an ancient land of love and romance, and it would be my first real step toward becoming who I was meant to be.

Chapter 6

CROSSROADS

Not much survives of my brief, unlikely modeling career. If I dug around deep enough, I could probably find a few yellowing pages from old newspapers and magazines, featuring me in ads for a Liberty House clothing line. I might also occasionally turn up on your TV screen, in reruns of *Jake and the Fat Man* and *Fantasy Island* (look really hard: I was a barely there extra in a few episodes of those cheesy '80s dramas). But aside from that—and the grainy tape of my beauty-pageant fiasco—very little exists, thankfully, to remind me of my awkward glamour stage.

It ended altogether when I graduated from high school and decided to devote myself to academics. An education was going to be my salvation, my ticket out of Hawaii—and away from my father. I was always a good student, in part because I was practically obsessive-compulsive about studying. I'm not sure if I would have been officially diagnosed with OCD, but even as a child I had to face all my Lego creations a certain way and avoid stepping on sidewalk cracks. In my teens I read and reread my school assignments until I was absolutely positive I had memorized everything. As a result, I wound up with a 3.9 GPA and a solid score on my SATs. I was qualified to get into pretty much any college of my choice; my plan was to go to Stanford University, sign up for premed studies, and eventually become a doctor. This plan was twofold: to get me far away from my father, as I mentioned, but also to provide me with a good enough living that I could stay away from him forever.

But then my father tossed a big wrench in my plans. "Tough shit, you cannot leave the islands," he told me one day. "You are too young. If you're going to go to college, you have to do it here." I was only sixteen years old, so I had no say in the matter; I needed his approval to enroll anywhere. I finally settled on the best public school in the islands—the University of Hawaii. As a freshman, I didn't undergo any major transformation. I still dressed as a sort of bland approximation of a woman. I didn't make a whole lot of friends my first year. I kept to myself, studied hard, and enjoyed the feeling of freedom and possibility that is part of the college experience.

But everything changed after my freshman year, on a summer trip to France. Incredibly, my father allowed me to go, probably because I explained to him that it was crucial for my French studies and that it wouldn't cost him anything. I was seventeen, and it was my first time out of the United States—and my first time traveling alone. It was just me and a few other French students, and two French teachers to supervise us all. We spent two amazing weeks in Paris, then set up shop in a town called Annecy in the French Alps. I was absolutely floored by everything—the scenery, the culture, the people. It was all so different for me, such a change from what I was used to in Hawaii. Best of all, I got to see castles, just like the ones in my drawings and fantasies. Those three months in France, away from my father and more or less on my own, were a huge step in my development.

One of the most memorable moments of the trip came from a fellow student. She was a plain-looking, middle-aged woman from somewhere in the South—Alabama, maybe, or Tennessee. She was older, and she didn't stand out in any way. But then one night we all went out on the town, and a couple of students showed up with locals they'd started dating during the summer. When I noticed that the Southern lady was there with another woman, I was taken aback. The Southern lady wasn't especially pretty, but she was definitely feminine, and the woman she was with was heavy-set and kind of rough looking. By then I knew what a lesbian was, or at least I thought I did—I'd somehow concluded that all lesbians looked like this butchy woman. It never occurred to me that a feminine woman could also be a lesbian. Yet here was this Southern lady, holding hands and stealing kisses with another woman. I was totally shocked, and I realized that this was the very first time I had actually *seen* a lesbian. In an instant, my concept of boyfriends and girlfriends was rendered obsolete. This was something different, something else, and it immediately expanded my understanding of human sexuality. I didn't reach any spontaneous conclusions about my own sexuality—it wasn't that kind of "aha!" moment—but seeing this lesbian couple mingling easily with everyone else opened my eyes to a reality I had never fathomed previously.

Then there was my University of Hawaii French teacher—I'll call her Marie. She was in her thirties and small, five-foot-one or so, with curly, light brown hair and a muscular, athletic body. She was into martial arts, and her husband was also an athlete. I remember that she could do a lot of push-ups, which really impressed me. I wasn't sexually attracted to her, or at least I didn't know that I was, but there was definitely a connection between us. During our trip, she gave me a little pin as a present for being such a good student. For me, it was an incredible gesture, and I thought of her not just as a teacher, but also as a friend. I remember wanting to be around her—to spend as much time with her as I could. I was a bit of a teacher's pet, but I didn't care. I was just *drawn* to her. In the past, I had had similar feelings about some of my baby sitters. When I was really little I had a baby sitter named Blythe, who looked just like Blair on *The Facts of Life*: blond, petite, pretty, and curvy. She reminded me of my mom, and I felt an attraction to her. I would crawl all over her, hang off her arms, climb up on her lap—her body was like a magnet to me. Suddenly, in France, I was feeling something similar toward Marie. I didn't recognize it as sexual attraction at the time; I just thought there was something different and special about this feeling I had for her. I remember thinking I had a real crush on her, in a way I had never had on any of my "boyfriends." It was a nonsexual crush, though—I was still a virgin, and I still had practically no awareness of my own sexuality. But it was a real, honest-to-goodness crush, and my attraction to Marie was a wonderful, positive thing.

That summer with Marie marked the beginning of my sexual awakening. My understanding of what it meant to be a lesbian was broadened, and my own feelings of attraction to women came into sharper focus. All those fake kisses that I had shared with Byron and Jason and Mark meant nothing at all to me. But my time around Marie was special, meaningful, *real.* I finally knew what it meant to feel real attraction, real chemistry.

❖ ❖ ❖ ❖ ❖

After France, I decided to travel around Europe on my own. I was seventeen and reveling in my new independence. I bounced around from Austria to Amsterdam, Czechoslovakia, Hungary, Germany, Belgium, Venice—everywhere. In Italy I met a local boy named Luca; he didn't speak any English and I knew no Italian, but within a day of our meeting he let me know he wanted to marry me. He wrote me letters for years after that, but once again my only reaction to a boy's deep feelings for me was puzzlement and disinterest.

One day, on my way to Hungary, a man came up to me in the Munich train station. He sat right next to me and pulled out an English dictionary. He was older, in his thirties or forties, and he didn't speak English very well. He told me his name was Marco and he kept thumbing through his little dictionary and pointing out various words. "Virgin," he said, pointing to the word in his dictionary. I didn't know what to say or do, so I just waited for my train to arrive and then walked away from him. He followed me to the platform and pulled me behind a large sign, out of sight from other commuters. He grabbed my hand roughly and stuck it down his pants; I struggled to get away but he just held me there. I knew I was in a bad situation, but I didn't know what to do. I didn't feel like I could overpower him, so instead I decided to be nice to him, to talk to him and make him think I was interested. In his badly broken English, Marco told me he wanted me to get on a train to Yugoslavia with him. I acted excited and said that I would, but first, I told him, I had to go back to the station to go to the bathroom. I promised him I would be right back, and I sensed that he believed me. As I walked away from him he followed, but at a distance. When I got the chance, I jumped on a departing train. I had no idea where it was headed, and I didn't care. As the doors closed, I saw Marco standing on the platform and I waved at him. I caught myself in that moment, waving without any malice or irony, and I suddenly felt mad. I was relieved that I had escaped him, but I was also mad at myself for having been so nice, for feeling that I *had* to be nice. Here was a man who had accosted me, who might very well have intended to kidnap and even kill me, and there I was, waving at him like he was an old friend. I was frightened by how vulnerable I had been, and I hated that I had been so passive.

As soon as I got back to Hawaii, I started taking karate again. It was a decision that would land me in one of the most important relationships of my life.

❖ ❖ ❖ ❖ ❖

I had already made up my mind to get back into karate as a result of my confrontation with Marco, but that wasn't the only thing. I knew I had to learn how to defend myself better because of my ongoing relationship with my ultimate antagonist, the one who had harmed me most of all—my father.

After my mother's suicide, my father sued the hospital for negligently giving her penicillin. The courts in Hawaii split the suit into two cases, separating my father's grievance into one case and giving my brother and me our own suit against the hospital. My father had trouble winning his case; the hospital's attorneys painted him as villainous and abusive, and thus the reason for my mother's downward spiral. He wound up getting next to nothing, but he was awarded some money to spend specifically on his children. Our case never went to trial; it was settled out of court by a supervising judge. He awarded Anthony close to $400,000, while I received less than a quarter of that. The judge reasoned that Anthony, who was believed to have had attention deficit disorder, would have a harder time making a living and thus needed more help, while I, as he put it, not only was smart but also would likely "find a husband to take care of you." It was as if the inequality of the judge's decision had come directly from my father's mouth, but once again I was powerless to fight back. The best I could do was get a college education—something I knew my mother would have encouraged.

But the settlement money took six years to materialize, and I had to work hard to scrape up around $1,200 to study in France. Of course I spent every nickel of it while I was there, and wound up back in the airport in Hawaii without any money to get home. My father said he would pick me up, but when I arrived he was nowhere in sight. I was dirty, exhausted, and physically burnt out, and all I wanted to do was take a shower and sleep in my own bed. I had bought a heavy faux-marble chess set in Venice and for weeks had carried it around in my backpack, and I felt like I couldn't even lift my bag anymore. I waited an hour or so, without any sign of my father. Finally, I rooted around in my bags for a quarter to call him with. I came up empty, though, and had to panhandle for it. I called home and my father picked up, sounding surprised to hear from me. He clearly hadn't made note of my return date. When I told him I needed a ride, he said he was on his way to the movies with his girlfriend, and that I'd have to make my way home on my own. I cried and pleaded with him, but he told me to shut up and finally just hung up on me. I knew why he was acting this way. He resented me for taking the trip; he always felt that I thought I was somehow better than everyone else, that I had some misguided sense of superiority. "We live in paradise," he'd say. "Besides, I already went to Europe for you." Leaving me stranded in the airport was his way of bringing me back to earth.

Fortunately, Marie saw me bawling and offered to drive me home. Things remained tense between my father and me for weeks. I think both of us sensed that our long, difficult relationship was inexorably coming to an end, but I was still his daughter and I still depended on him for many things, including money. Though I was in college, I was still wearing outfits I'd worn back in seventh grade. I needed to buy new clothes, and since my settlement money hadn't yet arrived, I went to my father's bedroom and explained to him that I needed new clothes. Then I asked him for a loan. My father muttered something, but it was clear he didn't want to give me any money. I kept asking; he kept hemming and hawing. Finally,

I brought up the settlement. I knew that he had been awarded some money that he could use only for my care. "What about that money?" I asked him. "You're supposed to use that money for me." My father stood up from his chair, grabbed me by the shoulders, and started to push me out of his bedroom. Money has always been a sore subject for him; many of his relatives have had issues with him about finances. All I was doing was asking him to be a father to me, but he saw it as an accusation that he was hoarding money, and that was like pressing his rage button. His grip tightened on my shoulders and he pushed me into the hallway, toward the top of the stairs. I struggled, but that only made him push me harder. I grasped the bedroom doorframe and held on for dear life. I felt like if I let go, he would push me right down the stairs. My father—strong, sinewy, relentless like a shark and scary as that moray eel—pushed as hard as he could, and finally my fingertips slipped from the frame. Now there was nothing for me to grab on to but the railing of the stairs. I reached for it, but my father gave me one final push, and then I was gone.

I tumbled down seventeen stairs and landed in a heap at the bottom. It happened as if in slow motion—I knew that I had flown right over the top four stairs before landing hard and tumbling over and over; I felt my head smash against the railing and my left foot turn in a weird way beneath me. When it was over, I looked up and saw my father at the top of the stairs. The man there was, to me, a demon—the devil himself. He was flushed, face red, chest heaving, breathing heavy. He looked perfectly capable of the ultimate sin of man—murder. This was the stuff of my nightmares, the ones in which my father would chase me and stab me or punch me or shoot me until I was dead. I cried, but no sound came out, at least not for a few seconds. Finally I sobbed, because I didn't know what else to do. My neck was sore and my foot was throbbing. I wailed, as much out of fear of his rage as from the terrible pain I felt. "Shut your fucking mouth," my father said.

When it all subsided, I tried to get up but I couldn't. I told my father that I needed to go to the hospital for my ankle. We drove in silence to Kaiser medical center, where X-rays confirmed that my ankle was broken. My father told the doctors that I had tripped, and when they asked me what had happened, I confirmed his story. I had been in this position before. I had once told some police officers who came to our house that my father beat me, and that's how I learned that if I complained too much, I would wind up in foster care. That seemed an even worse fate than being beaten, and so here I shut up and played along. I was put in a cast and given crutches to hobble home on. The look on my father's face at the top of the stairs that day is the look he now wears in my dreams. It is a look of pure hatred, an evil, killing look. As soon as my ankle healed, I went straight to the Marina Athletic Club in Honolulu and signed up for karate classes.

❖ ❖ ❖ ❖ ❖

My instructor was a short, stocky black belt named Ron. He had trained under Chuck Norris, and had even done stunt work in martial-arts movies like Jean-Claude Van Damme's *No Retreat, No Surrender.* He brought a flashy new style of karate with him from Hollywood to Hawaii, and he was able to attract a lot of students to his studio at the athletic club. Physically, he wasn't all that formidable. He was half-Italian with lots of thick brown hair, lots of hair on his chest. He was thirty-five years old, around five-foot-seven, and he was burly, not lean, with a barrel chest and a little stomach paunch. He looked like he could have been a longshoreman, or maybe a taxi driver.

But on the mats, he was incredible. He had freakishly large calves, so big that people accused him of getting calf implants. And he had slightly webbed toes—the result, he claimed, of his mother's drinking throughout her pregnancy. He also had impossibly sturdy shins; when I kicked them to try to get his feet out from under him, it felt like kicking a fire hydrant. He had exceptional balance, and he was nearly impossible to take down. I don't remember anyone ever getting him off his feet in hundreds of sparring matches. What's more, he was deceptively quick for such a stocky man. He could move from side to side, change directions, and execute a spinning kick with astonishing speed, and his hands shot free from his body as if they were spring-loaded. On top of all of that, Ron was cocky and self-assured. He had a way of walking on the balls of his feet that made him seem taller than he was. He had an aura about him, a palpable charisma, and he liked to spout slogans and phrases to emphasize his dominance. "I am the master of time and space," he would proclaim. He was, indeed, a master of movement, and as a teacher he knew how to maximize time and get his point across efficiently. He had a reputation for taking students into tournaments and producing winners. Ron was dazzling to his students and he knew it, and his swelled head and robust confidence were part of the whole Ron package. I must admit it: I was dazzled by him, too.

Even though I had studied karate for three years in grade school, I started over as a white belt in Ron's class. Still, I was able to pick up the old skills quickly and progress much faster than the other students. Ron took notice of this, and he paid special attention to me. He'd watch me closely, correct my movements, and pull me aside and show me techniques. I appreciated the attention, and it felt good because it meant I was doing something right. Before long, Ron had me breaking off with some of the students and teaching them moves and techniques. I became his second-in-command. Then one Saturday, after a long and grueling class, Ron pulled me aside.

"Do you want to go on a date with me?" he asked. "Come over to my house, and we'll watch a movie or go out and eat."

I was shocked. I was only seventeen, and he knew it. Besides, he was my sensei, and the idea of dating seemed weird and wrong. Whatever feelings I had for him were not sexual; I was impressed by his mastery and I enjoyed his attention, but I felt no attraction to him beyond that. Still, my history had been to say yes whenever any boy asked me out. Part of it was not wanting to be rude or mean. Part of it was feeling like I was being accepted. Ron's asking me on a date felt different, though, far more serious than some grade schooler begging to be my boyfriend. I wanted to say no, but I also didn't want to upset my sensei. I reasoned that there wasn't any danger in saying yes, and I agreed to the date.

The next weekend, I made my way to his apartment in downtown Waikiki. It was actually his grandmother's apartment; she was letting him stay there while she lived somewhere else. It was a small, bare one-bedroom, with a kitchenette, a tiny TV, an old sofa, and not much more. I was beyond nervous; I didn't know what to expect or what I was getting into. I wore blue jeans and a white top, and I don't remember if I tried to make myself look pretty. Most likely, I didn't. Ron and I sat on the sofa and watched TV and talked. He told me that I was his most special student, that I had real talent, that I was able to do things that no other female student had ever done. Looking back, he was circling me, grooming me, softening me up. But at the time it felt good to hear those things. That night, Ron paid me a compliment that remains among the greatest of my life.

"You fight like a man," he said.

That was exactly what I wanted to hear. Inside I felt like a man, and I wanted to be able to defend myself like a man. Ironically, in flattering me this way, Ron was breaking down my defenses, too.

Our third date started just as the first two had. He pulled his rusty two-door compact Honda Civic out of his grandmother's slender parking stall and left it on the street so I could wedge my gray-blue station wagon into the space. We sat on his sofa and talked about karate. About an hour or so into the date, though, Ron suddenly put his hand on mine, leaned toward me, and kissed me on the lips. I can't say I was shocked; all of my previous boyfriends had made the same move. So I kissed him back. As usual, I didn't feel anything— no explosions, no fireworks. I was simply playing along.

But then Ron took me by the hand and led me into his cramped and stuffy bedroom: two crummy twin beds pushed together, mismatched sheets, a closet with no door and dirty shirts spilling out of it, a rickety lamp, a little fan, an old stained sheet instead of a window shade. The walls were cinder block, painted a dull white and host to not a single poster or picture. The whole place had a worn, stale smell. Fazed not a whit by such a miserable setting, Ron laid me on the bed and lowered himself on top of me. He lifted off my shirt and kissed my tiny breasts. I was hyperaware of everything, yet also removed from the moment, as if I were watching it all happen from the sidelines. I knew what was coming next, and I knew that I would be submitting to it. Sure enough, Ron lowered my pants and began to go down on me. I stared up at the cement ceiling and wondered what he was doing. Who had told him to do such a thing? What was it supposed to accomplish? I felt some physical sensation down there, but overall the effect was unsettling. Before long he stopped what he was doing and lowered his pants. He didn't take them off; he just kept them bunched around his ankles. Then he was on top of me, and he pushed himself inside. I was shocked and ashamed but I just lay there, betraying nothing. The pain was excruciating, and the way he was pressing on me, pushing, grunting, made me want to cry. He kissed me again and I turned my head away; he kissed my neck and his stubble felt rough, like sandpaper. This went on for a minute or two—he thrusting, prodding, taking, I lying there and wishing it were over. Soon enough, with a throaty groan, it was over. Ron rolled off me and lay there, half-naked but unembarrassed. With his pants around his ankles, and in the strained silence of that dingy bedroom, he fell asleep.

I figured this meant I was supposed to spend the night, and I did. The next morning he scrambled eggs and told me he wanted to be in a committed relationship with me. After all, he now owned a part of me.

"It's better if we keep it a secret from everyone at the club," he said. "You're underage, and it's better that no one knows."

And so I became Sensei Ron's girlfriend. Why did I agree to everything if I felt nothing for him? Why did I so passively slip right into the role of his latest conquest, especially since I wasn't getting anything out of it? I suppose because I *was* getting something out of it. Ron had a lot to teach me, and I wanted to learn it all. Karate was helping me feel confident again, and the better I got under Ron's tutelage, the more quickly I would be able to defend myself against my father. I surely would have learned and improved under any qualified sensei, and I didn't stay with Ron merely to get top-notch instruction. But his obvious mastery, and his attentiveness to me, made me vulnerable to him. I wanted to be as good and strong and masterful as he was. I felt a real urgency to be able to overpower my father, because I truly believed that one day he would try to kill me.

I also felt that Ron had a good, solid plan for his life, and I was flattered that I was now a part of it. He was so confident, so cocky, and I got swept up in his oratory. I look back and I feel disappointed in myself for not being stronger—for being so vulnerable that someone like Ron could take command of me the way he did. But I also realize that I was only seventeen years old, and it's hard to have a good, critical perspective of what's going on at that age.

I wound up moving into Ron's grandmother's apartment. I got so wrapped up in Ron's life—I was his girlfriend, his workout partner, his karate assistant—that I even neglected to enroll in classes at the University of Hawaii for the fall semester of my sophomore year. I ended up taking two entire years off. I had the feeling that my life was out of control, that I was merely hanging on to Ron by a shirtsleeve while he lived his busy, full-speed life packed with things that only he wanted to do. I helped him when he decided he wanted to get into film production; I went with him to rehearsals and gigs when he put together a band. When the first installment of my settlement money finally came through, I used it to pay for rent and food and clothes for Ron. I kept stacks of $100 bills in a tiny toy safe, with a combination lock that didn't even work and a door that was barely on its hinges. Ron, the master of time and space, couldn't seem to keep his weight down, so I paid for him to have liposuction. He was drastically concerned with his body image, and shedding his stomach paunch was vitally important to him. Never mind that he liked to sit on the sofa and eat a whole bag of miniature Chips Ahoy cookies out of the bag with chopsticks. He wanted the liposuction, so I got it for him. I even took him to Europe because he wanted to meet his distant family in Germany. I paid for everything, and actually believed him when he promised to pay me back. Ron always had money problems because he refused to work for anyone or hold a typical job. He wanted to live by his own rules, and he wanted to be the boss. That was one of the reasons why he was attracted to me: He liked me because I was Asian, and because he believed all Asian women were submissive.

In this way, I fell effortlessly into Ron's routines and totally out of my own. He watched *David Letterman,* so I did too; he loved football, so I tried to learn its rules. We did have a few things in common: He spoke some French, so we practiced the language together. And, of course, there was karate; we constantly worked out and honed routines. I respected Ron, and I thought of him as a friend. I had never had a man in my life offer me positive attention, and because of that I developed real feelings toward Ron. I became emotionally dependent on him and on his compliments and attention. Naturally, when I told my father that I was moving in with Ron, he put his particularly ugly spin on it. "Finally, you're with a man," he said. "I knew all you needed was a little cock."

And the sex? I hated it, but I felt like it was the price of being in a relationship. It was a chore, just like sweeping or washing the dishes. Never once in my three-plus years with Ron did I feel any romantic attachment to him. I endured the sex as best I could, though I also tried to avoid it whenever possible. But Ron was insistent. He liked having sex, and having it often; he also enjoyed sex that had an edge of hostility. I noticed that he liked throwing me down on the bed and being rough with me. One time he had me dress up in my old Girl Scout uniform before ripping it off. Occasionally I would merely be standing near the bedroom when he'd grab me and push me into the room and toss me on the bed. There was never any foreplay; Ron liked getting right down to business. And because I was never, ever aroused, the sex was always miserable. There was no lubrication, and my privates were always bruised and often bleeding.

Yet the more I resisted—the more I told Ron that I didn't want to have sex, or that it didn't feel good—the more inspired he became to take me forcibly. Sex between us became unmistakably antagonistic, and that played right into Ron's dark side. I don't remember precisely when it happened, but Ron became abusive to me, and not just during sex. Our relationship dynamic changed into one of dominance and submission. He would push me and pin me down, crush me with his weight, and take my breath away. Sometimes he would punch me; sometimes his rough play left my knees and thighs bruised. I was miserable in the relationship, and I grew more and more depressed. For all the things we had in common, and all the simple satisfactions that I found in having a boyfriend, I always sensed my potential to move beyond the glass ceiling of our relationship. I wanted to finish college and go places, live a big, bold life. Ron was happy teaching karate and playing in his garage band. I knew I had to get away from him—I just didn't know how.

Incredibly, I escaped to—of all places—my father's house. I reenrolled in college and began spending nights at home on the pretense of having to study or get up early for class. Gradually, I spent fewer and fewer nights with Ron. I got back into the groove of meeting new people at school, and slowly some of my appetite for the outside world came back. Ron saw these changes in me, and he wasn't happy about them. I became distant, colder, less friendly toward him, and some weeks I spent only a night or two at his apartment. What's more, I stopped dressing in the feminine way that he preferred. When he insisted that I wear something feminine so we could go out, I always picked the same pink dress and high leather boots; I felt like a prostitute in that getup. I always kept my hair long for Ron, too, the way he liked it. But part of my distancing myself from him involved my wearing blue jeans or workout pants and simple T-shirts—sometimes I even wore Ron's clothes. Then, one day, I cut my hair really short. I showed up at his apartment and Ron's face just dropped. He shook his head, resigned, angry, frustrated. That may have been the moment he realized we were finished as a couple, that he had lost me, or perhaps never had me to begin with. Sadly, we were not quite through.

Ron's aggressiveness toward me got even worse because of the way I dressed. He would belittle and berate me more often, handle me even harder. "Why are you wearing that?" he'd demand. "Why are you dressing like a man? Are you attracted to women? What are you, a lesbo?" One day when Ron was over at my father's house, he looked under my bed and found a journal I was keeping.

Everything was in there, all my negative thoughts about him and about our unhappy relationship. "He calls me bitch, respect is fading. He gets upset if he can't control me," read one entry. "With him I am by myself. I feel like I am drowning. I've become someone else. I've become him." Ron locked himself in the bathroom and read it while I pounded on the door and begged him to stop. Finally he came out and tossed the journal on the floor. He lashed out at me, called me names, then stormed out. We didn't speak for several days. I figured the relationship was over.

Still, I had to return to his apartment to get the remainder of my things. When I got there, Ron sat me down and said he wanted to talk to me. He told me how disappointed he was in me, how he had made me the person I was, and how I was now betraying him. But he also said that he wanted to try to make things work, that he didn't want to lose me. I felt compelled to soften the blow, so instead of saying we were through, I agreed that we would have a trial separation. Before long, both of us were crying, but I thought the worst was behind us, and that our final breakup was right around the corner.

I was right, but not in the way I expected. I went into the bedroom to gather some of my things, and suddenly Ron was standing in the doorway. He moved closer to me and had me cornered. He told me he wanted to have sex; I answered that there was no way that would happen. Ron, so quick and clean with his chops, balled his fist and gave me a swift uppercut to the stomach. I never saw it coming, and it knocked the wind out of me. I doubled over, gasping, unable to catch my breath. When I could finally breathe, it hurt like crazy to even draw in air. My mind filled with images of my father pushing me down the stairs. Here it was, happening again, a man trying to grind me into submission.

All the work that I had done to learn how to defend myself was not, at this crucial moment, helping in any way. I was crumpled over, crying like a baby, completely vulnerable. I tried to get up to leave, but Ron just pushed me back onto the bed and jumped on top of me. I struggled against him, pushed as hard as I could, but it was no use. Halfway through the rape, I stopped struggling at all.

When it was over, Ron grabbed some sleeping pills from the bedside table and forced them into my mouth. I swung meekly at him, tried to spit up the pills, but I was already broken. He wanted me to fall asleep and spend the night, like I used to. Every ounce of my being wanted to leave, but I couldn't; I was powerless. This was my nightmare come to pass. I drifted off into a groggy, anxious sleep.

Ron had left me bruised and bloodied many times before. He would take sex whenever he wanted it and then say, "I can't rape you—we're boyfriend and girlfriend. No one will believe you." But this assault was the worst one yet. When I came to in the morning, I tiptoed around Ron's slumped body and grabbed as many of my possessions as I could. I didn't want another scene; I just wanted to get out of there. But then he was up, yelling again, trying to stop me from leaving. I managed to slip past him and out the front door, and for a few seconds it looked like he might not chase me. The minute I hit the street, I started running as fast as I could; I took a look behind me and saw Ron at the bottom of the building. I watched as he took two small steps and started running toward me. His first chilling burst of speed was feral, predatory; I knew in that instant that I was going to be hurt some more. I ran as fast as I could, but with every glance backward I saw that Ron was gaining quickly. Finally, I just stopped and turned toward him, figuring that he would stop running, too. But instead he leapt into the air and executed a perfect flying side kick into my stomach. I crashed to the ground and saw him standing over me, just as my father had. Before he could pounce again, though, I rolled to my side, got on my feet, and ran straight across four lanes of traffic on Ala Wai Boulevard. I dodged cars, yelled for help, pointed behind me at Ron. He was sprinting again, relentless, determined. I ran back toward his apartment and tried to quickly get into my car, which was parked on the street; Ron jumped on its hood, kicking the keys out of my hand. I took a defensive stance and tried to stop the punches and kicks, but he was too good, too fast. I picked up my keys and stuck them between my fingers; Ron tried to kick them away again and I cut his shin. Finally, as cars screeched to a stop in the street and pedestrians yelled at Ron to back off, a police car pulled up. I told the officer I was trying to leave Ron, and that he wouldn't let me. I was a twenty-year-old woman, 135 pounds; Ron was thirty-eight and 205—clearly the aggressor. But because the officer noticed blood on Ron's shin, he arrested us both.

Ron and I sat in adjacent jail cells, saying nothing. Before long, we were released. A few months later, the arrest was expunged from my record. Looking back on those difficult days, it's easy to see the symbolism of walking out of that jail cell. I was doing more than just leaving Ron behind; I was turning my back on the person I had become as well. For far too long I had locked myself up in an inauthentic persona, one based more on other people's expectations of me than on my own feelings and desires. When I walked out of that jail cell, I left all that behind. I was—at last—free to be myself.

Chapter 7

PASSION

The entry to my brave new world was a stuffy little room in the Honolulu YWCA. One Wednesday night in 1994, I took a deep breath and walked in, knees wobbling with nerves. A few people had already gathered for the lesbian support group, which I'd read about in the University of Hawaii's campus newspaper, but I kept my head down and waited for whoever was in charge to get things started. Soon there were a dozen of us milling about, and we were instructed to arrange our chairs in a circle and sit down. For the next hour I did nothing but listen, but with each passing minute, the world as I knew it cracked and crumbled a little more.

The way the women were sharing that night—the deep, nuanced emotions they were struggling to articulate—was like a new and exotic language that mysteriously made sense to me. I still wasn't sure I was one of them, but I knew that I could be, that these women's stories might well forecast the way my own story would unfold. The journals I had been keeping were already full of urgent but vaguely expressed thoughts not unlike those of the women surrounding me. It was as if these eleven other women were speaking directly to me.

Many of the new friends I'd been making at the University of Hawaii were women, and in the aftermath of my summer in France, my friends were almost exclusively women. I suddenly became aware of the way I would notice women around me—the way I would look at a woman across a classroom and feel, I don't know, something. I'd never focused on a guy that way; men were just part of the scenery for me. But women were different—I *noticed* them. I paid attention to how they moved, how they smiled, how they dressed. The more I broadened my world and invited in new experiences, the more observant I became about the allure of certain women. And, for the first time, I realized that my interest in women, and my attraction to them, was unequivocally sexual in nature. Yes, I'd had a couple of crushes on women in the past. There was Marie, my French teacher. And there was an aerobics instructor I worked with on a fitness video when I was in my teens. She was tall and strikingly beautiful, with lush dark hair and a personality that was larger than life. She was famous in the fitness community, and I did everything I could to be near her before and after the filming of our video. But I never questioned or tried to understand my feelings for either of those women. I was too young and too naive to realize what was truly happening.

But now, in college, there was no denying it: I was starting to realize that women stirred something in me that men never had. In the past, I had left my feelings unexamined and buried myself in my books, rather than dwell on the matter of my sexuality, whatever it might be. I had the sense that it was time for me to address my sexuality head-on. It was time to examine these feelings and figure out exactly who I was and where I was heading—which was what led me to a lesbian support group in the first place.

At the end of that first group, I still wasn't completely comfortable calling myself a lesbian, though I suspected I was. But I had been inspired to find out the truth once and for all. I knew that kissing boys did nothing for me. What would it feel like to kiss a girl? The support group turned out to be an important step for me in my path to figuring out my own sexuality. I had a lot of questions, after all: What would it feel like to actually be with a woman? What if I simply wasn't attracted to men *or* to women? What if I never found a girlfriend?

But the second or third meeting I went to, I noticed a girl I knew sitting in the circle of chairs. She was in my history class, even though we'd never spoken to each other before. I'd noticed her plenty of times, and had paid attention to her as she walked into our lecture hall on campus; she was short, just under five feet, but she had a curvy body. She had amazing, puffy blond hair—so long and curly and boisterous, it seemed to walk into class a few feet in front of her. She also had an air of confidence. It was the way she walked: directly and sure of where she was going. She wore big black military boots and didn't seem to mind that she attracted unwelcome stares. At first I wasn't all that attracted to her, but rather was intrigued. At the end of the support group that night, I decided to talk to her regardless. I liked the idea that someone from one of my classes—someone like me—was here in the group, looking for help, searching for answers. So many of the women in that circle were longtime lesbians who talked about their relationships and other issues; I sensed that Jody was a lesbian I could learn something from: She was secure, confident, and also the same age as me. We talked for a while that night and became instant friends.

After a week of having lunch and working out together, Jody invited me to her house in Kailua, where she lived with her parents. We were only friends, but because I knew she was a lesbian, the dynamic was different—there was a strange and exciting charge in the air. It seemed inevitable that we would kiss. The night unfolded slowly, with our talking and getting to know each other better. We lay in her bed for hours, and eventually, sure enough, we kissed.

Kissing Jody was, in a word, amazing. I felt a weird, electrical charge shoot through my body, instantly warming me from head to toe. I got butterflies. Lots of them. My butterflies got butterflies. I felt a little woozy, dizzy almost, as if my brain were about to explode. I was afraid but also thrilled, confused but also giddy. It was real, honest-to-goodness emotion, raw and unfiltered, and it was overwhelming. All of those kisses I had shared with past boyfriends had been so cold and absent of feeling that I was wholly unprepared for what happened to me when I kissed Jody. I was *consumed* by that kiss, and I surrendered to it without thinking or reasoning or doing much of anything besides *being*. Afterward, my only thought was: *Wow, what a difference from kissing guys!* No scratchy stubble, nothing aggressive about it. Jody's lips were soft and her kiss was gentle, and in that remarkable kiss I was able to put the final seal on my sexuality. No more denying or ignoring what was real for me. In that moment I discovered myself.

Jody and I stopped hanging out shortly after that first kiss. It had been a powerful thing, but at the same time I wasn't truly attracted to Jody, and the kiss had been more about a mutual curiosity. I don't think either of us believed we were each other's soulmate. I wrote Jody a long letter and a poem, telling her how much meeting her had meant to me. I'm sure she'll never know how much that single kiss changed my life. It was one of those markers in life that I can pinpoint as a catalyst, an event that helped me to better understand myself, and to start my new life.

❖ ❖ ❖ ❖ ❖

I met Christine at the Metropolis, a lesbian bar in downtown Honolulu. I was there with four friends I'd met through an acquaintance at the gym. I was still uncertain about how I was going to go about expressing my sexual orientation. I felt less than clear about the protocol around lesbian dating, and yet here I was, eager to explore my curiosity about women. I could only hope that my instincts would kick in and that there'd be a woman I wanted to talk to at the bar.

I'd been to Metropolis a couple of times before, and I had mostly enjoyed the sensation of being in a room filled with lesbians. I wanted to see what was out there, and what better place than a gay bar? I watched a tall blond walk by me hand in hand with another woman, and then I realized that I knew her—it was Alison. She worked with me at Costco. I had a mad crush on her, but had only dreamed that she was gay. Now I was not only shocked to realize she was, but also disappointed that I didn't have a chance with her.

My mood dropped, and I ordered a Zima and sat morosely on my stool. It was one thirty in the morning, a half hour before closing. I had time for one more drink and maybe, if I were lucky, a dance. But truthfully, I didn't feel like doing much of anything.

And right then, as I was stewing over my predicament, she appeared. I heard her before I saw her—a soft voice with a hint of a Southern accent.

"Do you wanna dance?"

I looked up. She was blond and gorgeous, with a friendly face and a shy little smile. She was wearing blue jeans and a maroon long-sleeved shirt with what looked like a Mexican tapestry on it. The shirt was unbuttoned low, and I could see her white sports bra peeking through. Against her tanned skin she wore a necklace with a silver dolphin charm. Her hair was down and long, past her shoulders. She seemed innocent, uncomplicated. It took me several seconds to catch my breath.

"Sure," I said, trying to sound nonchalant. Actually, I was stunned that someone so beautiful would ask me to dance. She took me by the hand and led me to the far side of the floor.

"Do you know how to dance?" she asked when I didn't join her in her movement to the beat.

"Yes, I believe so," I said. How formal of me. How stupid. But I was lucky that I managed to say anything at all. I started to move my feet. The song was midtempo, and we swayed to the rhythm, the strobe lights bouncing off her silky hair.

"My name's Christine," she said.

I wasn't dancing at all like myself; I felt awkward, dazed, out of sync. Maybe it was the Zimas, but more likely it was Christine. I fell into some kind of trance while staring at her necklace. I wanted desperately to reach out and touch it and take a better look. She pulled my face close to hers and leaned into my ear so she could be heard over the music. "I'm gay. Are you?"

I nodded. So there it was. I was a lesbian.

After the dance Christine gave me a warm, close hug that lingered for a long moment. The feeling of her hair brushing against my cheek made me weak. I simply couldn't believe that this was happening—that someone whom I actually liked, who was my type, was also interested in me. She asked me if we could meet again at the bar the next night, but I had to work, so we agreed to meet the following Friday. We slowly let go of each other's hands, but neither of us looked away. We held each other's gazes as we stepped farther and farther apart, until finally we each disappeared into the crowd. *Is this a dream?* I thought to myself. The bar was closing, and the bright lights flickered on. But then the DJ announced there was time for one more song, and the lights turned down and the strobe came back on and a good, slow song blared over the speakers.

Time for one more dance.

I didn't dare chase after Christine and ask her for the last dance. But then Sachi, one of the friends I'd come with, grabbed me by the hand and pulled me across the bar, practically knocking over stools in her haste. She led me right up to where Christine was talking with two friends, then turned on her heel and left me there.

"We don't have to dance if you don't want to," I said to Christine, embarrassed by the way Sachi had dragged me over to her.

"No, I would like to," she said.

We rocked slowly from side to side, completely off the beat. We held each other close, my hands around her waist and hers on my back. Her touch was soft, tender. Quietly, she whispered to me, "I think I'm getting used to being gay."

I looked straight into her eyes and said, "So am I."

After the last dance, outside the bar, I got up the courage to touch her necklace and look at it more closely. It was actually two dolphins intertwined. In the harsh streetlight outside the club, Christine was even more beautiful, more alluring. "Next Friday," she said as we said our goodbyes again. "I promise, I promise," I told her. "I'll be here." We hugged one last time and I walked toward my car where my friends were already waiting. When I turned my back, I heard her say, "Please, God, let her get home safely."

❖ ❖ ❖ ❖ ❖

I still couldn't believe what had just happened. Christine and I had been so instantly attracted to each other—it was exhilarating. I don't think I stopped smiling for a second on the drive home. I thought about her nonstop the rest of the week and couldn't wait for Friday to arrive. My feelings were so new, so strong, that I feverishly wrote a poem for her. My plan was to give it to her at the bar. "Her beauty called my soul to smile," the poem began. "I pinched myself/How could this be?/Why would she/Look twice at me?" put on black, pleated dress pants and a blue silk top and pulled my hair back. I was trying a new look at this point. This was my "tweener" phase, when I was sporting a *GQ* look of sorts, trying on androgyny and masculinity and figuring out what kind of style I was going for

in my newfound identity. Looking back, I looked more like someone who was trying to figure out who she was, but on that Friday
I tried to look extra hot, and I spent a lot of time fussing over my
appearance.

When I finally got to Metropolis, I nearly ran inside to look for
Christine. I saw her right away and snuck up behind her. I tapped
her on the right shoulder, then ducked to her left. Then, just like
a little kid, I tapped her on the left shoulder and ducked the other
way. I immediately felt embarrassed about the way I was acting,
but I was excited, and I felt giddy and not completely myself.

Finally I spun her around and said, "It's me!"

"Me who?" was her reply.

I am sure I visibly crumbled. My beaming, weeklong smile
fell away. I wondered if she'd been in a drunken stupor the week
before. She didn't even remember me, and all I'd done all week
was think about her incessantly. I had never gone from elation to
devastation that quickly in my life.

"Oh, Tracy, it's you!" she said. "You look so different with your
hair back."

My smile returned. My heart bounced off the floor and back
into my chest. True emotions, I quickly learned, are *really* intense.
This was going to be interesting.

Christine and I spent the whole night talking and dancing. I
finally got up the courage to give her my poem, and she slipped away
to the bathroom to read it. When she came back I expected her to be
bowled over by the depth of my feelings, but all she said was, "It's not
bad for an amateur." I would soon learn that Christine liked to mix
things up, to be challenging. She was a bit of a trash talker, especially
when she played pool, and she could be sarcastic. But I was already

smitten. Christine was beautiful and feminine, yet not too dainty or demure. She wasn't curvy or a bombshell; she was a surfer, and her body was lean and athletic. She was like me in many ways, except she was the opposite of me—blond to my brunette, blunt where I was shy. "She has me bound by magic spell" went another line in my poem. And it was true. For the first time, I was in love.

On our second date, we walked along Waikiki Beach and stayed up all night looking up at the stars. In a bath of moonlight, we shared our first kiss. It was electrifying, a jolt to my every sense. We talked all night, about our feelings, our lives, our hopes, everything. The chemistry was incredible—I had never been in a relationship like this before, in which both people felt the same way about each other. Yet here we were, both of us clearly smitten. What thrilled me most of all was the way she expressed her affection for me, the way she looked at me and played with my hair. I noticed that sometimes she was nervous to be around me, as if she, too, couldn't believe her good fortune. This was a feeling I could certainly relate to. Sometimes she was jittery, unsure of herself, as if she was overly anxious about being liked. She tried hard to show off for me, cooking for me and planning romantic evenings. She was wooing me, and I felt incredibly flattered. Part of me felt bad to see her so intense and nervous in my presence, but part of me felt wonderful, because I felt the same way about her. I wanted more than anything for her to like me, so we were a perfect match for each other at that point in our lives—both of us tentative in our newly discovered sexuality and both of us marveling at being with someone we were so intensely attracted to.

After two weeks of full-blown infatuation, we finally found ourselves alone in the small two-bedroom apartment she shared with her brother in Kailua. Christine was going to be starting at the University of Hawaii in the fall, where I'd be resuming my junior year. It was exciting to think that we were going to be in college together; it made us feel even more like a couple. Still, I had never had sex with a woman, and though Christine had, she was still figuring out her own sexuality, too. I was really nervous that night in her apartment. I had no idea what to do or what to expect. But once we lowered the lights and started kissing, instinct took over. Every move I made felt right, every time we touched felt magical. I stopped thinking and started feeling. I allowed myself to be completely consumed by what I was doing. It was unlike anything I had ever experienced. There was a rawness to it, an urgency, and in that way it was just like my poem—overheated but sweet. More than anything, I felt alive—truly alive. We made love for hours, straight through to morning, and I can't remember how many times we said we loved each other. Any doubts I might have had about being a lesbian, or about wanting to be with Christine, vanished. I knew I wanted to be with her, not just that night but forever. Was this just a case of over-the-top, impossibly sappy puppy love? Perhaps. But on that night I felt like I was part of a great epic romance, and I truly believed Christine and I would do everything in our power to feel this way for the rest of our lives. We weren't tied or devoted to anything other than each other. We would just follow this love, wherever it might take us.

❖ ❖ ❖ ❖ ❖

Passion awakened is a powerful thing. It not only transforms the way you feel but also the way you think and see and live. It changes everything. For me, these were more than welcome changes; I felt in touch with myself and my body in a way I'd never been before. Passion remakes you into a whole new being—fuller, more robust, more alive. But one thing passion does not make you is clear-eyed about what is real.

When school started in the fall, Christine and I moved into a dorm room and started our lives together. We pushed the two single beds together and turned the tiny room into a home. All we had was a small TV, a primitive computer, a couple of wire racks to hang clothes on, and a bunch of framed photos of us. But the feeling of setting up house as a couple was wonderful. We'd walk to classes together and help each other study; I was majoring in health science and Christine was focused on psychology. I was finally in a relationship that was based on mutual attraction and respect, and I couldn't have been happier. I believed I had found something pure, precious, and perfect, and that all I had to do to enjoy it was wake up every day.

About a year into our relationship, though, I began to notice cracks in the perfect illusion I'd been so invested in. One problem in particular was potentially a big one. It started when we were at Fusion, a gay bar in Honolulu, late one night, enjoying the club's raucous energy. Male strippers and other people were performing, and the music was loud and pulsing. For a while Christine and I got separated, dancing with different friends, until I finally went looking for her. I turned a corner in the crowded club and I saw her pressed up against a wall, kissing someone else—a man—quite passionately. Her eyes were heavy-lidded and nearly closed. I stood there, rooted to a spot, in absolute shock. I could not believe what I was seeing, and I felt a surge of anger that made me want to punch the wall. Not even Ron had cheated on me in such a blatant way, and as I watched Christine and this strange man together, I felt as if my world were being turned upside down. All of those big, bold, powerful feelings I felt for her turned, in an instant, into equally powerful negative emotions. How could she do this to me? How could she do this to us?

We went home together that night but didn't talk about what had happened. The next morning, Christine apologized and said it meant nothing. She explained that she had had too much to drink and had just been having fun. I didn't think that what had happened was insignificant, but I still wanted to fix things and move on with our life together. So I forgave her, and I promised I could put it behind me. But just a few days later I saw her kissing someone else— this time a woman—in a nightclub. Once again, I felt a terrible, disorienting blast of pain, as if I had been kicked flush in the stomach. My legs felt weak and I feared I might just slump to the ground. And then I felt angry again, like I wanted to fight back. I didn't like feeling hurt; I had vowed long ago not to sit idly by while someone tried to do me harm. But all of the skills I had learned in karate class—all of the moves I had practiced a thousand times so that they would protect me from my father's punches—were utterly useless to me in that moment. I didn't know how to protect my heart, and a blow to the heart hurts more than any other wound.

Of course, Christine apologized again and swore the kiss was meaningless. "We were just having fun, that's all," she said. "You know I still love you." I did believe that she still loved me, but somehow that wasn't enough. I told Christine that I didn't want to see her for a while, and I moved out of our dorm room and back into my father's house. I didn't see or talk to Christine for several weeks. She left me messages saying how sorry she was, and that she wanted me back. She left notes, begging me to reconsider, on my car in the parking lot at Costco when I was at work. Part of me wanted nothing more than to bring Christine back into my life. I loved her more than anything, and I wanted us to be together forever. But another part of me was terrified of the unstable feelings I was starting to have when I was around her. Suddenly I didn't feel like my footing was firm; instead I felt lost, confused, helpless. At any moment, it seemed, Christine could change into a person I didn't know at all.

The root of the problem, I knew, was Christine's drinking. I always knew she liked to drink, but at first I didn't pay much attention to it. After all, we were in college, and we had met in a bar—drinking seemed like part of the deal. And in our first few months together, Christine didn't drink very much because she was, like me, swept up in our relationship. Or perhaps it was just that I was so swept up that I didn't notice what was going on.

Eventually, though, I did realize that Christine's personality changed when she drank past a certain point. She'd become more aggressive, more confrontational. But lately it seemed as though it took only a couple of beers to instigate a change in her. I didn't know how much she drank or why she drank so much—only that when she drank she became a person who was capable of hurting me deeply. During our weeks apart, I still didn't know the extent of her drinking problem, only that I had a choice to make. Would I just kick Christine out of my life, or would I bring her back in and try to help her stop drinking?

I chose to bring her back in. I still loved her with all my heart, and I hoped that we could somehow overcome her drinking. And, for a while at least, it seemed to work. Christine drank less, and we went back to being a happy couple. But Christine kept on drinking. It took me some time to realize that she had never really slowed down, but rather had just learned how to hide her drinking better. She always carried a backpack that I noticed was unusually heavy; inside it, I would later learn, was a giant mug filled with beer. She also worked at a pizza place, and some nights she wouldn't come home at all, explaining in the morning that she had worked very late and fallen asleep in her car. Another time she told me she couldn't sleep and just drove around until the sun came up. I didn't want to believe she was cheating on me again, so I didn't push too hard to find out the truth. But one morning, she straggled home wearing a pair of men's pants. She told me she had gone to some guy's apartment after work and just had a beer with him. But it was clearer than ever that her drinking was driving a wedge between us that threatened to end our relationship.

I spoke with Christine's parents about her drinking. Her father knew how much I loved his daughter, and he knew she had a problem. We had several long heart-to-heart talks, and we both vowed to do whatever we could to help Christine get better. Everyone who loved her pushed her to get help, to address her drinking issue once and for all, but Christine was running from something that no one else could see or understand. I was as close to her as anyone outside her family, and I didn't know what demon was inside her driving her to drink and destroy her life. Her dream was to be a dolphin trainer or a marine biologist, and she worked extremely hard to make that dream come true. The academic requirements were brutal, and her drinking got in the way, which only made matters worse. The more difficult her life became because of her drinking, the more likely she was likely to drink. Her drinking was her escape, but it was also the thing that was stopping her from achieving the life she wanted.

For me, this was the most painful realization of all—that whatever was driving Christine to drink was something only she could overcome. No matter how much other people loved her and supported her, she would have to conquer her demons on her own. I felt helpless, powerless, not at all like the brave superheroes I created as a kid. I had gone through something like this before with my mother, and I had learned a hard lesson—that I could not protect or save her from the dark forces that overtook her. And now I was helpless again, watching as someone I loved dearly lost her grip on life a little more each day.

Christine and I stayed together through it all, battling every day to make things work. We graduated from the University of Hawaii, a crowning moment in each of our lives. In 1997 we traveled to Europe, but for much of the trip Christine was hostile and cynical. She had always been a little biting, playfully confrontational. I loved that about her, that she challenged me. But over the years this side of her began to emerge more and more. Christine and I opened a business together—a company that made custom T-shirts. The idea came to us when we couldn't find any T-shirts that made a statement about being gay in college. I read everything I could find about making T-shirts and, with Christine's father's help, we built a small wooden T-shirt press, and we started our own business. Our first job was making shirts for Christine's pizza parlor. We earned $200 for that job and realized we could make a go of it. Yet we also fought. I felt Christine wasn't really committing herself to the business. We were trying to move forward with our lives, but in truth we were merely sliding backward.

Finally, we decided to move to California and continue our T-shirt business there. This was my dream—to finally escape Hawaii and begin anew. But as the date of our departure grew closer, Christine and I became even more anxious around each other. Nothing felt sure or certain; everything felt wobbly and weak. I had a terrible sense of doom, not only about our relationship but about Christine herself. I began to worry that nothing could save Christine, that she might never be able to overcome what plagued her, that she was sliding inexorably toward some terrible fate. Suddenly, a future that had once seemed so bright and beautiful seemed likely to be full of sorrow and pain.

Yet I didn't want to give up on us. I loved Christine, and I didn't want to just let her walk away. But surely she, too, sensed that we weren't going to make it together. One day she simply announced that she was going to go to California ahead of me, to set things up. I think she may have picked up on my hesitancy about the move. We were always on edge, and we had a lot of issues to deal with, and we both thought that the move to California might give us a fresh start. But something was keeping me from throwing myself into it. It just didn't feel right. The irony was that leaving Hawaii and starting a life with someone I loved was all that I had ever wanted to do—yet I simply could not take the first step. When Christine called me from California, I told her I wouldn't be coming to meet her.

She cried and cried and said she would stop drinking forever if only I came out. And yet I knew she would never stop drinking for me; she had to do it for herself. I wanted more than anything to be with Christine; God, I wanted to *save* her, to be her superhero, to sweep in and make everything better. But I knew I couldn't do it; it was simply beyond my power. The choice I had was to continue in a situation I feared would be just as troubled and dysfunctional as the one I was trying desperately to flee in Hawaii, or to get out once and for all, as painful as that might be. It was not an easy decision, and that conversation was one of the hardest I have ever had to have. But I knew deep inside what I had to do. I couldn't chase her anymore. I had to let Christine go.

   We didn't speak for about a year, although we did eventually reconnect, both of us acknowledging that we didn't want to lose each other as friends. She kept me posted about her progress in quitting drinking, and I even went to visit her in California. Things were okay between us, for the most part, but there was also a strange tension and sadness. After all, Christine was the first true love of my life, and at one time she had been my entire world. I remember holding her tight against me as we slept, determined to never let her slip away. But there are things we cannot keep simply by pressing them to our chests. The world just doesn't work that way.

Chapter 8

LOVE STORY

The telephone rings, noisy and unwelcome. I disregard it, hoping someone else will answer it, but no such luck. My father doesn't like to be bothered at home. Over the years I've become convinced that he thinks phone calls deliver only bad news. Anthony—eighteen years old now—is surely sound asleep after a full night of partying. I am in bed at my father's house, enduring the tail end of a bad case of the flu. My head feels heavy and detached from the rest of me, and my forehead tingles with sweat. My feet are swollen from working a long shift at the Paradise Bakery in Honolulu, where I am mired in the dead-end position of assistant manager. When I swallow, my throat feels as if it's lined with sandpaper. I have a rare day off from work, so I have stacked my soft pillows just right and poured myself a hot cup of Kona coffee and drawn my curtains tight. All I want to do is lie there, as far away from the rest of the world as possible. But the damn phone just won't stop ringing, and finally I straggle upstairs to answer it.

"Hello, I'm trying to reach Tracy?" says the voice, uncertain and pitched at the end like a question. I know that voice well.

"Speaking."

"Hi, this is Nancy from the gym."

Nancy? From the gym? Of course, Nancy. And yet, wait—Nancy? Is calling me at home?

Suddenly my brain snaps into focus. I have no idea why Nancy is calling, but just to have her on the line with me is exciting, to say the least. I had been aware of Nancy for more than eight years by the time she called me that February day in 1998—a day I will never forget as long as I live. She was the receptionist at the Marina Athletic Club, where I taught karate. Her physical beauty and electric personality were magnetic and alluring. She had the ability to draw me into her sunny, cheerful world with nothing more than a bright smile, a silly joke, and a warm gaze. Over the years we'd gone from being mere acquaintances to being gym friends.

I'd felt an instant connection to Nancy the first time I met her, but over time I started to figure that pretty much everyone had that experience, since there were always guys loitering around the front desk, trying to flirt with her and get her phone number. Nancy was a bodybuilder, and her body was strikingly sculpted yet still amazingly feminine. Photos of her in bodybuilding poses were everywhere in the club; she had been written up in national bodybuilding magazines like *Flex* and *Shape,* dubbed a rising star in article after article. She was the pinnacle of strength and beauty. I admired Nancy because I knew how much sweat and devotion it takes to change the shape of your body, and I aspired to one day be as in control of my physique as she obviously was of hers. But beyond her incredible body and sensuous looks, there was something about her personality that had me mesmerized. She was open and inviting in a way I wasn't used to; she liked to talk and laugh with everyone, and her sense of humor was down-to-earth and self-deprecating. I noticed she could disarm pretty much anyone who walked into the club; within minutes they'd be sharing intimate details of their lives. I'd seen big, beefy bodybuilders come in with tons of attitude and be reduced to hugs and giggles by Nancy's unstoppable charm.

That, more than anything, drew me to her; there was a lightness to her, a very contagious optimism. It felt good to be around her, and my life just seemed more fun whenever she was in it. She was at once mysterious and an open book.

One incident left me particularly intrigued by her: It was 1994, and I saw Nancy coming out of a gay bar called Hula's Bar and Lei Stand one night when I was hanging out at another nearby bar. She was walking with a woman who had her arm around Nancy's waist. Instinctively, I ducked into the shadow of a doorway, my heart pounding. The idea that she was with a woman was thrilling to me, but witnessing her with another woman made me think she wasn't attainable to me. Nancy was quite a few years older than I was and she had two children. She was impossibly out of my league.

Ultimately, as Nancy and I got to know each other a little bit better, my curiosity got the best of me and I worked up the courage to ask her about that night and the woman she was with. She seemed embarrassed at first, but, as was her way, she soon opened up and told me everything. She had split up with her abusive husband and found herself in a relationship with another woman, Danielle. She told me how she'd spent a lifetime looking for love, so far in all the wrong places. I sensed that she had endured hardships and overcome them. She was both vulnerable and strong, two opposing yet compatible qualities that only endeared her to me more. We became friends to the extent that we shared our personal lives with each other when we saw each other at the gym. She also invited me over to her home a few times to chat. When I confided in her about the abuse I suffered at the hands of my sensei, Ron, she was one of the people who gave me the courage to stand up for myself and get out of that relationship. Over time, we bonded over another sad reality in each of our lives: that my girlfriend, Christine, and hers, Danielle, had problems with alcohol.

Still, life took us our separate ways, and there was a long stretch of time when I was away from the athletic club and never saw Nancy. But in 1998, I decided to go back to a regular routine there. When I walked in, there she was: with her sun-bleached hair tumbling all the way down to her curvy waist, Nancy was as irresistible as ever. She looked different than I remembered: more womanly, somehow, more assured, and even more stunning. I, too, had changed—I had packed on pounds of muscle, cut my hair short, and matured a lot. I was coming out of my tweener phase and looking a lot more masculine; I'd even bought a black Kawasaki Ninja motorcycle. I'd finished college and was more myself than I had ever been before. When I walked into the gym and saw Nancy behind the front desk, I saw her notice me and hold her stare for what seemed like quite a while. Memory is a funny thing, though; it puts a pretty sheen on your favorite recollections. But I swear I remember Nancy and I staring at each other for a small eternity. All of the chemistry and attraction that had existed over the years was, in this moment, transforming into something else, something deeper. I left the club that day thinking about Nancy, and she was still on my mind when I was forced to stay in bed with the flu. Her eyes and her body and her laugh were wonderful things to contemplate as I curled up in my bed that day with my Kona coffee, longing to be able to return to the gym for regular workouts and conversations with Nancy.

Nancy would later tell me that she fell in love with me the day I strode back into the Marina Athletic Club. Her reason for calling me was simple: She wanted to make sure I was coming back.

❖ ❖ ❖ ❖ ❖

When Nancy was little, she and her friends liked to pack as much bubble gum into their mouths as they could—wads of gum puffing out their cheeks, tears of laughter running down their faces. This is still the Nancy I know—packing as much living into her life as she can, and laughing every step of the way.

Her grandparents on her mother's side were Midwesterners with lots of money. Her grandfather, Duke Rufus Gaskins, was a brilliant doctor who played golf with Frank Sinatra and Bing Crosby. Her mother, Nancy Juliette—or Julie, as she's been known since junior high—was gorgeous like Nancy, with dark brown hair and bright blue eyes and an easy, happy laugh. But she was also spoiled; by the time she was fifteen she had her own Cadillac convertible.

Julie was always a fun, boisterous person to be around, but she was controlled by men, one of whom came to be her husband and Nancy's father, Marvin. Nancy grew up witnessing the way her father dominated her mother by putting her down and beating her up. Marvin was very smart and made it through medical school thanks to Duke Rufus's generosity, but before long his access to drugs got the better of him, and he became hopelessly addicted to morphine and Demerol. Duke Rufus paid for his rehab, too, but Marvin never lost his appetite for pills.

Marvin was also abusive to Nancy, the third of four children under his roof. He once locked her in a small room while he took her brothers out for a bike ride. The worst of him would come out when he'd wake up after a night of drinking; reeking of vomit, he would call his children unspeakably vile names. When Nancy was in her twenties, Marvin remarked that she would make a fine high-class call girl. It was as close to a compliment as she would ever receive from him.

After Julie and Marvin split up, Nancy drew another short straw with her stepfather, Alan. He used Julie's money to buy a fiberglass-boat business, demonstrating to Nancy yet again the ways in which her mother was at the whim of the men in her life. Alan had a bust of his head made out of white plaster and put it on a pedestal in the hallway of his home. Nancy remembers having to fight off a constant urge to tip the bust over and watch it shatter. Alan was arrogant, demanding, and fond of caviar and oversize rings—but these were hardly the worst of his faults. When Nancy was fourteen, her mother took her to see a psychiatrist because she was doing so poorly in school. With Julie and Alan in the room, Nancy told the psychiatrist that Alan had been sexually abusing her for years. Julie kicked him out of the house, but Nancy and her mother never discussed what was said in that psychiatrist's office.

Depressed, confused, and alienated from just about everyone, Nancy proved to be more than her mother could handle. One day Julie told her that her grandmother was sick and dying, and that they needed to get on a plane to go see her. Nancy remembers the plane landing in the middle of a desert—that was when her mother told her she was going to boarding school for three months. Nancy ran into a bathroom at the airport and threatened to swallow a whole can of aerosol hair spray if she wasn't allowed to go back home. She hadn't been given the chance to say goodbye to her boyfriend or her brothers, or even to pack her clothes. Before long, though, her mother subdued her with 20 milligrams of Valium and a shot of vodka to calm her nerves.

Nancy lasted just one day at the boarding school before threatening to kill herself if her parents didn't come to take her home. It was Marvin who showed up in his Cadillac to bring her back. Once again, however, she wasn't going where she thought she was going. Marvin gave her more Valium and walked her into St. Luke's mental hospital in Arizona. There, Nancy recalls, she realized how institutions like that can tip someone over the edge. She felt more determined than ever that the only person she could rely on was herself, and she submitted to her parents' wishes, knowing that she would find a way out of there and figure out how to make it on her own. As it turned out, the hospital had no room for her in the youth program, so for the first thirty days, Nancy lived among adults. What she witnessed during that first month—men screaming in the night, women wailing for hours on end, patients walking lifelessly through dingy gray halls—changed her life and served as further evidence that she was, in fact, far from crazy.

Nancy finally did make it back home, but she didn't stay for long. When she was fifteen and a half years old, she ran away with her boyfriend, Barry, and married him in Tijuana, Mexico. That was, in effect, the end of a childhood that Nancy likes to say was not "fluffy-bunny stuff." Yet life with Barry was only different, not better. She married Barry in the hope of being saved from her broken home. She looked to him as her knight in shining armor, but trusting her fate to Barry was like jumping from the kettle into the fire. Barry was a young blond surfer, handsome and reckless, fond of booze and drugs, and wary of jobs and responsibility. When Nancy was sixteen she got pregnant; her son, Shawn, died of crib death at just three months old. Nancy was the one who discovered him face down in his crib; she picked him up and cradled him, sobbing giant tears that washed down her face and onto his. Nancy recalls just how cold Shawn's body felt to her touch—like a Popsicle—and she is brought easily to tears when she remembers the day she watched his undersize casket being lowered into a hole in a hill in a special cemetery section known as Babyland.

Nancy and Barry went on to have two daughters, Amber and Jen, and the family of four struggled to find firm footing. They moved from town to town to stay ahead of the police, who were always on Barry's tail for some offense: stealing, drug use, disorderly conduct. Nancy remembers moving close to one hundred times in eleven years. For long stretches the family lived in a car, a beat-up old gray Nova. One day, Barry ran off with his daughters, leaving Nancy alone and in a panic. That was the wake-up call she needed to take control of her own life. She got into fitness and bodybuilding, developing her body so that no man could ever beat it down again. She worked multiple jobs—as a cocktail waitress, a house cleaner, whatever she could find. She was just in her twenties, yet she had lived enough life for someone twice as old. Finally, she went to Colorado to get her daughters back. It wasn't easy; Barry fought her off and gave her the last beating she would ever endure at the hands of a man. Then Barry's mother begged her not to go to the police, pleaded with her to just take the girls and go. And that's just what Nancy did, moving them far away from their past—all the way to Hawaii.

Nancy checked into a hotel and quickly lined up two jobs— one cleaning private homes and the other at the Marina Athletic Club. Then she got involved with Danielle, a talented artist who liked to drink and who would eventually land in rehab three times. Nancy tried to help Danielle stop drinking, but she soon learned there was little she could do. She finally left Danielle and decided to be on her own for a while; she would spend her time working, lifting weights, and being there for her girls. Nancy's biggest test was believing she deserved to be with someone who loved her the way she wanted to be loved.

By the time I reappeared in 1998, Nancy had turned her life around. She wanted to be with someone who was kind and loyal. She wanted to be with someone she could trust, not just on her own, but also with her daughters. She and I had bonded over shared hardships and a similar sense of humor. She claims to have fallen in love with me that day I came back into her life, and I think that's because she was finally ready to experience a love that had been eluding her all her life. She had spent a lifetime looking for someone to love her the way she deserved to be loved, and I recognized the way she ought to be loved early on. It took eight years for us to be on the same page, but no one ever said that the journey of our hearts' desires is a clearly marked path.

❖ ❖ ❖ ❖ ❖

Holding the receiver to my ear, I tried to think of the most likely reason Nancy would be calling me. I had probably forgotten something at the gym, and she wanted to let me know. For some unfathomable reason—perhaps I can chalk it up to having had the flu—all I could think to say was, "How did you get this number?"

"I got it from Information," she said, unfazed.

I told her that my number was unlisted. "Okay, you got me," Nancy said with a lilt to her voice. "I got your number from the membership database. So, what are you doing?"

"I'm just getting over the flu," I said, realizing there was no way to not sound whiny. "I'm not feeling all that good and . . . "

"So, do you feel like eating?" she interrupted. "I'll treat you to a bagel and coffee. I'm at work right now, but I have a fifteen-minute break coming up."

The last thing I wanted to do was get dressed and hop on my motorcycle and be blasted by cold air as I hurtled toward the gym, but that's exactly what I did. I had been thinking about Nancy for days, and here she was, inviting me for coffee. How could I pass that up? When I pulled into the parking lot in front of the Hole-in-One bagel shop next to the gym, I saw Nancy sitting outside on a cement stool. She watched as I killed my engine, knocked out the kickstand, and walked toward her with my helmet tucked beneath my arm. I tried to look as cool as I could, even though my face felt cold and clammy. The sun lit up her smoldering teal eyes, and when she put up a hand to shield them I noticed they changed color to a deep ocean blue. I stumbled onto the stool next to her and took a good hard look at her face, just to make sure that she was really there. She wore a bluish-green silk blazer, sleeves rolled up, over a black leotard. A golden phoenix medallion hung from a chain around her neck. I just wanted to stare at her strong forearms and shoulders, and I had to literally shake my head to stop from doing so.

"So, how are you?" she asked in a low voice. Nancy always speaks in soft tones, making you want to lean in closer.

"I'm feeling better now," I said. We chatted like this for a while, idly, before Nancy drew a breath and said, "You know, after you came into the gym I couldn't stop thinking about you. I don't know, you just look different. I like your hair. I like how you look. I guess you just look...you look more like I always imagined you should look."

What an incredible compliment. I hardly knew what to say. I'd never even imagined that Nancy would take notice of me, but here we were, flirting and talking the way two people do when they're interested in each other. Nancy told me that she had split up with Danielle, and that she was on her own for the first time in a long while. I explained that I, too, was focusing more on myself and less on finding someone to be with. I was aware that something was being left unsaid, and while I hoped I knew the answer to my question, I asked it nonetheless, perhaps afraid of what might happen if I assumed too much.

"Why did you call me?" I asked.

She suddenly got nervous and fidgety. "Do you want to come over to my place for dinner tonight? How does steak and lobster sound?" And then she smiled at me, and I was a goner. She could have offered me cardboard and shoe leather and I would have said, "Sounds delicious!" I told her I would be there, and she scribbled her address on a napkin before hugging me goodbye. I took a deep breath of her hair and smelled fragrant conditioner. That night, I got dressed up and rode to her house, completely forgetting that I was still sick. I enjoyed the most wonderful steak and lobster dinner imaginable.

I didn't tell Nancy until much later that I was a vegetarian.

❖ ❖ ❖ ❖ ❖

Babies love Nancy. Don't ask me to explain it—they just do. We'll be walking in public and we'll come across a mother pushing a baby in a stroller, and the baby will absolutely fixate on Nancy, locking eyes and smiling a big baby smile. Children often spot Nancy and hide behind their mothers' legs, peeking out shyly and looking back at her once we've passed. One neighborhood girl comes over just to hug Nancy; she once confessed that her own mother isn't much of a hugger. Even dogs are drawn to Nancy. It's something to do with the energy she puts out toward small creatures. And I know it's something about her, because children and babies and dogs do not respond to me this way. She just has this aura about her, an advertisement for her giving, playful soul.

Seeing straight through to her beautiful, generous heart was the thing that made it easy for me to decide to move in with her after just a few dates. A little sudden? Sure. But I cannot overstate just how quickly we bonded, once the timing was right. I knew over bagels and coffee that first morning that we were meant for each other, that we fit like pieces of a puzzle. Of course, chemistry and compatibility alone do not ensure that a relationship will work out. But I never doubted for a moment that Nancy was worth risking everything for. True, I worried about being with someone who already had two teenage children. It is, to say the least, a little daunting to walk into something like that. What if Amber and Jen didn't like me, or didn't like having me around? What if I didn't like having an instant family? And what about my masculine appearance—what would Amber and Jen think of that? None of this was clear to me, or to Nancy, or to the girls. But one thing was totally clear—Nancy and I were going to take our chances and try to build a life together.

I moved into her three-bedroom, one-and-a-half bathroom townhouse in Hawaii Kai in February 1998. It was a two-story building with a kitchen and living room downstairs and the full bath and small bedrooms upstairs. The townhouse was part of a complex in which all the homes looked exactly the same, where we shared thin walls with our noisy neighbors. Nancy didn't have much furniture; she was still struggling to make ends meet. She had an old glass-top dining table that she had gotten from someone in exchange for cleaning services, and she had a king-size mattress on the floor of her bedroom. There was no dresser; instead she had cardboard boxes stuffed with clothes and covered with a towel in her closet. She hadn't been able to buy curtains yet, so the windows in the girls' rooms were covered by a sheet. Downstairs she had an old TV and a couple of framed paintings, one of boats and one of tropical trees. And that was about it. Still, the place was immaculate; Nancy worked hard to keep it clean, despite spending hours and hours cleaning other people's homes. She was proud of what she had, even though she had so little. Something about that touched my heart and made me love her even more. She was a fighter, and she was determined to give her daughters a good life. When I walked into her house—and into her life—I vowed to do whatever I could to help her dream come true.

Our first days as a new family were strange and awkward. We all sort of stumbled around a suddenly more crowded house, trying to figure out the new family dynamic. But the girls were busy, and I was up and out at 2:30 AM every day to open up the bakery. And the girls didn't resist my being there. They both knew me from the gym, and they could see that their mother was happy to be around me, and that, for the moment, was good enough. I tried to stay out of their way and never assumed the role of a parent; instead, I became a kind of mediator between them and their mother. They would come to me and complain about her, and I am sure they had the impression that I was 100 percent on their side. In fact, I made it a point to always subtly lay out Nancy's side, so that in the end they always seemed to meet her halfway. I was a good listener, and the girls came to see me as someone they could talk to and trust, and in this way we functioned as a family—we hashed things out, talked things through, rarely got into serious arguments, and generally were there for each other. Strange as it may seem, for both Nancy and me—and for Amber and Jen as well—this was the first positive family scenario any of us had ever known. It was clear to everyone that I believed in Nancy, and that she believed in me. What we had was *working*, and it was good for everyone. Nancy got more serious about her bodybuilding and we worked out together. We motivated each other. I encouraged her to compete again, and she brought home some trophies. I ran around the house fixing things—hanging a new towel rack, tightening loose hinges, whatever was needed. Bit by bit, Nancy and I added furniture—a chair here, a dresser there. The girls could see that my arrival brought order and happiness to their home. Looking back, our first months as a family opened all of our eyes to what was possible—to what a truly loving family might look like.

One day, on my day off from work, Jen stayed home sick. She walked into the kitchen to tell me she wasn't feeling well, and she fainted right in front of me. I put a cold washcloth on her forehead and rushed to call 911. When the ambulance came, one of the nurses asked me a question that made it obvious she believed I was Jen's boyfriend. Sick and ghostly as she looked, Jen managed a smile, and so did I. I was her mother's girlfriend, and yet I was being mistaken for a teenage boy. The whole thing was a crucial bonding experience for us all—our first crisis survived as a family.

As Nancy and I watched countless couples we knew fall by the wayside, we just kept getting stronger. Nancy supported me in a way no one ever had; she complimented me constantly, and stressed every day that I was capable of achieving anything I set my mind to. It was hard for me to believe that she was sincere in her compliments, coming from the background I'd come from—strict father and a string of not-so-great relationships. But she did indeed believe with all her heart that I was special, and I believed the very same thing of her. Together we were unstoppable, stronger as a unit than apart. There was nothing we wouldn't try, nothing we couldn't handle. In our early days I realized that we would be together forever—that there was nothing that could ever drive us away from each other. And today, over a decade later, I still feel that way. I remember the day, not too long after our coffee-and-bagel break, that Nancy looked me in the eyes and said, "I love you." I said it right back to her, and wished that I had said it first.

In our minds we felt as if we were already married, but legal recognition for that had long been nonexistent. When we moved in together in 1998, same-sex marriages were still against the law in every state. Because we knew that someday we wanted to officially declare our love for each other, Nancy and I became active in the fight to legalize same-sex marriages. It was important to us that we not only be allowed to live as a lesbian couple without discrimination, but that we also be afforded all the rights of a married couple. It seemed archaic to us that at the dawn of the second millennium, gays and lesbians were still seen as second-class citizens. We do not choose whom we fall in love with; none of us has that much control over our feelings. We simply fall for whom we fall for, man or woman. Why in the world should two adults who clearly love each other be shunned and denied the legal rights of any other loving couple?

Through our activism in Hawaii's civil rights movement, Nancy and I became a fairly well-known couple in the gay and lesbian community. We lobbied legislators, testified at Senate hearings, and organized numerous protests. We would go to nightclubs and soon be surrounded by people wanting to talk about the issues. Nancy and I were among many hardworking and dedicated activists who helped get the Hate Crimes Law passed in Hawaii in 2001. That law was the state's first hate-crimes law to include gays and lesbians (and ultimately transgender people, in 2003). Nancy and I both shook the lieutenant governor's hand the day the bill became a law.

Still, the goal of legalizing same-sex marriages seemed distant. Nancy and I and countless others kept up the fight. For us, the issue could not have been more personal. We wanted to share our lives with each other, and we wanted to one day be legally married. We vowed to never quit protesting until that day arrived.

And so in 2001, we helped organize the March for Equality, a seven-day, 110-mile march around the island of Oahu. For part of the march we helped carry a coffin symbolizing all the victims of hate crimes. Nancy and I walked all 110 miles, and covered much of the route with a couple of dozen other marchers. We had people scream obscenities at us, hurl bottles at us, threaten to kill us. Finally, after seven long days, we arrived at the steps of the state capitol building—the last stop of the march. There were hundreds of marchers there for that final leg. Everyone gathered in front of the state attorney general's office for a special preplanned ceremony. A nondenominational minister took his spot at the head of the crowd, and, two by two, five couples made their way toward him to pronounce their commitment to each other.

Nancy and I were one of those couples. I stood across from her and stared into her eyes and told her that I would love her forever. We were both still in our sweaty marching clothes, but that didn't matter one bit.

"Do you take this woman to be your partner for life, to love and cherish now and forever?" I was asked.

"I do" was my reply. Nancy replied that she would love and cherish me, too, and then we kissed and I lifted my head and I screamed to the heavens, as loudly as I could. It was an incredibly emotional and cathartic moment, and all of the pain and frustration and hopes and dreams that we had inside came pouring out. Symbolically, we were joined as a couple, and no one could ever take that away from us. I felt stronger, fuller, and happier than I ever had before. I had found Nancy, and she had found me, and as we stood before that minister and the four other couples, we were two broken halves that had become one beautiful whole.

❖ ❖ ❖ ❖ ❖

I have a couple of pillows that are my favorites. They are soft and silky, and they remind me of the tattered baby blanket that I slept with for many years. I love having these pillows close to my body, and I am very protective of them. And yet every night, when I come to bed, the pillows are missing. And then I see Nancy, and I can tell that she is lying on the pillows, hiding them from me. And then she smiles, a mischievous smile—the same smile, I imagine, that was on her face when she stuffed it full of bubble gum. And so I have to jump in bed and wrestle with her and get my pillows back, and after we laugh and roll around for a while, I finally snatch them away. Night after night she hides my pillows, and she never gets tired of making me wrestle with her to steal them back.

This woman in my bed, this thief of pillows—she is the heart that I call home.

Chapter 9

BECOMING THOMAS

I had my back to the front door of our warehouse, off Sand Island Access Road in the industrial area of Honolulu, when I heard a familiar voice call out my name. "Hey, Tracy." It was my father.

I was training two new employees for my T-shirt screen-printing business, Define Normal.

My father did not normally visit me at work; once in a very rare while he would stop by if he was in the neighborhood and needed to use the bathroom. And yet here he was, in his pocketed polo shirt and blue jeans. I turned to face him—then stopped abruptly, catching myself. I turned my back to him and said, "Jeez, Dad, you scared me, Give me a minute, I'll be right with you."

And then I ran off to the bathroom without another word. He must have thought I was acting strangely, but I could handle that. I hadn't seen my dad in a while, and I was worried about what he'd say if he saw my face. I locked the bathroom door behind me, looked at myself in the small mirror, and tried to come up with a plan. I half expected to hear my father banging on the bathroom door and demanding that I come out, as he had done so often when I was young. But no knock came. I turned on the cold water and fumbled around the cabinet, looking for the one thing I knew could save me. I held the razor in my shaky hand, knowing that eventually I would have to confront my father—to let him see what I had done. But I wasn't prepared to do it at work, especially in front of new employees. This was the new me, the real me, and yet rather than confront my father in that moment, I splashed cold water on my face and did what I had to do.

Being with Nancy not only brought me more happiness than I had ever felt, but it also gave me confidence and courage beyond what I'd ever imagined. The way she supported me and believed in me made me a brand-new person. We all dream of finding a place where we feel safe and loved and encouraged to chase our dreams, and I was lucky enough to have found such a place, right by Nancy's side. In her presence, I felt emboldened to reach for the moon and pull it right down.

For starters, I quit my job at the bakery and focused on my custom-T-shirt business. I asked Nancy to stop cleaning homes and come work with me. Nancy and I rented a 1,200-square-foot warehouse and bought a $35,000 silk-screening machine. We shelled out about $10,000 per month on TV, radio, and phonebook advertising. Before long, we had a long list of clients, including many in the gay and lesbian community. Nancy and I worked long, hard days—sometimes fourteen hours or more—doing everything ourselves and enjoying the time together, building our little business. As the business grew and our profits increased, so did the bond between Nancy and me. We were partners in every sense of the word, devoted to the grand adventure that was our life together.

But Nancy also gave me the strength to take a giant leap I'd been wanting or needing to take for some time. For years I had been drifting away from my birth gender—female—and toward an identity that felt more right. I cut my hair short and had moved from my tweener phase straight into wearing exclusively men's clothes. I began working out and building up my body, and I felt more masculine than feminine. I had never forgotten how it felt to wear makeup as a teenager, and how embarrassed I felt when I looked at my made-up face in a mirror. All of these rituals of womanhood were, to me, terribly uncomfortable. Now, as an adult, I felt free to stop trying to be someone I wasn't. I dressed how I wanted, rode a motorcycle because I liked it, and lifted weights because I enjoyed feeling strong. In so many ways, I was already living my life as a man and I knew the way I felt went above and beyond what many of my friends in the lesbian community felt. It was a feeling of being more comfortable in my skin as a man than as a woman, and Nancy was the first partner I had who helped me talk through some of these more complicated feelings about my identity.

As I started living more and more in a male identity, I knew that there was another step I could take—a big step. I could choose to officially turn myself into a man. The state of Hawaii requires only two things of people before they are allowed to legally switch genders. First, they must produce a letter from a therapist or medical doctor attesting that they're living full-time as the gender they intend to switch to, and that they're undergoing treatment;

in other words, the decision to switch genders cannot be a rash or impulsive one. The second requirement is that a person undergo some sort of irrevocable surgery to alter their gender; in my case, that would be the surgical removal of my breasts.

My reason for going forward with the decision to change my gender identity wasn't that I needed official approval—I already felt like a man, and I knew that I was living the life I should be living. Rather, I knew that officially switching genders would make life easier for me. It would allow the world to see me as I wanted to be seen.

I remember a time when Nancy and I checked into a hotel. My driver's license still read "F", but I had begun living my life as a male. The receptionist pointed to the stark little letter with a critical look of confusion. "But this is not the way you look," he remarked. This was the type of exchange I was looking forward to living without, and changing the gender on my legal documentation would ensure that these types of things would never happen again.

Once I fell in love with Nancy, I felt the courage and freedom to finally take this big step. I knew that she loved me inside and out, regardless of my gender, and I knew that nothing in the world would change that. I would like to think I would have taken this step even if I had not met Nancy, but I can't imagine I would ever have felt as good about doing it without her by my side.

In 1998, Nancy and I sat down with Amber and Jen and told them what I planned to do. Ironically, Jen had teasingly said to me a few months earlier, "Tracy, you would make a really ugly man." She had no idea that I was thinking about becoming a man, but she was apparently aware of my masculine presence and perhaps mulling that over in her fifteen-year-old brain. I had never considered whether or not I would be a handsome man—that seemed beside the point to me. But her comment made me think about the actual repercussions of changing my gender in a way that I hadn't really considered before. What would I look like? How would other people react to me? Just how would I change, or would I change at all? Suddenly, it all became that much more real to me.

Nancy and I explained to Amber and Jen that I would take steps to transition from a female to a male. We assured them that it wouldn't change our relationship, or any of the dynamics of the family we were building together. I told them it was not a decision I was entering into lightly; I explained how, for most of my life, I'd felt more like a man than like a woman. And I said that because of Nancy's love for me, I finally felt strong enough to make the physical changes I needed to make. The girls asked a couple of questions about the procedure, and then essentially shrugged. They were teenagers and they had their own busy lives. Their mother's girlfriend wanted to change from a woman to a man? Whatever.

I began testosterone therapy soon thereafter. I received injections of 200 milligrams of testosterone intramuscularly every two weeks. For the first few weeks I checked my body in the mirror all the time, anxious to see the changes. I hoped I would develop the defined, masculine chest I dreamed of having. After just a few injections, my voice started to crack like a teenager's. My shoulders broadened, my hips narrowed, and—sure enough—the muscles in my chest filled out. My skin began to feel coarser, and my feet seemed to grow an extra size. The hair on my arms and legs thickened, and to my amazement I started growing facial hair. It was like going through puberty all over again. I remember the first time I noticed a few whiskers on my chin. I was astonished and thrilled. Having a beard was very important to me—it was a symbol of masculinity. Even so, as soon as those whiskers sprouted, I ran out and bought shaving gear—a nice razor and some shaving cream—and I went into the bathroom, lathered up my face, and took the razor to my new facial hair with great deliberation—my very first shave. No one had ever taught me how to shave, so I figured it out as I went along. Shaving was like a sacred ritual to me—a rite of manhood. I wanted to let my beard grow, but I also enjoyed the act of shaving, so I was a little torn. Eventually I let it grow, and for a while my beard was very whiskery. Nancy hated it, and I must admit that it didn't look very good in the beginning. But in time I came to have a beard that was full and thick—thicker, even, than my father's beard.

And those were just the physical changes. The testosterone also made me feel mentally unstoppable. I found that I was able to focus more clearly, and I felt more productive at work. All of my senses felt sharper, and all of my goals seemed closer at hand. I took more measured risks in my business, confident that they would pay off and provide a better life for Nancy and me. I was more upbeat, more optimistic, and I began to welcome challenges as learning experiences. I also became more analytical and less emotional in my decision making, and because of that I found that my life was far less complicated. All of these changes were all inherent and seamless, so after a while I wasn't sure if the testosterone had caused them or not. I was simply growing, changing, maturing—getting better. I was different—and yet I was more myself than I had ever been. When I was younger there were times when I doubted myself, when I was far too eager to please other people. I did things that I thought would make others comfortable around me. But thankfully, I came to the realization that life is too short to ignore your dreams and passions, and to pretend to be someone you're not. I wanted to be able to wake up in the morning and be proud of the person I was. I was finally doing that—and it was the best feeling in the world.

After a year of being on testosterone, I looked very much like a man—lean, defined, hairy, muscular. When I looked at myself in a mirror, I felt pure elation. For the first time, the way I looked was starting to match the mental image I had long had of myself. But I still had to wear baggy clothes to hide my breasts. Soon it became clear that the next step was to have my breasts surgically removed. It wouldn't happen until 2002, but ultimately that surgery would eliminate the last obstacle to my being accepted as a man in the world. When the time came, Nancy and I talked it over at length and agreed that the time was right. My insurance wasn't going to cover my sex-reassignment surgery, so Nancy and I had waited until we could afford the cost of the chest-reconstruction surgery, and to take the time off work. Our business was making enough money, the girls had moved out of the house, and Nancy and I were solid. For the most part, I had assimilated myself into society as male—except, of course, for the visibility of my breasts.

In March 2002, Nancy and I flew from Hawaii to San Francisco to see Dr. R., a reconstructive surgeon I had chosen after weeks of online research. It was a chilly morning, with cold winds pushing off the bay, and I tried to hide my nervousness as best I could. I had fasted the night before, and my veins were hiding well below my skin; Nancy sat by my bed as a nurse struggled to hook up an IV. I could tell that Nancy was nervous too, and that made me want to be strong for her.

"Don't worry," I told her, "everything's going to be just fine."

"That's what my dad said before they wheeled him in for a quadruple bypass," she reminded me. "He died."

I took another tack. "This is the beginning of a new life for us. When I wake up, I will be a new man." I smiled at her, and she took my hand and gripped it hard. I watched as tears filled her eyes.

"Don't forget that I love you," she said. "I'm going to be right here for you when you wake up."

I felt a cold sensation in my arm as the anesthesia trickled through my body. I vaguely remember a nurse pushing me through the hallway and into an operating room, and people in scrubs darting in and out, paying no attention to me at all. I felt far away as a nurse strapped down my arms so that I was laid out like a T. I felt vulnerable, exposed. My eyelids were impossibly heavy, and the chatter and bustle of the operating room slowly faded away. I was in their hands now. No turning back.

Four hours later, I opened my eyes. For a moment or two, I had no idea where I was. I looked up and saw a man with a bandage on his head, sitting on his bed across the room from me.

"Hey, dude," he said. "Welcome back."

I didn't feel any pain, and I initially thought they might have canceled my surgery. But then I looked at my chest and noticed a large white binder wrapped around my torso. I smiled a wide smile as the reality of what had happened dawned on me.

"Whatcha in for?" the man in the bandage wanted to know.

"Chest surgery" was all I could think to say.

"Well, now you got a good heart, man," he said, and he gave me a big thumbs-up.

I didn't correct him and tell him I had had a bilateral mastectomy, followed by nipple and areola shaping and grafting. Instead I just gave him a big thumbs-up right back. He had called me "dude" and "man." I was now a he.

❖ ❖ ❖ ❖ ❖

D r. R. told me the surgery had been a success. He looked at my chest and said I had an incredible amount of muscle tissue, and that my chest was naturally contoured and masculine. He asked if he could use before-and-after pictures of me for his website. I was happy to oblige. I couldn't wait to check out of the hospital and get back to the gym.

Before I left, Dr. R. drafted a letter attesting to the reasons for my reconstructive surgery, which would later serve my purpose in changing my legal gender from female to male. "Psychological and medical testing has been carried out to determine this patient's true gender," he wrote. "In this case, this was determined to be male. Tracy has undergone extensive hormonal and psychological treatment and has been referred for and undergone surgical procedures performed by me to irreversibly correct his anatomy and appearance. This should qualify Tracy to be legally considered male." Dr. R.'s letter remains one of the most important documents of my life.

The following week, once Nancy and I got home from California, I went to the lieutenant governor's office. I filled out all the necessary paperwork, and I legally changed my name. I had never minded my first name, Tracy, which means "fighter" in Gaelic.

I decided to keep a variation of it, Trace, which is what Nancy used to call me, as my new middle name. For my new first name, I chose Thomas. Oddly enough, why I chose it is still a mystery to me. It didn't come to me in a dream, or in the shower, or any other time. It has simply always been there, as if it chose me. I simply knew that my male name should be Thomas.

Finally, I changed my last name, too, to Beatie—my mother's maiden name. In doing so, I not only freed myself from my father's name and legacy, but also honored the memory of my mother, whose values and goodness had always been dearer to my heart. My fifth great-grandfather, John Beatie, escaped religious persecution in Ireland and sought his paradise in America, at which point he dropped the second "t" in our original name, Beattie, so as to leave a new legacy in his chosen homeland. His grandsons trudged across untamed plains to carve out brand-new lives. To me, the name Beatie symbolized freedom and courage, and I felt an obligation to uphold my ancestors' legacy. And so, in a government office with overhead lighting and plastic chairs, I became Thomas Trace Beatie.

Following the legal name change, I changed my passport and driver's license. My passport features a photo of me in a blue sweatshirt and a mile-wide smile. The passport reads: "M" for male. My driver's license, too, reads: "Sex: M." I even had a new birth certificate generated, and changed my social security record. Changing my passport and social security meant that every state, not just Hawaii, would accept my male status. One simple word—heck, sometimes a single *letter*—would now make all the difference in how the world treated me. Literally and figuratively, a great weight was lifted off my chest when I had my breasts removed. Before the surgery I wore baggy clothes and walked with a pronounced slouch to hide them. Afterward, however, I walked straighter, with my head held high and my chest thrust out. I was proud of my body and proud of who I was. And now I had the documents to prove it—official government documents with that wonderful letter, M. I had become a man.

After my surgery, a lot of people asked me if I was going to go back in for what is sometimes called "lower surgery." Some of my brother's friends used to tease me and ask if I was going to get an "add-a-dick-tomy." The actual medical term is "phalloplasty," and it involves forming a penis out of tissue taken from other parts of your body. I have seen photos of people who've undergone this surgery, and even when it's gone well, the results aren't good. In some cases, forearm grafts fail and fall off. Some men suffer life-threatening infections. No attempt to replicate a male organ looks even remotely natural. What's more, nerves are damaged and sensation is sacrificed. Sexual pleasure becomes nothing more than a memory. It is a brutal, barbaric operation, and I've never seriously considered having it. I simply did not feel I needed to undergo any more surgery to feel like a man. I had already done everything required of me by state and federal guidelines, and legally I was fully a male. Even less destructive and barbaric procedures, such as an operation that fuses the labia and implants silicone testicles, did not appeal to me. And the metoidioplasty, where a ligament is cut and lengthens the clitoris, didn't seem necessary. I already had everything I needed to be happy with my body. Size doesn't matter.

In addition to that, more surgery seemed beside the point because testosterone therapy had enlarged my clitoris by inches, giving it the appearance of a penis. I can use it to have intercourse with Nancy, and she has told me that it isn't much smaller than the "organs" of some of the men she has been with. I wouldn't change the rest of my body for anything in the world. I did what I needed to do to become a legal male, and to move past what I considered the burden of my breasts. Some men may feel they need to have a penis and endure a phalloplasty to truly feel like a man, but the prospect of transferring skin from one part of my body to another wasn't going to achieve that for me.

I also chose to keep my reproductive organs. Some transgender men opt to have them removed, believing they need to sterilize themselves to be considered a different gender. But I didn't feel this way at all. In fact, I couldn't help but wonder about the logic: How could having *no* reproductive organs make someone any more of less a man or a woman? It just makes you sterile. Thankfully, there are no state-sponsored sterilization requirements for transgender people, and I had no desire to opt out of the possibility of procreating. Nancy and I had talked about having children one day, and I felt it was important for me to retain my reproductive organs. If we used a surrogate mother, I would be able to donate an egg and have a biological child. What was important to me was that I did exactly what I needed to do to be perceived as a male in the world, and for me the facial hair and removal of my breasts were enough to align my outside identity with what I had felt on the inside for so many years.

❖ ❖ ❖ ❖ ❖

When my father surprised me at work that day, I hadn't told him that I had started taking testosterone, or that I had had my breasts removed, for that matter. The only solution I could come up with in that moment was to do a quick shave, which I did with a disposable razor and no shaving cream. I got my chin and cheeks as smooth as I could, leaving only a couple of nicks. The sides of my face felt raw from the rough razor, so I kept splashing myself with cold water. I toweled down and looked in the mirror. This was the person my father knew—the same face that, when I was little, he had said was beautiful. I took a deep breath and walked out of the bathroom, ready now for my little charade.

The charade felt important in that moment, in part because of my new employees, and in part because I knew how he would react, and I dreaded having to tell him and face that reaction. Being a disappointment to my father, no matter how strained our relationship may have been, was not something I was looking forward to dealing with. After all, I had been his only daughter. But I knew I couldn't be his son, either—I knew he would never, ever think of me that way. And that was exactly why I put off telling him about my transition for as long as I did. I was careful to shave thoroughly whenever I knew I would be around him. I was just waiting for the perfect time, but it never came. It took me years to realize that it would never come, because my father would never change his way of thinking.

One of my father's most damaging flaws was his misogyny. He had been raised to believe that men were strong and dominant, and that women, by nature, were frail and submissive—objects of beauty but little else. When I graduated from college, he encouraged me to be a clerk at Longs Drugs. He didn't believe in me when I expressed interest in becoming an entrepreneur. It's hard to look back now and not feel satisfied about being his most successful child. He never encountered anything in his life to shake him from those beliefs. And as long as he held on to them—and he did, with blinding ferocity—he all but ensured the destruction of our relationship. The problem wasn't just his ingrained misogyny, though; we might have been able to survive that, and come at least to some tolerant, hospitable understanding of each other. The bigger problem was that I posed a direct, daily challenge to his basic worldview. I did not fit into his conception of what a woman should be—and I certainly wouldn't fit into his notion of what makes a man a man. This was the key fissure that doomed our relationship—who I was, at my core, was someone my father could never understand or tolerate.

It's natural, then, that I developed strong defenses against his dislike of me. This meant abandoning any hope that we might have a real, meaningful relationship, and settling for something that was superficial at best. The decision to have this kind of relationship with him was difficult, but things between us had been strained for years. Still, I longed for my father's love and acceptance. In nearly every important moment in my life, I wished that I could invite my father into it, as much for his benefit as for my own. I suffered not only for the closeness to him that I was being deprived of, but also for his loss—a staggering loss, I felt—in not being able to know the real person who was his daughter. But I knew that I had no other option. Without some evidence that my father could make concessions, there was nothing I could do but present him with a safer, sanitized version of myself, while keeping the real me as secret from him as I could.

Even after I transitioned—even after I was no longer Abraham's daughter but was instead his son—I stuck to this protective approach of shielding him from the full truth. My father was aware of my masculine ways—that I wore men's clothes, that I worked out hard, and that I rode a motorcycle. He did not approve of these things; to him, my behavior was an aberration, an act of petulance, something he should ignore. I was never under any delusion that he would understand my decision to have gender-reassignment surgery, and so, even though it was the most important decision of my life, I kept that from him. If just acting like a man was despicable to him, what would he think of someone's surgically altering the work of Mother Nature?

As soon as I saw my father, sitting on the corner of my desk in my front office, I immediately felt that he was suspicious of something. I had a strange sensation that we were in the very moment I had been dreading, that this was the hour when he would finally learn the truth. My father didn't say anything when I walked in, and for a second or two neither did I. But then I couldn't bear the tension any longer.

"What brings you here, Dad?" I asked.

"I was in the neighborhood," he said. "The coffee goes right through me, you know."

I took another deep breath and spoke. "Well, what can I say? You caught me. I guess now is as good a time as any."

My father seemed confused. Just then, I realized he wasn't wearing his glasses. Without them, there wasn't much of a chance he would have picked up on anything that would have led him to suspect that I'd transitioned. I felt like laughing at the way I had panicked, but instead I steeled myself to keep going. The moment had already begun—by accident, perhaps, but we were both in it now. The room was warm and stuffy; I felt a tiny bead of sweat trickle down my reddened cheek. The silence was like heat. I had to say something, anything, to keep the moment going. I might never be able to summon this nerve again.

"I meant to tell you sooner, Dad; I just didn't know how to do it. I'm sure you already suspected something like this."

"What is it?" said my father, an old man now but still lean and strong and dominant, still capable of shrinking me with his gaze. I was gagging on the words, trying to gather a few that might make sense, anything besides "surgery" and "transition" and "gender reassignment," hard, clinical words that would bruise my father like blunt objects.

But there were none. And so I reached down and grabbed the hem of my T-shirt and pulled it over my head in one quick movement. I could already see my father's expression as I pulled my shirt over my head. Even without glasses he could see the twin red crescents on my chest, my surgical scars, longer and brighter than I had hoped, inescapable testaments to what had happened. He could surely see that my breasts were gone, and that my chest, thanks to testosterone injections, had gained musculature and definition. He could see that his little girl was now a man.

"What are you doing?" my father stammered as I pulled up my shirt. And then a small, guttural gasp.

"My god, Tracy, what have you done?"

I stood there and let him take it in. There was nothing I could say to make it any worse or better. I knew to give him time to process what he was seeing. I thought I might not say anything more at all, even once he started his inevitable tirade about how I had shamed and betrayed him. But what he said next surprised me.

"You look," my father said, "like me."

I felt suddenly confused. Rather than dismay, here was a vague trace of a compliment. What child doesn't want to be told he resembles his parent? It was the sort of thing I had wished to hear from him my whole life—a suggestion of connection, a link between us, some fundamental familiarity between my father and me. Even now, in this surreal, supercharged moment, it felt like a warm, comforting thing for him to say. But the better part of me knew it was more likely just his way of grasping the reality of what he was seeing. It was a stammered observation, devoid of any emotion. My father braced himself against the desk, slouching a bit, as if the only way he could retreat from me was to slump to the ground. But his eyes stayed on my chest, and on my crescent scars, and the great weight of my secret left me then, like a giant wave that keeps you in its tumbling power until, all of a sudden, it washes away and is gone.

"I know you've been noticing a change in me for a while now," I said.

"I'm not blind," answered my father.

"This is the person I want to be," I told him. "This is the person I've always felt I was. I'm just getting the outside to match the inside." And then, "I'm happy now, Dad. I'm finally happy."

My father kept his stare but scrunched his face into a frown. "You were so beautiful, Tracy," he said. "You could have had any man you wanted."

"It's not about that, Dad. I'm in love with Nancy. My sexuality has nothing to do with my gender."

I was losing him now; he couldn't digest anything else. But I had to say as much as I could, and before the moment passed I had one thing to add. "My name is Thomas now, Dad, not Tracy. I am Thomas Beatie."

And so my father learned that I had changed not only my identity from female to male, but also my first and last names, from the ones he had bestowed on me to ones he had not chosen. I had abandoned not only the gender he knew me to be, but also the first name he'd picked out, and the middle name, Lehuanani, too. Worst of all, I had cast off his surname in favor of my mother's maiden name. The entirety of his conception of me, as a person and as a daughter, had been obliterated, not through chance or circumstance but by design. I had changed the very things he understood about me—my feminine beauty, my family name. I had fashioned myself into a new person, wholly different from the person he had created.

"I cannot stop you, Tracy," my father said. "You have always been strong-willed and done as you pleased. As long as you are happy."

I was astonished. Did he really mean it? Or was he just telling me what he thought I wanted to hear? Either way, it was a miracle— he had not, in his confusion, lashed out or tried to hurt me. He had spared me, and for that I felt unbearably grateful. I felt guilty for having denied him for so many years, and for having, perhaps, underestimated his capacity, at the least, to tolerate me. I think I felt closer to him in that moment than I ever had before. We had come through this thing I so dreaded—the telling of the truth, the big revelation—and here we were, both of us, still standing, still okay. Of course, he had called me Tracy rather than Thomas, but that was fine; he would need time to adjust. Perhaps he might go away and marshal all of his venom for me in time, and then return to pour it on me when he had occasion to, but that, too, was fine. At least in this moment, he had not been a monster. At least now he had been human—frightened, confused, vulnerable, wounded. And for that, I was thankful.

"Well," he finally said, "as long as we're sharing secrets, I might as well tell you this. You have a sister."

I had no idea what he was saying. It made no sense to me. It was a garble of words. A sister? That wasn't possible. All my life I had pined for a sister. I was sandwiched between two brothers; I dreamed of having someone to talk to and share things with, someone who might, just might, understand what I was going through.

"Say that again," I told my father. "Say that again. What do you mean?"

"Didn't I tell you this before?" he asked with feigned innocence. "Her name is Lori. Her mother's name is Leimomi. She's a couple of years older than you."

I felt blindsided. Now it was I who felt the need to brace myself against something solid. A sister? A flesh-and-blood sister? Could this be true? Had I lived my whole life without knowing this crucial, precious thing? Had I passed this woman on the street and not recognized the resemblance? This bright new strain of family, available to me and yet kept secret, a source of vital nourishment so close and yet a million worlds away. Could anyone be so callous, so cruel? And then I realized—this was my punishment. This was how my father chose to bludgeon me—with his own long held secret, wielded now like a weapon.

"I saw her a few years ago at a carnival. I think she has children. That's all I know." And with that my father left, turning quickly on his heel and walking out the door. He said something about not wanting to be late for work; I weakly lifted my hand to wave goodbye. I slowly put my shirt back on, glad to cover up my scars. Later on, from my brothers, I learned how my father really felt about my name change. He took it as the ultimate betrayal, a terrible slap in the face. My brothers told me he said I was a disgrace to the family. I wasn't even ashamed of myself, as I should have been. Instead, I clambered onto rooftops and shouted out my story with glee; I felt compelled to share my perversity with the world. This, to my father, a man of decorum and quiet hatred, was abhorrent.

My father indeed found a way to lash out at me that day. He found a way to hurt me, and the hurt still lingers today, an intermittent sadness about all the years of warmth and closeness I lost with my sister, Lori. My father struck at me in my weakest place of all—in my heart, which had been ravaged by a lifetime of family disappointment.

That day in my office, as I stood shirtless and exposed before my father, whatever tiny shred of family I still clung to dissolved completely into the air, like fading wisps of smoke.

To this day, I still haven't met my sister. And my father refuses to call me Thomas. He will only call me Tracy.

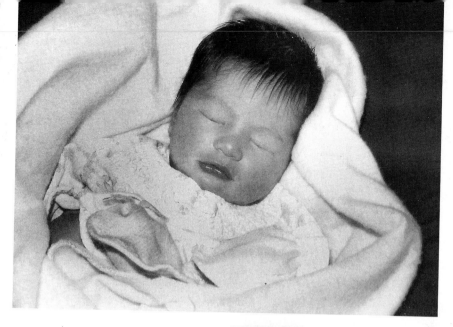

▲
me as a
newborn, 1974

me and ➤
mom, 1974

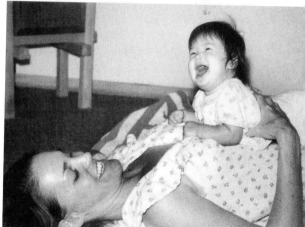

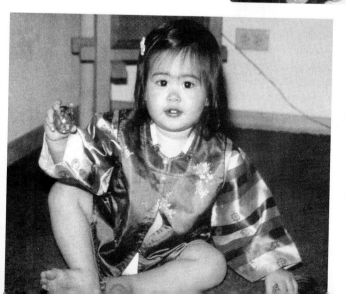

◄ me in a traditional
Korean outfit, age
18 months, 1975

▲ 2nd grade, age 7, 1981

▲ me with broken arm,
Christmas, 1981

▼ me and mom, Thanksgiving, 1978

▲ mom, age 15, 1959

▲ my Cocker Spaniel,
Biscuit, and me,
age 10, 1984

▼ brown belt, age 9, 1983

▲ modeling photo,
age 13, 1987

▲ modeling photo,
age 15, 1989

▼ Basic Training exercise
video shoot, 1990

▼ practicing martial arts,
1995

▲ me at Christmastime, 1995

▼ on my Kawasaki,
   Ninja motorcycle, 1995

▼ me and Christine, 1995

▲ Nancy, 1985

▲ Nancy, 1996

▼ on Christine's parents' boat, Kaneohe, HI, 1996

▼ in Las Vegas, 1999

▲ Nancy and me, Waikiki, 1998

▼ Nancy and me at home in
   Honolulu, 1999

▼ in Waikiki, 1999

▲ on the Big Island of Hawaii, 2002

▼ in the men's bathroom, 2002

▲ commitment ceremony between Nancy and me, Honolulu, January 2001

▼ Nancy and me taking marriage vows, Honolulu, 2003

▲ post-wedding dinner, Waikiki, February, 2003

▼ my mother's gravesite, Kaneohe, 2004

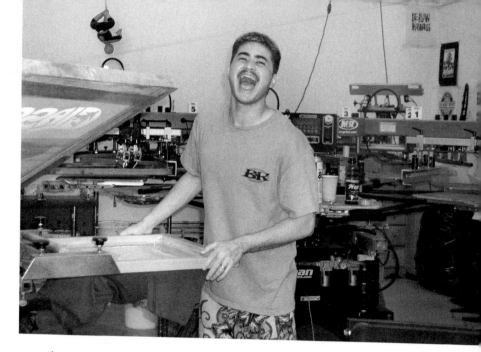

▲ Define Normal Warehouse, Honolulu, 2004

▼ Mt. Bachelor, Bend, Oregon, 2004

▲ Nancy and me in Bend, 2005

▼ Winter 2004 — purchase of first home, Bend

▲ Nancy's daughters, Jen and Amber, with me in Bend,
March 2007

▼ Thomas, Amber, and Nancy at baby shower, Bend,
May 31, 2008

▲ me at 6 weeks

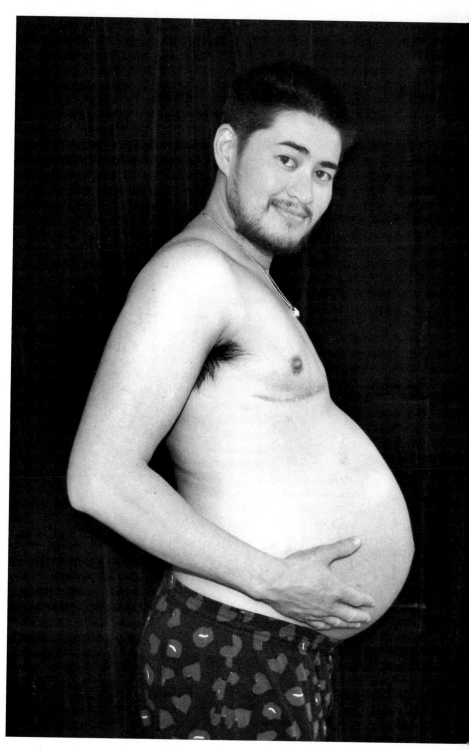

▲ me at 36 weeks

▲ Thomas, Nancy, and Susan Beatie, July 2008

Chapter 10

THE DECISION

On a perfect moonlit evening in 1999, I had Nancy jump on the back of my motorcycle and I drove us to the overlook above Makapuʻu Bay, a romantic spot on the south shore of Honolulu. We walked along the hardened lava and listened to the waves of the Pacific crashing against the cliff below us. When I stopped, I pulled a box out of my pocket. I knelt on the jagged lava and opened the box. The liquid light of the moon shimmered on the diamond ring.

"Nancy, will you marry me?" I asked.

Nancy drew a deep breath and slid the ring onto her finger. "Yes, Tracy," she said, with tears in her eyes. "I will marry you." Then we kissed and held each other and stared at the million twinkling stars in the sky.

When I asked Nancy to marry me, I meant it with all my heart, but I also knew that it was a largely rhetorical question. That same year, the Hawaii State Supreme Court made a final ruling denying same-sex couples the right to get married. The idea that I could ever legally marry Nancy was little more than a fantasy. Even so, I wanted to propose to her because I wanted her to know that if I could marry her, I would. I know full well that the issue of same-sex marriage is a divisive one, and that smart, good people disagree on whether this country should recognize it or not. But to me, it boils down to fairness and equality. Why are two women or two men who are clearly in love and in a stable relationship be denied the rights and benefits afforded to different-sex couples? Federal laws prohibit discrimination against and intolerance of anyone based on their sex—yet denying these same people the hundreds of federal benefits that flow from legal marriages seems like a clear case of sex discrimination. Our system of governance is based on the separation of church and state, but religious convictions against homosexuality play a huge part in the government's denial of rights to same-sex couples. You will often hear the fight for same-sex marriages referred to as a "homosexual agenda." In fact, it is a civil rights issue, plain and simple. Gays and lesbians aren't seeking any special rights or privileges based on their sexual orientation; they are merely seeking the *same* rights and privileges afforded to everyone else in society.

This is anything but a symbolic fight. The benefits of a legal civil marriage are enormous. Legal marriage offers a couple hundreds of state benefits and over 1,100 federal benefits, legal standing, property rights, access to courts, hospital visitation rights, contract rights, health decisions, workplace benefits, social security, Medicare, insurance breaks, tax breaks, inheritance rights, military privileges, and on and on. All of these rights and benefits are being denied to same-sex couples because another group of people feels they pose some sort of threat to the fabric of this country. Yet it is impossible to argue that affording all of these benefits and rights to same-sex couples would in any way harm or threaten different-sex couples who already receive those benefits. Depriving people of these rights, therefore, amounts to one group discriminating against another based solely on its personal and/or religious beliefs. Thirty years ago, interracial marriages were not recognized in Hawaii; today, more than 50 percent of Hawaiian marriages are interracial, and civilized society is no worse for it. Our choice seemed simple: Wait around until people's fears about same-sex marriages slowly dissipate, or speed up the process by fighting to eliminate hurtful stereotypes—and finally be granted the rights, protections, and benefits we deserve.

For Nancy and me, the issue became a personal mission. We wanted to buy a house together, and we knew that would be harder as a same-sex couple. We wanted to be each other's legal next of kin, should anything happen to either of us. I wanted Nancy to get my workplace and social security benefits, and we wanted to be able to sign contracts together as legal spouses. If I died, I wanted money to pass to her unadulterated by inheritance tax. We were activists in this fight for several years, highlighted by our March for Equality, when we were "married" in a symbolic commitment ceremony. Our motto was based on a quote from the cultural anthropologist Margaret Mead: "Never doubt that a small group of thoughtful, committed citizens can change the world; indeed, it's the only thing that ever has."

Nancy and I are proud of everything we accomplished. We raised a lot of money for gay and lesbian causes. Nancy, named Ms.

Gay Pride 2000, raised more money for the event than any other winner ever had. We volunteered thousands of hours to the gay and lesbian community. We had many good friends in that community, and many others who looked up to us and admired our dedication.

When I began to transition to a male, however, all of that changed. The more I began to physically resemble a male, the more lesbians began to shun me. "You're not one of us anymore; you're one of them now," I would hear. Or, "How could you betray your womanhood?" Nancy and I began to be excluded from events and were no longer seen as one of the community's power couples. I was still the same person inside, but I became just another "man" whom many of our former friends and acquaintances would rather not have to deal with. Being rejected by a community we had become such a big part of truly hurt Nancy and me. We were stunned by this reaction; we never dreamed that we would be seen as traitors to the cause. I believe now that my transition confused many of our friends and acquaintances about their own orientation. They were proud to be either gay or lesbian, and they wanted to categorize me, or have a vision of me they could easily understand. For many of them, accepting which gender they were attracted to had been a hurdle, and they were invested in the safeness of like-minded people who didn't threaten to blur the lines. Not fitting into people's preconceived notions was then, and remains now, a major theme of my life.

The gay and lesbian community started to turn away from using Define Normal. We had been the official merchandiser for Hawaii's gay pride parades, but suddenly we were viewed as just another straight couple trying to take advantage of gays and lesbians. Ironically, as soon as I changed my gender and my name, the straight business community embraced me with open arms. I was no longer seen as a lesbian trying to make a go of her little T-shirt business; I was now a capable man running a tight shop. Potential clients reacted differently to me on the phone after I became Thomas; I was given automatic respect without having to prove myself. And so, despite the painful rejection by people we had considered friends, our business began to flourish.

One thing was missing in our American dream, however. In January 2003, I called Nancy's mother and asked to speak to Zino, her current husband. Zino had met me when I was Tracy, but knew that I was now Thomas. We weren't exactly crazy about each other, but I still felt I had to make this call to him. Marvin, the man who raised Nancy, was dead now, so I decided to call Zino and fulfill a tradition I valued. "As you know," I started, "Nancy and I have been together for five years. I am in love with her. May I have your permission to marry your daughter?"

"Now, that's a class act," he said, his voice cracking. "Nobody has ever asked me that before. Yes, Thomas, my answer is yes."

In February 2003, I took Nancy on a stroll in a secluded area in Portlock, not far from our home in Hawaii Kai. We walked near an underwater volcanic tube called Spitting Caves and watched the tide shoot foaming waves against the rocks and into the air like geysers. In the near distance, migrating humpback whales bobbed up and down. We laid out a picnic: smoked sausages, brie, and berries; we popped a bottle of riesling. Right there at the edge of the magnificent coastline, I once again got down on bended knee and produced a box from my pocket.

Just then, a man with a pair of goats walked right past us and Nancy and I both burst into laughter. Looking back, I like to think that the two goats were an omen—a happy, inseparable pair. Once we regained our composure, I opened the box and pulled out an even larger diamond ring than I'd given her the the first time. "Will you marry me?" I asked her again. Nancy cried and laughed and said, "Yes, yes, I will," she said. "And now," she added, "we can really do it."

A day we could have never dreamt of in 1999 had now, at last, arrived. Nancy and I would soon be man and wife.

❖ ❖ ❖ ❖ ❖

I have been criticized for switching genders so I could marry Nancy. I have been told I want to have my cake and eat it too. I have been accused of toggling back and forth between genders to suit my current mood. None of this is even remotely true. If I could have married Nancy when I was still Tracy, I would have in a heartbeat—and then I would have transitioned to a male after we were married. By the same token, once I transitioned, what purpose would it have served to not go ahead and legally marry Nancy? My love for Nancy and my gender identification are two separate issues. I do not feel I betrayed the gay and lesbian community by becoming a man—when I was Tracy, I fought long and hard for the rights of all of us, before following a path that I was born to follow. And now that I am Thomas, I am still the same person inside; my values, my beliefs, my convictions are all unchanged. I am a realist, though, and while I don't like the negative feelings that people seem to have toward me, I have, to some degree, learned to live with them. That does not mean I am ready to stop fighting for acceptance and tolerance. I want this society to one day accept all of us who are different from the norm, and to realize that we just want what everyone wants—full, authentic lives.

A couple of days after I proposed to Nancy, we decided to tell my family. My older brother, Barry, and his wife, Char, and my younger brother, Anthony, and his girlfriend, Kim, met up with us at a karaoke bar in Honolulu. My father showed up, too, with his young girlfriend, Cindy.

"I have important news that I'd like to share with all of you," I announced between songs. "Nancy and I are getting married."

I let the announcement linger in the air, waiting for a burst of excitement that, deep down, I knew was not coming. For the longest time no one said anything, until Barry finally broke the uncomfortable silence. "That's great news," he said. My father simply said, "Great." Anthony said nothing.

"It'll be this Wednesday at 3:00 PM," I told everyone. ""It'll be a small civil ceremony with a justice of the peace. You're all invited. This has been our dream for so long, and it's finally coming true."

I had not even finished speaking when Anthony interrupted me. "This seems like a good time to share our good news," he blurted out. "Kim and I are getting married, too."

Cindy erupted in peals of congratulations. My father's stone-cold face crumbled into a broad grin. Everyone patted Anthony on the back and started asking about his wedding plans. Once again, a family member had wielded news like a weapon against me. I felt like one of the happiest moments of my life had been destroyed. Only later, at home, did Nancy convince me that no one could ever diminish the beauty and splendor of our decision. This was our dream, our moment, and no matter what, we would always have each other.

On February 5, 2003, Nancy and I went to a government building in downtown Honolulu. Nancy's daughter Amber was there with her then boyfriend (now her husband), Josh. Our friend Scott Clark was the witness. I wore beige slacks and a periwinkle shirt; Nancy had on a simple lavender dress to match me. She wore her long dark hair down, and she was stunning. A single white rose and a vine-themed backdrop were the only decorations in the justice of the peace's office as Nancy and I read our vows to each other. The judge, in his black robe, was nice enough not to rush through the incantations.

"Do you, Nancy, take this man to be your lawfully wedded husband, in sickness and in health, till death do you part?"

"I do," said Nancy, staring into my eyes.

"And do you, Thomas, take this woman to be your lawfully wedded wife, in sickness and in health, till death do you part?"

"I do," I said, tears trickling down my cheeks.

"I now pronounce you man and wife."

And with that, we were married. We sealed it with a passionate kiss, and later we had a lovely dinner at an American Asian restaurant. It was our first meal as a legally recognized couple, afforded all of the rights and benefits that had been denied to Tracy and Nancy. We had always felt we were a real family, but now the rest of the world validated that, too. Both of us hoped that somehow our marriage might help shoot down all the weak arguments against same-sex marriages. People were terrified of Tracy and Nancy getting married, and yet they were fine with Thomas and Nancy getting hitched.

But that night was not a night for politics. Nancy and I went home and savored every moment as the proud owners of an official marriage license. In the weeks and months ahead, dramatic events would change our lives forever and steer us straight into a dizzying and surreal global spotlight. We couldn't have predicted any of what would come to pass on our sweet, tender wedding night, but Nancy and I—husband and wife—were on the cusp of our greatest adventure yet.

❖ ❖ ❖ ❖ ❖

Hawaii is a beautiful place. It is the dream of people everywhere to live in or visit the islands. Hawaii conjures up images of mild and balmy breezes, gently swaying palm trees, gleaming white-sand beaches, shockingly blue skies, air as clean as you've ever breathed, and days as magical as a fairytale. Sometimes when I gazed at the outer islands, close as lily pads, or at the rain forests of Manoa Valley, I felt like I had walked onto the set of some amazing movie. To many who were born and raised in Hawaii, the problems of the world seem to skim past the islands. Tornadoes, ice storms, epidemics, gang violence—we are immune to such problems, people say. My father is one of these people. He believes he lives in a perfect biosphere, with everything he could possibly need on the island he calls home.

While Hawaii may be a paradise for some, it was not one for me. For as long as I can remember, I itched to leave Hawaii and find

out what else was out there. I suppose I am like my ancestors, des-
tined and driven to move away from the place where they started.
I was tired of the high humidity and temperatures, and I dreamed
about enjoying a winter's snow. My plan had been to attend college
on the mainland and thus escape Hawaii, but my father forbade me
to pursue that dream. Even after I graduated from college, something kept me from leaving. I can't explain why I didn't just pack
up and go the minute I turned eighteen. For years I just felt trapped
and marooned, held back by forces I couldn't quite understand.

Nancy and I wanted to buy our own house somewhere, and
to get out of the townhouse we were renting when we got married.
It was infested with termites, resistant to any and all measures to
exterminate them. Buying a townhouse in the area where we were
living would have cost us close to half a million dollars in Hawaii's
drastically inflated real estate market. We knew that for much less
than that, we could own a beautiful, termite-free home—as long as
it wasn't in Hawaii. Both of us wanted the same thing—a big house
with a white picket fence and maybe a deck where we could snuggle
under the stars, and a lawn we could mow and a chime outside and
a bird feeder in the back. You know, the classic American dream.
We started talking in earnest about leaving, and we couldn't come
up with many reasons to stay.

Emotionally, I wasn't moored to my homeland in any way.
When my mother died, I lost the only true family I had ever had
there. My father and I had virtually no real connection, and my
brothers were distant presences in my life, at best. Both of Nancy's
daughters had grown up and moved to the mainland. Old friends
married, divorced, drifted away; the gay and lesbian community
turned its back on us. We realized that we were a circle of just

two—and our seven beloved pet parrots. If we were ever going to leave Hawaii and start a new life somewhere else, now was the perfect time.

For several hours each week I worked as a day trader, buying and selling stocks from my home computer. One day I was reading my *Investor's Business Daily* when I came across an article about a boomtown in Oregon called Bend—a former logging town just minutes away from Mount Bachelor's ski lifts and the hundreds of breathtaking lakes off the Cascade Lakes Highway. A lot of California corporations were relocating to the area, which promised beautiful mountain views, affordable homes, and quaint, old-fashioned living with a hip, modern edge. I showed the article to Nancy, and both of us felt a little giddy. A month later, in October 2004, we bought a home in Bend online, without ever seeing it.

On our last night in the old townhouse, we slept on the carpeted floor. All of our furniture was on a Matson cargo ship somewhere in the Pacific Ocean. We hated shutting down our business and saying goodbye to our loyal customers. Dismantling the big silk-screening machine and packing it into crates for shipment was difficult and a little painful. We had absolutely no guarantees that we'd be able to get the business up and running, or make it successful, for that matter, in Oregon. We didn't even know if we'd ever see our belongings again. But we had a home waiting for us across the sea, and that was all we needed to feel happy and excited as we drifted off to sleep.

The next day, November 30, 2005, I finally left Hawaii.

Getting settled in Oregon was a little crazy, and not just for us. Our parrots—Davinci, a baby Scarlet Macaw; Hobbes, an Umbrella Cockatoo; Einstein, an African Grey; Dante, a Bluefront Amazon;

Darwin, a Solomon Island Eclectus; and Chip and Dale, two half-moon conures—somehow survived their scary several hours in the hull of a giant Boeing. Nancy and I drove our rented Budget van, all seven birds in tow, through the slick and narrow Santiam Pass, on roads so steep and packed with snow, we had to stop to buy chains for our tires. Unfortunately, they sold us the wrong size and we slid off the road into a ditch. Finally, though, we arrived at our brand-new home, which we'd designed online as if we were playing a real-life version of the Sims video game. When we pulled up, we confronted three feet of snow in our driveway, and had to borrow a shovel from neighbors to even get to the front door. Never mind all that, though—we were home, at last. No one in Bend knew our history; to them, we were just Thomas and Nancy, another happy couple settling into a new town. This was the fresh start I had been dreaming of. Nancy and I dove into decorating, painting rooms, hanging pictures, picking out new furniture, and choosing different themes for different parts of the five-bedroom house. I can't think of many things more thrilling than decorating a new home. Nancy and I were nesting, big time, and we'd never been happier in our lives.

Just one thing was missing.

❖ ❖ ❖ ❖ ❖

I pushed hard on the emergency stop button, shutting down the giant, whirring, six-armed T-shirt press. Nancy looked at me, wondering what was wrong.

Something had suddenly occurred to me—a flash of insight I couldn't ignore. "Marvin's nose was way too large, and your mother's nose is way too broad," I said, out of the blue. "Who else could your mother have slept with?"

It may sound odd that I brought this up to Nancy in this way, but like I said, it was almost an intuitive feeling. The only question is why it occurred to me right then and there, after years of being with Nancy. I have always been hyperaware of facial features. I used to stare at my face, and then at my parents' faces, for hours, trying to figure out why I looked the way I looked. Because my appearance was so different from my mother's, and because people always told me I looked nothing like her, I paid a lot of attention to eyes and noses and lips and everything on a face. Anthony would tease me that I had a big nose like my father's, and wrinkles on my neck just like he had, and a round face, again, just like his. He was the lucky one, I thought. He didn't look anything like our father. My features became a mystery to me—why did I look nothing like the parent I loved and exactly like the parent who didn't love me? It seemed so unfair, and the puzzle of inheritance mesmerized me for much of my life.

That day, as Nancy and I printed T-shirt after T-shirt—a repetitive and noisy task that allows us both lots of time to think— Nancy's nose entered my consciousness in a new way, for some reason. Her nose didn't look anything like her father's or her mother's. I had seen photos of Marvin, and he had a really big nose. So did Nancy's brothers. I started wondering how she wound up with such a pretty, perky nose—and how it could possibly represent the middle point between Marvin and Julie.

It took Nancy only two seconds to blurt out an answer to my question, "My godfather! Jimmy! The last time I saw him I was three years old!"

My little "eureka" moment set into motion events that changed both of our lives. Nancy immediately called her mother, who was in the middle of preparing for a dinner party.

"Mom, this is going to sound weird, but did you ever sleep with Jimmy?"

Julie was quiet for a moment, before saying, "Of course I did."

Nancy drew a deep breath. "Could he be my real father?" Julie was quiet again, then told Nancy to call her back after the party. I could tell from Nancy's face and Julie's reaction that my hunch wasn't harebrained after all. Later that night, when Nancy called her mother back, she got right down to business.

"Mom, is Jimmy my father?"

"Yes," said Julie. "There's no doubt in my mind."

Nancy was crying now. "Why didn't you tell me? What were you waiting for?"

"I didn't feel like you were ready."

"Ready? I moved out when I was fifteen! I got married, had three children, I own my own house! When did you think I'd be ready?"

Julie told Nancy to calm down. "I want to talk to him," Nancy said. "I want to meet him. Where is he?"

"I need to talk to him first," Julie replied.

Nancy and I cried and hugged and tried to digest everything that had happened. She didn't sleep a wink that night. She had always wished she had a different father. She dreamed she had been adopted, or somehow dropped into a family not really her own. She knew that she was a good person, kind and caring, and she couldn't understand how she could have come from a man as cruel and callous as Marvin. Realizing that he wasn't her father after all was an enormously emotional discovery for her. Now she just had to prove it—and then see if the man who really was her father would accept her as his own.

Julie gave our phone number to Jimmy, who'd started using the name Jim after his college years, and we waited and waited for him to call. I knew it had to be excruciating for Nancy. She had so many questions. Had he always known? Would he want a relationship with her now? Was he even a decent person? Finally, Jim called. He had a deep, kind voice. At first, he seemed guarded and unsure. But as he and Nancy spoke, he became more sensitive to her emotions.

"I can't be completely sure that I am your father," Jim told her, "but I am open to meeting you in person."

We immediately booked a flight to Phoenix to meet him. One day before Nancy's forty-third birthday, we showed up in the ornate lobby of the Phoenician resort in Scottsdale to wait for Jim. I looked at Nancy and saw that her eyes were glazed over. "I'm scared," she said. "What will I say?"

"How about 'hi?'" I joked. "Look, you're getting a second chance at having a father. Do you know how many people would love to have that?"

"I'm scared he's going to reject me. And I'm not ready to be rejected by another father."

"He will love you," I said. "*Strangers* love you. If he truly is your father, he's going to walk in here and scoop you up with open arms."

But Nancy couldn't stop crying. "I don't even know this man," she said, "and I love him already."

We looked up and saw a man with gray hair and blue jeans walking toward us. From fifty feet away, I knew it was him. As he got closer, I looked at his nose—it was a match. Jim was nearly with us now, and I looked at Nancy. She knew it was him, too. I could tell she recognized the man she had last seen when she was just three years old. Jim stopped in front of us. He didn't say a word. He simply scooped Nancy up with open arms.

They hugged for a long, long time. Then they separated and looked each other over. Nancy gave him a long-stemmed rose she had bought for him. Jim handed over a package of presents he had picked out for her. I remember thinking he looked like Santa Claus. In our hotel room, we all talked for hours, and I pulled out a DVD of photos I'd made of Nancy, starting with images of her as a child. I could see that Jim was crying as he watched it.

"I'm sorry I didn't try to find you," he told Nancy. "Julie never told me things were bad. I thought you were having a good life without me."

Then Jim hugged Nancy again and said, "I want you to stop looking. Let's just say I am your dad."

"I need to know for sure," she said.

The next day I accompanied Jim and Nancy to a clinic that performed paternity tests. In the waiting room, Nancy felt the urge to touch Jim. She reached across and took his hand in hers. He smiled, and they held hands as they waited. An attendant finally arrived to swab Nancy and Jim's cheeks; when it was done, he came back limping and holding his jaw and joking, "Man, that was hell!" He had the same irreverent, playful sense of humor as Nancy.

A couple weeks later, we got a phone call from the clinic. They had the results. I grabbed my camcorder and filmed Nancy listening to the technician on the phone. Every now and then, I watch the tape because it is so beautiful.

"There is a 99.9968 percent chance that James is your father," the clinician said.

"What are you saying?" she asked. "What does that mean?"

"Honey, he's your dad."

We jumped and laughed and cried and hugged. Something remarkable was unfolding right before our eyes. Neither Nancy nor I had had a good father-daughter relationship; in fact, they had both been lastingly destructive relationships. And now, Nancy's greatest fantasy—that she had a good, kind father waiting somewhere to meet her—was actually coming true. I can't come close to describing the emotion we felt in those days of discovery. For both of us, it was a magical gift.

Jim embraced the news just as he'd embraced Nancy. Never a big phone talker, he ran out and bought his first cell phone just so he could communicate more regularly with Nancy. He called her "baby" and "sweetheart"—names no father had ever called her. He fell in love with Nancy's two daughters, thrilled to have his twelfth and thirteenth grandchildren. As it turned out, Amber was his first biological grandchild. And he watched the DVD I made of Nancy so many times that it wore out and started to skip. I've since made two replacements for him.

Beyond my joy at seeing Nancy's reaction to finding Jim, there was something about him that made him very dear to my own heart. From the moment we met, Jim accepted me as a man, and then as his son. We became wonderful friends, and he has told me he is proud of me because of the way I treat his daughter. He has called me his hero. I had never had that sort of relationship with another man—a relationship based on respect and admiration. Nor had I ever experienced the attention of a father whose fortitude came not from the power of his hand but from the tenderness of his heart. Jim became an invaluable male role model for me, as well as an example of what a true father could be like. For both Nancy and me, having Jim in our lives was a huge eye-opener. In his short time as Nancy's official father, he made us believe that a strong, healthy father-child relationship can indeed exist, and he taught us that fathers can be trusting and loving in a way neither of us had ever known. He was the kind of father that I wanted to be.

Not long ago, Jim sent me a tattered and well-worn 1939 edition of Rudyard Kipling's verse. One of Kipling's poems, "If," is Jim's favorite, and over the years he has asked his sons to memorize it and to try to live by its meaning. Now he was asking me—his son—to do the same. I was filled with a bursting sense of honor and pride. He was giving me a gift far greater than he could have possibly known. I have indeed memorized the poem, and its last lines always give me chills.

> " . . . If you can fill the unforgiving minute
> With sixty seconds worth of distance run,
> Yours is the Earth and everything that's in it,
> And—which is more—you'll be a man, my son."

❖ ❖ ❖ ❖ ❖

Leaving Hawaii and buying our first house, and then meeting Nancy's real father, were two profoundly impactful events in our lives. Moving forced Nancy and me to consider exactly what kind of life we wanted to live together, now that we had the opportunity to start from scratch. And meeting Jim convinced us that we wanted to have a family of our own, that we weren't at all doomed by the bad examples of fatherhood from our pasts.

Nancy and I had many heart-to-heart talks about our future. We knew we wanted to have a baby, and now we knew something else— we knew we wanted the baby to be biologically our own. Nancy could no longer have children, because of a hysterectomy she'd had, due to endometriosis, in her twenties. We discussed the ideas of hiring a sur-rogate mother, but there was a long list of cons that were difficult to dismiss. Besides, I had specifically opted not to remove my reproduc-tive organs. Physically, I was more than capable of carrying my own child. At the very least, it was a possibility we had to consider. Both of us knew from the very beginning that my getting pregnant would open us up to untold scorn and criticism. We knew the world would not be ready for the sight of a pregnant man. But we both decided that this hardship alone wasn't reason enough for me not to carry my own child. Ultimately, we talked about what would be best for our child, and we decided that no child would want its parent to pass off the responsibility of giving birth just because of what other people think. The more we talked about it, the closer Nancy and I got to deciding to have a child the natural way—with me getting pregnant.

One of the first people I chose to tell about our discussions was my old girlfriend Christine. Breaking up with her had been painful for me, and I still cared for her deeply. We spoke often on the phone, and when I called her to tell her that I was thinking of getting pregnant, she was supportive. "Your baby is going to be beautiful," she said. "And you are going to be such a wonderful papa."

On a lovely summer Sunday, July 16, 2006, Nancy and I spent an afternoon picnicking by a tranquil stream in the Cascade Mountains, and I got the urge to call Christine. Nancy and I had talked about how important family and friends are, and we both agreed that Christine was one of the few truly special people in our lives. I had been trying to reach her for a week, but we had been missing each other; I felt a strangely urgent desire to hear her voice. But that evening her machine picked up yet again.

"Hey, it's me. What are you, dead?" I said. "Call me, I miss you. I love you."

Two days later, Nancy picked up a call on my cell phone. I watched as all the color drained from her face. It was the mother of one of Christine's friends, telling us that Christine had rented a Dodge Magnum and had been driving from a friend's house to a bar late Sunday night. She had been drinking most of the day. She was on a dark two-lane road in the middle of the desert in Barstow, California. Perhaps a car in front of her started to turn and she didn't notice. Perhaps a car coming from the other direction caused her to swerve. Her Dodge screeched across the opposite lane, hit a dirt berm, and flipped. The impact threw Christine from the car. The first person at the scene saw her lying on the road near a stain of blood on the asphalt. Her face looked fine, but inside, her injuries were devastating.

We never knew if Christine died instantly or later, at the hospital. Nancy and I flew to Barstow for her cremation memorial. We drove to the spot where she had crashed, and the bloodstain was still there. Though it was California, "Arizona hot" was the term Christine always used to describe the unimaginably hot weather there. Standing there in the place where she'd met her end made my stomach drop. To think that this arid desert was the place where the life of someone I loved dearly had come to an abrupt end was too much for me to bear. After all, Christine and I had known the tropics of Hawaii together, and she'd been so free and alive. My associations with her were blue skies and sandy beaches, not the vast desert landscape we confronted that day. The small church in Barstow was filled with so many people that some had to stand in the back. There was no coffin, just a photo of Christine's radiant face next to some flowers on a table. I had brought the photo with me, and carrying it from Christine's parents' place to Barstow on my lap made me feel like she was there with me, riding "shotgun"— like she'd always liked to call out.

I didn't think I could do it, but I made it up to the podium to say my final words in remembrance of Christine. I didn't speak of the little things, like her love for surfing or that her favorite music group was Journey. Instead, I spoke of how much love she shared with others. When I first learned she had died, I broke down sobbing—deep, wrenching, unstoppable sobs. Here on the podium, I was afraid I would break down again. But I kept my composure as best I could, and I read a poem I'd written for her when we were a couple, on a day when I missed her desperately and all I had was a photo of her to look at.

"For then this breath about my ear

Says nothing to my wordless tear

That drips upon your paper face

Where lips instead should be in place."

❖ ❖ ❖ ❖ ❖

hristine had always told me that if she were to die, she wanted her ashes sprinkled into the sea so she could be with the dolphins she loved so much. And so Nancy and I accompanied her parents to a beach in North Carolina on a blustery but bright November day. Colorful shells were everywhere on the shoreline, and some black, fossilized shark teeth had washed ashore. I remembered how Christine had described these very things to me—the beauty of the beach and the pretty shells. She had vowed that one day she would take me with her to her hometown in North Carolina. This, sadly, was that day.

A reverend said a few final words before Christine's father and brothers, clutching the box that bore her ashes, marched toward the sea. We all followed and watched as they sprinkled what remained of Christine into the lapping water. In the distance, we could see dolphins swimming by, arching their bodies and spraying mist. We said goodbye to Christine, there at the ocean's edge. She could now swim with the dolphins and surf for eternity.

The truth is, beyond the devastation I felt, I was also very angry with her. We had fought so many times about her drinking, and this was the exact fate I'd always dreaded for her. I was angry that she didn't love herself enough to stop drinking, and that she thought she was invincible. I cried for days after her memorial service because, among other things, it reminded me so much of my mother's funeral. I never got to see my mother after she died, and now I was reliving that experience with Christine. I hurt so badly that I even tried to blame myself for her death. Just a few days after she died, I got a phone call and saw the name Christine flash on my phone. I was stunned. But it was only Christine's brother calling me from her cell phone, which he had found in the bushes near the crash site. There was just a single message on her phone, and it was the one from me, wondering if she was dead. I realized then that I had called her around the very time that she crashed. Had she been reaching for her phone when she swerved? Was it my fault that she died?

I knew it wasn't, but I still wrestle with my pain and anger. I dream about her more than I dream about my mother—I see her wearing her familiar teal jacket with her hair down, the way she always wore it, and sometimes we talk and hug and I try to somehow fit her into my life. But then I wake up and the pain and anger come back.

The very day we found out that Christine had died, I was due to take my bimonthly injection of testosterone enanthate. It had been my ritual for eight years now, and it was a central part of my life. But on that day, I held open the refrigerator door and just stared at the half-full 10-cc bottle of testosterone on the shelf. I stared at the bottle for a long, long time. I felt intense sorrow at losing Christine, and intense guilt at being able to go on with my own life. *What is the meaning of it all?* I thought. Life is so precious, so fragile, so fleeting, that to waste even a minute of it is a terrible crime. Christine's death was so stark, so final, and now all I had left of her were memories. How do we remember and honor those we lose? We honor them by living our lives in a way that would make them proud.

Though it took her some time to come around, in the end, Christine had been supportive of my transitioning to a male. She had also been there for Nancy and me when we'd told her we wanted to have a child. I knew that I would have to stop taking testosterone if I wanted to get pregnant. Losing Christine made me realize how much family meant to me. Life has a higher meaning and purpose for us all, and for Nancy and me that meaning and purpose were becoming increasingly clear: We were going to have a child together. I knew that if Christine were there, she would tell me once again that our baby would be beautiful, and that I would be a wonderful father.

I shut the refrigerator door and went to find Nancy.

"It's time," I said to her. "Let's have a baby."

Chapter 11

COMPLICATIONS

I am bleeding.

It is October 9, 2006, and I am having my first period in more than eight years. I had always thought of my menstrual cycle as a curse, so I was relieved when I started taking testosterone and my periods went away. But that October day, the sight of my blood filled me with such intense positive feelings that I was caught by surprise. I wasn't just happy to be having a period—I was ecstatic. My reproductive organs were just fine.

Getting my period scared me a bit, too. Both Nancy and I were well aware that my getting pregnant would change our lives in ways we couldn't possibly foresee. And, like any expectant parents, we had a lot of natural concerns about bringing a baby into the world. Nancy would be experiencing this pregnancy from a very unique perspective, as the mother of the child but not carrying it herself.

She had two beautiful daughters already, but Nancy had also had some difficult experiences: She'd had an abortion at a young age, endured a miscarriage, and lost her son to crib death. She had been married to an unfeeling man who had punched her in the stomach while she was pregnant; who had not been fit to be a father to her children; who had torn her down with insults and beatings until her self-image had eroded. She was older and wiser now, and far surer of herself. And now that she had a loving husband and a stable home, she was embracing the idea that this pregnancy experience would be joyful.

I had other concerns. For one thing, I wasn't sure how I would handle the loss of a certain portion of my masculinity. When I stopped taking testosterone, I noticed drastic changes right away. I saw signs of muscle atrophy, and at the gym I had nowhere near the same strength or vitality as I was used to. Even though I weighed a little less, my body felt heavier. I used to be able to knock out a whole bunch of pull-ups, but now I was able to do only fifteen, then ten, then five. I was also becoming more emotional as my natural testosterone and estrogen levels returned. How would I handle all of these changes? Psychologically, was I ready for all of it?

Of course, there are no guarantees in life; all expectant parents have fears and concerns. I knew that I was mentally strong—I had to be to have survived my upbringing. Sacrificing some of my masculine physicality, which I had fought so hard to obtain, was ultimately okay with me—it was, after all, just temporary, and a small sacrifice to make to achieve this higher dream of ours. Instead of building muscles, I would be preparing my body for a different kind of challenge. But my determination and devotion to the task would be no less fierce.

I didn't feel that carrying a child would compromise my identification as a male. I was a man who was renting out his body to perform this one miraculous feat. I was not switching back to being a female; I was still, in my mind, fully male. I've always felt that the desire to have a child is neither a male nor a female desire—it is a human one. So why not carry the child as a male? Why couldn't I be a pregnant man? It was important for me to come to terms with what I was doing, and to be sure of how I felt and what it all meant to Nancy and me. Ultimately, I spent hundreds of hours thinking about it, and talking it over with Nancy. We further discussed the idea of hiring a surrogate mother, but the cons outweighed the pros for us. The stress, the money, the increased risk of multiple births, adoption issues—all of it was more than we felt we wanted to take on, particularly since we didn't have to. After all, how many couples hire a surrogate if they can carry the child themselves? Why hire a surrogate who won't have the same commitment to the pregnancy that you would? Would a surrogate do all the things I was planning to do for our baby—take prenatals, avoid drugs and alcohol, listen to classical music?

Eventually, we felt sure of our decision and ready to move forward. We were secure in our relationship as husband and wife, and now we'd be parents—and have the classic nuclear American family. The only difference would be that I—the male and the father—would be the one getting pregnant and giving birth. Once we made our decision, Nancy and I never looked back. We felt that we were doing the right thing, and we steeled ourselves to face a world that was sure to challenge our steadfastness.

The temperature gauge on my truck read two degrees Fahrenheit the day Nancy and I kicked off our baby-having business.

Powdery snow kept the windshields busy. Nancy was bundled in layers: mismatched T-shirts, her black leather jacket, and fuzzy black gloves. She slid into the truck and scrunched up her shoulders, shivering. We blasted the heating vents and fishtailed out of our driveway.

"I dreamt of babies last night," Nancy said.

"Me too."

❖ ❖ ❖ ❖ ❖

We were off to visit Dr. M., the fertility endocrinologist we had selected to help us get pregnant. We'd signed up for a $350 initial consultation, hoping to get as much information as we could about our unique situation. I had trolled hundreds of websites, looking for some precedent for what we were doing. But there was nothing. As far as I could tell, no legal male and husband had ever had a baby before, so we were hoping that Dr. M. could help guide us through the process.

The waiting room smelled of nothing, neither antiseptic like a hospital nor scented like a medical office. A bible sat on the table near our chairs. Finally, Dr. M. emerged. He was tall, around six-foot-five, with almond-shaped eyes. "Right this way," he said as we shook hands; we settled into an office at the end of a hallway.

"So," he began, "when did you last take your medication?"

I told him I had been off testosterone for nearly seven months. I explained that my menstrual cycles were four or five weeks apart, and that before I started on testosterone they had been six weeks apart. "Your hormones seem to be out of balance," he said. "Your ovaries were probably dormant from the years of taking testosterone." Dr. M. looked at us both contemplatively and asked why Nancy couldn't carry the baby herself.

"Well," I said, "she would love to but she can't. You see, she used to be a man."

Dr. M. reeled a bit before realizing I was kidding. Nancy patiently indulged him, telling him about her hysterectomy. Dr. M. proceeded to ask us if we'd considered using a surrogate. "God knows, that's more acceptable than you carrying the baby," he said. "This is a small town. People will talk."

Dr. M. had other reservations as well. Would I, as a male, be able to get insurance that would cover my pregnancy? How would the birth certificate read—would it say that "Thomas" was the mother? What about the baby? How would we tell the child about our situation? Weren't we worried that our child would be teased mercilessly at school? Was I psychologically capable of going through this difficult process? "Don't worry about me," I told him. "Yes, I can feel my body changing, but it's only temporary. I have no desire to become a woman again. When I want something, I do whatever it takes to get it. That's just me. I am fine with being a pregnant man." I didn't feel the need to go into the details of the birth certificate, but I mulled it over in the office for him nevertheless. "I will be the father, yes, but for the sake of argument, there are women whose names are Ryan and Michael and Kyle," I said. "It's just a name."

I could tell that Nancy was done indulging him. She was biting her tongue, trying to stay calm. We had come to get information from Dr. M. about the process, and instead, for $350, we were educating him. Finally, he said, "I'm going to have you speak to our counselor. We've never dealt with this situation before, and I need to make sure that our staff will be comfortable working with you. The counselor will get a good feel for where you are and how we can all deal with this."

Dr. M. told me to drive out to his Portland clinic as soon as my period started, so that I could take an FSH-level test to measure my follicle-stimulating-hormone levels. I'd also have an ultrasound to see the number of active follicles in my ovaries. He told us that he'd be scheduling an appointment with his staff psychologist when we came to see him. On the way out, he offered what I'm sure he felt was helpful advice.

He said, "You might want to consider shaving your facial hair the next time you come in."

❖ ❖ ❖ ❖ ❖

Because we were eager and excited, the time couldn't have passed more slowly. As soon as I got my next period, we took off work, drove the snowy Santiam Pass to Portland, and found ourselves sitting in Dr. M.'s waiting room. I still had my beard. I noticed giant-eyed goldfish swimming in a tank; one of them was hording pebbles, sucking them up and spitting them out behind a big rock. Sting and Enya played in the background. A sign read, "MALE PATIENTS ARE RESPONSIBLE FOR BRINGING IN THEIR OWN SAMPLE."

When the nurse came out to greet us, she immediately asked Nancy if she'd ever had a vaginal ultrasound.

"The appointment is for him," Nancy explained. The nurse's three- or four-second pause, and the nearly audible shifting of gears in her brain as she processed what was happening, was a reaction we would soon become all too familiar with.

I hopped up on a cushioned metal exam table and waited for Dr. M. Looking down at my hairy legs, I noticed the presence of muscle and absence of fat. *How different I must look compared with all of the doctor's other patients,* I thought. Dr. M. came in, took hold of a long plastic wand, and gently started the ultrasound. Dr. M. seemed distracted and fidgety, and the nurse actually had to remind him to sanitize the wand. Very quickly, we could see on the screen what looked like an oval horizontal sack with twelve large black dots.

"Here's your left ovary," Dr. M. said. "These dark circles are your developing follicles. It looks like you have twelve on that side. That's a good number to work with." He found another fifteen follicles on my right ovary.

"You have good-looking ovaries," he told me.

A blood test would show that my FHS level was 6.5; anything under a 13 was good. My estrogen level was 31, perfectly normal at that point in my cycle. Physically, I was in great shape to have a baby. "We're going to have you see the psychologist now," said Dr. M. "Chances are, your case will have to go in front of the ethics committee to see where we go from here."

That sounded ominous to me; I pictured a bunch of old men sitting around a long cherry-wood table, grilling me as I wilted under a harsh spotlight. Nancy gave me a nice firm hug.

Dr. D. was an attractive, unassuming, middle-aged woman, friendly and apologetic for keeping us waiting. Nancy and I sat on her leather sofa, and Nancy grabbed a pillow and clutched it tight to her lap.

"So, when did you realize you wanted to have a child?" she asked.

I liked her immediately. Her demeanor was soft and gracious, and she had asked me "when" and not "why." I told her that I had wanted to have a child since I was young, but I'd wanted to go to college and become financially stable first. Nancy and I had our T-shirt business back up and running in Bend; financially, we were in sound shape. I also explained how we were a strong and loving couple, ready to provide our child with an ideal home.

"I do realize your situation is unusual," said Dr. D. "Please be patient with my learning curve. Thomas, how will it feel for you to be pregnant? To be female again?"

"But I won't be," I said. "My gender identity will not be changing throughout all this. I will still be Nancy's husband."

"How will you feel if others in your community find out you are pregnant?"

"We are new to the area," Nancy jumped in. "Thomas will probably look like he's just gained weight. Everyone knows him as a man. It won't even occur to anyone that he could be pregnant. And if they do find out, then they will have to seek psychological help if they have a problem with it. We're not going to change who we are."

It always makes my heart beat faster when Nancy stands up for us, but I felt a small twinge of fear that the doctor might take her reaction as a defensive one. I hated knowing that our ability to have a child might be in her hands, but I loved Nancy's feistiness and I couldn't help feeling lucky that we were going through this adventure together. "What will you tell the child?" asked Dr. D. Nancy explained that we would be open, and that we were sure our baby would love us and be proud of us, but that we hadn't yet decided exactly how it would all unfold. This was a good, honest answer, and again I felt proud of Nancy. Dr. D. didn't speak for a long moment.

"You're right," she said. "Other people's prejudices are not good enough reason not to have this child. Not long ago, two lesbians having a child wasn't acceptable. You are certainly a special situation, but I don't see anything wrong with your having children."

Nancy and I practically fell over each other as we ran giddily back to our truck. That a professional doctor had seen things our way was a huge windfall, and we couldn't stop laughing.

"It's actually happening, isn't it?" Nancy said.

❖ ❖ ❖ ❖ ❖

We waited and waited for Dr. M. to call us back. Days passed, then weeks. Nancy and I had settled on a cryobank and had found the perfect donor, after looking at hundreds of profiles. We paid extra to get a photo of the donor as a child, and we hung the picture up on my computer—a happy, attractive blond boy. Nancy and I knew instinctively that this donor was the right one as soon as we found him. There were specific reasons why we chose him, but overall it was something bigger and deeper than just his statistics that drew us to him. I can't even explain what it was, just that both of us were sure he was the one. Now, all we needed was a doctor's signature on an Authorization to Release Semen form so that we could open our account with the cryobank and purchase sperm. Supplies of sperm are limited, and sometimes donors disappear, so the fact that we had to act fast was testing our patience with the ethics committee and Dr. M.

When we finally got a call from Dr. M., he explained the ethics committee wouldn't be meeting for another two weeks. That meant I'd have to miss yet another cycle, and every time I missed one it cost us about a month and a half. We wouldn't be able to buy the donor sperm we wanted, and we felt worried that the stock would disappear.

"A bunch of strangers are going to play God with our lives," Nancy said.

Nancy called Dr. D., the psychologist who seemed to approve of us, to find out what was happening. It was surprising to both of us to find out that Dr. D. had had a change of heart. Suddenly, she had concerns about my pregnancy. Even her tone of voice had changed. "I'm concerned about how you're going to explain all this to your child," she told Nancy. "And I'm worried about how it will all affect Thomas psychologically." My gender identity was the problem, even for someone who seemingly sympathized with us. The irony was that if we were still a lesbian couple, having a baby would be no problem. Here we were, a man and a woman, a traditional couple—and yet we were facing obstacles that two lesbian parents wouldn't be contending with. I was starting to feel some of the old pariah feelings that I'd experienced in Hawaii—

that I was somehow not normal; that I could make people hate me just by being myself.

Another two weeks passed; once again, Dr. M.'s office called us to tell us the board had yet to meet. "And even when they do meet, they might not have a decision for you right away," an assistant at the clinic told us. "They might even table your case." Table our case? That could set us back months! We would surely lose our donor. Nancy and I talked about going to another doctor and starting over, but we realized that would only waste more time—and cost us several more thousand dollars, to boot. We had invested this much time and money in Dr. M., and we figured we had no choice but to wait for his decision.

Finally, on March 14, 2007, my cell phone rang; I noticed the call was from Portland. It was Dr. M.

"Thanks so much for calling," I said, shocked and happy to finally be hearing from him.

"Well, I don't think you'll be thanking me by the end of this call."

I felt my heart cramp in my chest. "Thomas, the ethics committee met yesterday, and we all came to the consensus that this situation is just too different. It's never been done before. We have nothing to refer to. There are just too many outstanding questions and concerns."

I wasn't shocked to hear the news. I had no words to try to argue with him. So I held the phone to my ear, absolutely silent. I felt nothing.

"We're concerned about your gender identity," Dr. M. went on. "It's not fair for you to be female, change to a male, then go back to being female, only to be male again. We're concerned about your psychological health. We're worried about what you will tell the baby."

Still, silence on my end.

"I'm sorry, I can't help you," Dr. M. said. "I like you, but I can't assist you in this endeavor. We all feel it would be unethical for the reasons I already stated. You know, Thomas, just because you can have a baby doesn't mean that you should." And then, the final thrust: "Our staff just doesn't feel comfortable working with someone like you."

Nearly ten months had passed since we'd made the decision to get pregnant. We were not even back at square one; we were way behind our starting point. It seemed entirely possible that we would never find a doctor to sign the form we needed to have in order to have a child. Not long after that call, Nancy and I checked the supply of our donor's sperm online. The word "unavailable" appeared in harsh, square letters next to his number. He was gone now.

Chapter 12

THE LAST PORTAL

There weren't many people Nancy and I could tell about my decision to get pregnant. We told her daughters, Amber and Jen, and they were supportive, as usual. A few medical professionals knew, too, but that was about it. We didn't tell Nancy's newfound father, Jim, because we felt it would be a lot to lay on him so soon in their relationship. We didn't know how he'd react, and neither one of us was ready to risk losing him. I didn't bother to update my father or brothers about what was happening. I wasn't in a hurry to hear their disapproving comments. There was, in fact, only one other person I really wanted to share my decision with—my aunt Tyler.

I had always wanted to be close with Aunt Tyler, because she was my only real link to my mother. She and my mother were estranged; she didn't even show up at my mother's funeral. Even so, she had grown up with my mother, and she sort of looked like my mother, so it felt important to me to have a relationship with her.

I wrote her letters from the ages of thirteen to sixteen and finally met her again when I was seventeen, because we were able to arrange a meeting in France during my study abroad, which happened to coincide with a vacation for her. We met outside her hotel and walked along the Seine. It was a short, awkward meeting, however, and when I hugged her she didn't really hug me back. I left feeling like she had attended to some obligation to meet me because I was her niece, not because she was interested in getting to know me. Aunt Tyler wasn't anything like my mother. She barely laughed or even smiled, and offered no personal details about herself. She was sedate and guarded, and she didn't give off any energy—unlike my mother, who was a powerful and giving presence in the lives of everyone she knew.

Still, Aunt Tyler and I kept in touch. I visited her a handful of times over the years. When Christine and I visited San Francisco, I called her and asked if we could stay with her for a couple of days. When I revealed to her that Christine was my girlfriend, she was supportive; she and her husband even went out to a gay nightclub with us. I was thrilled that she was so accepting, and after that trip we became much closer, talking regularly on the phone and sharing our mutual interest in our genealogy.

The next time I saw her, though, my appearance had started to change. My hair was shorter and I looked more muscular, more masculine. I noticed Aunt Tyler seemed uncomfortable. When I finally confessed that I was taking testosterone and was planning on having my breasts surgically removed so I could transition to a male, she became distant. But still, our relationship survived my transition; if she didn't wholeheartedly accept my transformation, at least she hadn't cast me away or written me off like the rest of my family had. We continued to talk and trade emails, and I was happy to have her in my life.

Telling Aunt Tyler about my decision to get pregnant was about wanting to share one of the biggest things I'd ever do. Aunt Tyler was the only family I had left, but I still struggled with finding the right time to tell her. Finally, in one of her emails to me, she mentioned how the Beatie line had no more heirs to pass along the family name. I decided to take the opportunity to tell her that Nancy and I wanted to have a baby, which—since I had changed my name to Beatie—would perpetuate the line. I didn't say specifically that I was the one who was getting pregnant; I figured being vague was a good way to broach the subject. But Aunt Tyler knew that Nancy couldn't carry a child, and so she wrote back that she wanted to talk to me about the matter on the phone. On Super Bowl Sunday 2007, I called her from my upstairs media room, earmarked to become our nursery. "Hi, Aunty T, it's me," I said. As it turned out, she had already guessed that I would be the one getting pregnant, so she got right down to business.

"So, do you feel any different now that you're not taking your hormones?" she asked.

"Nothing drastic," I said, feeling a little caught off guard. "I feel a little more emotional, but overall I feel very stable and happy."

"How do you feel about living as a woman again?"

"Oh, no, I'm not doing that at all. I am very content living as a man. My gender identity is constant."

I could tell already that Aunt Tyler was less than open to the idea of my carrying my own child. But I had handled her resistance to other changes in my life. I felt that I could make her see my side of things. Yet she kept pushing. "How will you hide the pregnancy?" she asked.

"Hide it?" I responded. "Heck, I'll just say I'm fat!" A long silence followed, so long that I asked if she was still there.

"Thomas, as a family member I feel that it would be irresponsible for you to have a child," she said at last. Her voice was icy, monotone. "It would be emotionally and psychologically damaging."

"What do you mean, damaging?"

"You have a hard time dealing with death. The loss of your mother, then the loss of Christine. Having a baby to make up for them is the wrong reason to have a child. You have a lot of issues you haven't worked through yet."

I could hardly believe what I was hearing. A hard time dealing with my mother's death? You bet I did—who wouldn't have? And Christine's death? I would be concerned if someone had an easy time dealing with death. Imagine if only people with no issues could have children—the human race would die off rather rapidly. What exactly was Aunt Tyler trying to say? Why was she so opposed to my getting pregnant?

"A child needs to know who his or her biological parents are. How would you explain being a man who became a woman and who gave birth, then became the father? How would you tell that to the child?"

I was angry now. I had heard this argument too many times before. "Lots of children don't know who their biological parents are. Besides, we're going to be honest with our child."

"Thomas . . . "

"So, it would be okay for me to adopt a child? Wouldn't that child also not know who his or her biological parents are? Am I so horrible that you don't think I can create a loving, stable home for my child?"

"Then at least get another opinion. Speak to a psychologist."

"Why? Other couples who want a child don't have to speak to psychologists."

"You're not other couples," she said.

I couldn't hold back any longer. I was starting to understand that Aunt Tyler didn't have a problem with my having a baby. She had a problem with my being me.

"Aunt Tyler," I finally asked her, "do you think there's something wrong with me?"

In the silence that followed, in the interminable five or six seconds in which she could not muster an answer, my relationship with my aunt essentially ended. Perhaps I'd known this deep down long ago; perhaps I was only realizing it now. But I knew then that she had been lying to me during our entire relationship. She had not been supporting me, she had been *tolerating* me and not telling me how she really felt. It occurred to me after I hung up that she had never introduced me to family friends I would have loved to meet—my Aunt Virginia, for example, who was not really my aunt but who had been one of the two sisters who took care of my mother after her mother died. Aunt Tyler was embarrassed by me, and I was angry with myself for not having seen it. I had gotten to the point where I was rarely duped by anyone—I can usually tell what people think about me—but I was completely blindsided by my aunt's rejection. I had wanted her to like me so badly that I had ignored the obvious evidence that she didn't. But you can't force someone to love you and accept you. They either do or they don't. In that long and awful silence, I realized that my very last link to my family was gone.

"You know how I feel about this, Thomas," she finally said. "I'm not going to argue with you. I hope you make the right decision for everyone's sake."

"Thank you for talking to me about this," I told her, sincerely. "It's more than even my father would do."

"I love you," she told me.

"I love you, too."

❖ ❖ ❖ ❖ ❖

After Dr. M. turned us away—and balked at our suggestion that he return any of the thousands of dollars we had spent on medical tests and consultations—I went online and found a transgender-friendly doctor in the Portland area. Dr. B., I soon found out, had transitioned herself, from male to female. Nancy and I went to see her in April 2007, getting up at 4:30 AM to drive three and a half hours over the Santiam Pass to make our 9:00 AM appointment. Her waiting room was enormous, and there were a couple of transgender women waiting for appointments. Dr. B. was short, with wavy brown hair and obvious breast implants. She didn't make much eye contact, but she was gracious and friendly, and that was a relief.

"You are my 603rd transgender patient," she announced cheerfully to us. "And my 223rd female-to-male. Actually, you're the third FTM to broach the subject of fertility this month."

"Really?" I asked, amazed that there might be someone else out there doing what I was doing. "Have any of them gotten pregnant or given birth?"

"Well, no," she said. I felt let down that Dr. B. couldn't offer any more information. We explained to Dr. B. that what we really needed was a physician to sign an Authorization to Release Semen form so that we could begin the process of getting pregnant. Dr. B. said she no longer delivered babies, but would refer us to yet another doctor, Dr. J., who might be able to help. Dr. J. had performed gender-reassignment surgeries, and Nancy and I allowed ourselves to think that our luck might finally be turning. Two weeks later, however, after we made another long drive to see Dr. J., we realized it hadn't. He declined to sign the paperwork, and said instead that we should come back again when I had my period—the same tactic Dr. M. had used to string us along.

"And," he said, "we feel that you should see a psychologist before we decide anything."

How many times would I have to defend my sanity? How many people would I have to convince that I was normal? Was another doctor now going to waste another six or ten months of our lives before deciding that he wouldn't be able to help us, either? A sickening feeling of desperation was starting to sink in. Could it be that we would never find a doctor willing to help us? It seemed entirely possible. When we got back home, I dug up the name of the doctor who had originally prescribed testosterone for me, and I sent him an email telling him that I was ovulating, and that I wanted to have a baby. I practically begged him to sign the release form, which I attached. Dr. L. had a sad personal history—he had a lesbian daughter who committed suicide, and he had been very sincere and interested in me when I was his patient. It was a desperate move on my part, and I didn't hold out much hope that he would send back the form. At work, my stomach tied up in knots whenever I heard the whir of the fax machine, but it always turned out to be an invoice or an order. Neither Nancy nor I was anywhere close to giving up the fight, but I must admit that I was starting to think that our dream might never come true.

On May 1, 2007, the fax machine whirred. There it was, in the tray—the cryobank authorization form. Dr. L. had signed the form.

We were going to have a baby after all.

❖ ❖ ❖ ❖ ❖

Nancy and I wasted no time at all. We fired the form off to the cryobank and jumped back online to find another donor. Amazingly, our original donor had come back—and his specimen was available. Our luck was turning. We decided to see a sociologist who specialized in gender-identity counseling, hoping to get a letter of recommendation that might help us down the road. The goal was to have a letter from a professional saying I was stable and clear thinking. Sure enough, she wound up writing a supportive letter for us. "I recommend whatever medical procedures are necessary to bring about the desired pregnancy," she wrote.

Not much later, we got our donor sperm—it arrived in a giant dry-shipper tank that cost a fortune to ship to Oregon. Nancy and I had purchased fifteen vials of the donor sperm, in case our donor disappeared again. It wasn't cheap. Each vial costs about $500; then you have to have it shipped to you overnight from the cryobank, which costs around $300. There is a very specific protocol that you must follow to get your sperm at the optimum time: We had to keep track of my hormone levels with a fertility monitor, which detected changes in my daily hormone levels and indicated when I was ovulating. There is only a twenty-four-hour window of conception per cycle, so timing is crucial. The monitor lets you know which days precede your peak fertility with a "high" reading, giving you time to have your sperm shipment expressed to you. We got two vials shipped to us and kept the others in storage.

Our shipment arrived with less than twelve hours to spare. Normally, both preparations aren't done at the same time. Our initial plan was to inseminate me using one vial for each of the peak fertile days. Now we had to use them both at once.

We were surprised by how big the whole contraption was for a couple simple vials of sperm. The sperm is kept in a heavy tank cooled by liquid nitrogen; the tank arrives in a giant box stuffed with foam padding. Nancy and I put the tank in the back of our truck and strapped it in very carefully with a seat belt. I kept thinking: *Our baby is in there somewhere.*

We drove to the Portland office of a new doctor, Dr. V., to whom we had been referred. He agreed that he'd help with the insemination, but on paper called the visit an "examination." In his office, a nurse came around to help prepare us, but within minutes we could tell she hadn't been briefed on who we were. She looked at me, then at the tank, then back at me. Then she left the room. Soon another nurse came to take her place. I had been rejected many times before, but I felt irritated by this treatment at this point in the process.

When we got into the examination room, Dr. V put on gloves and opened the tank. The interior is so cold that it will burn your hands if they are unprotected. There was a long metal cane attached to a metal canister. Dr. V. pulled it up, and out of the icy fog of nitrogen emerged a small metal cup containing two vials of sperm. It looked like a scene out of a futuristic movie. Of the two samples in the cylinder, one would be injected into my uterus, a washed IUI with decreased motility; and the other would be injected into my cervix, an ICI. Dr. V. started with the IUI, but it was clear from the start that he had never performed an insemination before. Nancy and I basically had to talk him through it. He heated water to precisely 98 degrees, then dropped the IUI vial into the water, where it would thaw for exactly ten minutes. If the water is too hot, it can crack the vial or kill the sperm. Once the vial had been thawed and taken out of the water, we had thirty seconds to aspirate it into the syringe. Exposing the sample to the air for any longer than that would have probably rendered the sample worthless. I watched as Dr. V. took the vial from the water and used a syringe to draw it up.

It seemed to me that he was moving in slow motion. I watched the clock on the wall—couldn't he move any faster? At around twenty-five seconds, I nearly jumped off the table to grab the syringe myself. Finally, Dr. V. got into position. He had put a speculum in me so that he could clearly see my cervix—now he needed to put a catheter through the cervix and into my uterus. Then he said he didn't have the right equipment to actually get the sperm into my uterus; instead, he would simply fire it in the *direction* of my uterus.

As he did so, I thought, *This can't possibly work.* I looked at Nancy and could tell she was thinking the same thing. When it came time to do the ICI, he was as ineffective as he'd been with the IUI. Nancy and I left convinced that we had just wasted two perfectly good, and pretty expensive, vials of donor sperm.

Two weeks later, I went into my upstairs bathroom and took a home pregnancy test. I waited for three of the longest minutes of my life. The result: negative. No pregnancy. Nancy and I were crushed. Nancy and I were so emotionally invested, even though Dr. V.'s insemination had been disastrous, that I'd allowed myself to believe that there was a chance it had taken nonetheless.

Two weeks after that, after my period had come and gone, I felt a heavy, damp pull between my legs when I got out of bed one morning. I was bleeding. Why was I bleeding now? My first instinct was to take another pregnancy test. What did I have to lose, besides the cost of the kit?

This time, the stick showed two vertical pink lines. I was pregnant, but how could that be? I had just had my period, and the earlier test had been negative. I told Nancy about the results, and we both agreed that I would take another test the following day. We figured it was a false positive.

That afternoon, we went on an organized tour of new homes in central Oregon. At the very first home we visited, a ranch-style house with stunning views of the snow-capped Cascade Mountains, I started to feel nauseous. By the third home, I was curled up in the fetal position on the expensive downstairs couch.

"What's wrong?" Nancy asked. "Do you want me to drive us home?"

"No," I told her. "Take me to the emergency room."

Chapter 13

LIFE AND DEATH

Nancy helped me up off the sofa and out of the 6,400-square-foot model home. My stomach felt like I'd been stabbed, and sweat dripped down my face. On the drive to St. Charles Medical Center I was curled up into a ball, holding my head in my hands. Something was really wrong with me.

In the emergency room, there were at least twenty people ahead of us. "Nancy, go up and tell them you're having pain in your lower pelvic area, that you're bleeding, and you think you're pregnant," I said. I knew it would only complicate matters if I had to explain my situation. Plus, I worried about my predicament becoming public, since there is no patient confidentiality in an emergency room. Nancy stepped forward and told a heavyset nurse she was in pain.

"On a scale of one to ten, one being no pain, ten being excruciating pain, how would you rate your pain?" the nurse said.

Nancy looked at me. I didn't want to give a hand signal, so I focused really hard on the number eight.

"Eight," Nancy said.

"When was the last day of your period?"

Again, Nancy looked at me, trying to figure it out. "June 4," I blurted out. "Remember, Nancy? And don't forget about your pain. Lots of pain."

"Yes, I'm having pain right here," Nancy said, pointing to her lower left side. She looked at me and I motioned to my lower right side. She quickly switched her hand. Part of me wanted to laugh. Nancy didn't look like she was in pain at all. Meanwhile, I was close to passing out.

We waited for over an hour, during which time my pain subsided to about a three. "Why don't we just go home?" I said. "We can always come back if the pain starts up. If I'm not pregnant, my hormones are probably whacked out or something. Maybe it's the beginning of endometriosis." Nancy got up to talk to the nurse, but it didn't look like she was saying that we were leaving. The nurse grabbed Nancy by the hand and led both of us into a private office.

"What's this all about?" she demanded. "What are you not telling me?"

"Everything I've told you is happening," said Nancy, "except that it's happening to him."

It took the nurse several seconds to get her bearings, She looked around for a moment, perhaps thinking that there were hidden cameras waiting to catch her reaction. "You, you . . . " she stammered, "you used to be a female?" I nodded and smiled.

The nurse snapped to attention, much to my relief. "Hold on, let me push you through to the head nurse," she said. "I'll switch the info in the system from Nancy to Thomas. Let's get a doctor to see you." She was on our side now, working for us. She didn't think we were freaks. On her way out she said, "You two are gonna make great parents." These were rare and fleeting moments of encouragement we relished, and the people responsible for them will never know quite how much they meant to us.

A few moments after her departure, a male nurse in royal-blue scrubs walked in. The original nurse went over to him and told him why we were being admitted—and which one of us was sick. He, too, did a double take. "Do you get it?" the female nurse asked him. "Yeah, I get it," he mumbled. He pounded at a keyboard and produced a blue plastic wristband for me. I noticed right away that it read, "MALE."

They whisked us into patient room number 21, and I lay on a gurney as they drew blood. I can't bear IVs, so I squirmed as I watched the nurse arrange his ghastly paraphernalia: a giant syringe, rolls of gauze, antiseptic, plastic tubes. When he started feeling around with his fingers for a vein, I nearly bolted. The nurse sensed my distress and joked, "Nancy, will you please hold his right arm down? I don't want him to punch me."

Eventually, an elderly doctor, Dr. W., swept back the curtain to our room and said, "I hear you're quite a unique person." While he examined me, he asked us questions about our situation. He then explained that the initial results of my blood test were inconclusive— they didn't know if I was pregnant or not. How could they not know? I became even more convinced that the home test had been a false positive. But then, two hours later, the curtain swept open again and the doctor popped his head in.

"You're pregnant," was all he said before vanishing again.

I felt my face scrunch up, and before I knew it, I was crying. Nancy hugged me, but neither the tears nor the hug were joyful. This was supposed to be the happiest moment of my life; I had waited so long to get here, and fought so many battles. This was not how I'd thought it would all play out—not in an emergency room, doubled over in pain, afraid that something was wrong. No matter how carefully you lay out your future, life sometimes imposes its own plans on you.

When the doctor came back, he told us that the ultrasound had revealed a mass next to my right ovary. It was four centimeters, about the size of a golf ball. "You are bleeding internally," Dr. W. told me. "There are three possible scenarios here." He proceeded to tell us that the mass could have been an ectopic pregnancy; that there was a chance I was having a miscarriage; or that the mass itself was bleeding. "If this is the case," he told me, "it could be a harmless cyst, which sometimes form during normal pregnancy." He went on to tell us that they couldn't tell if it was a normal pregnancy, because it was too early to detect a gestation in my uterus. He asked if we had an ob-gyn. We didn't. Dr. W. set us up to meet with another doctor, Dr. J., who would monitor my hCG pregnancy hormone levels to determine exactly what was happening inside me. The idea that I could be having an ectopic pregnancy—in which the fertilized ovum is implanted somewhere other than the uterine wall—terrified me. Yet I was discharged casually, and the doctor simply told me I should come back if the pain got too severe or if I started to bleed excessively.

"How am I supposed to know what is too much pain?" I asked, feeling panicky.

"If you're doubled over," he said, "come in."

We drove back home, scared, exhausted, numb. What was supposed to be an exhilarating life experience now felt murky and full of dread. We had just come off of a couple of very important visits, too: Steve Waterfall—the man who went on that magical camping trip with us when I was younger, and who I desperately wanted to step in and replace my father—came to visit Nancy and me in Bend. We fished for trout, kayaked, roasted marshmallows, and talked about the old days. I knew that he had once loved my mother, and that made him very special to me. He had recently reentered my life after twenty years. In him I discovered a link to my mother I'd never imagined I'd have. After Steve left, Christine's parents came to visit us for the first anniversary of their daughter's death. They drove more than 1,100 miles from Kingman, Arizona, to be with us. Having them stay with us made us feel rich and bolstered by the love of our small extended family. Best of all, Steve and Christine's parents alike completely supported my decision to carry a child.

Because of those visits, Nancy and I could not have been higher. They had carried us through the insemination with the knowledge that we had an extended family unit that supported us. In an instant, however, all those good feelings felt far away. Was my pregnancy normal? Was I going to be a parent? Or was it a miscarriage? To not know was excruciating.

For one week, I had to go to the hospital every other day to have my blood drawn to measure my hCG pregnancy hormone levels. For it to be considered a normal pregnancy, the hCG levels would need to double every two days. My numbers were coming up slightly short, but were high enough to give me hope. The pain in my abdomen increased and subsided. Before long, though, it got so bad that I was keeling over. I knew I had to go back to the hospital—I knew something was terribly wrong. I was admitted immediately, and another ultrasound was performed. The ER doctor on staff that day relayed the results to us: I was bleeding internally even more than before. Blood was pooling around my internal organs. The mass outside my uterus, now assumed to be a fetus inside my fallopian tube, had grown significantly. I needed to be administered methotrexate, a chemotherapy drug, which was used in cases like mine to stop the replication of rapidly dividing cells. This would, in effect, cause a spontaneous abortion and terminate my pregnancy.

I had to make a decision: Take the drug and abort the fetus, or not do anything and hope that it was a benign cyst. If it weren't the latter, however, the consequences could be disastrous: My fallopian tube might rupture, and there was a strong chance I could die. I was in shock, and very reluctant to let go of my pregnancy. I had a baby inside me, my first baby. But the doctor had no words of comfort for me. I asked him a few questions about the chemotherapy treatment and how certain they were about the ectopic pregnancy. He replied, "You're not going to let me go, are you?" I didn't know what to say. Emotional and thrown by my circumstances, I began to sob. He turned on his heels and exited the room.

It was a gut-wrenching decision. I was basically being asked to kill my fetus without knowing whether it was viable or not. Nancy's face had gone white. I knew just what she was thinking. "What should we do?" I asked her once the doctors had left us alone. "I don't want to lose the baby," she said. "But I *can't* lose you."

Our emotions were swirling chaotically, making it even harder to reach a rational decision. We hugged each other close, and for the longest while said nothing. Deep down, we both knew what we had to do. They injected a dose of medicine into both sides of my butt. After an hour, they sent us home. The medication made me lethargic and sleepy, and I slept for twenty-four hours straight. When I woke up, I had the awful realization that the medicine inside me was actively working to kill the fetus. It was excruciating to know that soon my body would show the biological signs of a miscarriage.

I had to go back to the hospital to get my blood hCG levels monitored over the course of the next several days. For four days, my levels were dropping and returning to normal. Suddenly, though, on the sixth day, I got a call that my results had tripled. This meant that the cancer medicine hadn't worked—and that I still had a baby inside me. It was clear to the doctors now that the fetus was gestating in my right fallopian tube, stretching it beyond its intended capacity. It was on the verge of rupturing. I was told to go to the surgery center immediately.

What was happening inside me was threatening to kill me. In fact, I later learned that masses of more than 3.5 centimeters tend to be resistant to methotrexate, and that the most advisable course of action would have been to remove the mass immediately. Instead, I had reached a crisis point. I was sweating, and my stomach was throbbing. I gripped Nancy's hand tightly. I told Dr. J. that I was consenting to the emergency surgery. My pregnancy needed to be terminated.

During the emergency operation, my right fallopian tube, pregnancy included, was removed. This meant that I now had exactly half as much of a chance of getting pregnant again. I became a much higher-risk patient. Nancy and I had somehow surmounted all of the obstacles to get to this point, and now here was another one, slashing our chances of having a baby by 50 percent. What if this happened again, I thought, to my left side? What if I had no fallopian tubes at all? I wouldn't be able to get pregnant without the help of a fertility doctor. Having a general practitioner perform a simple ICI was one thing; finding the support of a fertility endocrinologist to perform in vitro fertilization was quite another. Our chances at a successful pregnancy were seeming increasingly bleak.

After the surgery, Dr. J. talked to us about what had happened. In her office, she asked if I wanted to see pictures of my surgery. I did. I wanted to know everything. The series of photos showed me from the inside out, including what they had removed. I was not prepared for what I saw: shots of my organs in varying shades of purples and maroons, and the fallopian tube they removed, containing my fetus. Doctor J. explained that the ultrasound indicated that there were three small sacs in my fallopian tube. They couldn't be sure, but it seemed very possible that I would have had triplets.

Nancy and I went home, devastated. We had invested so much time and heart, and so many resources, in having a baby, and now it had ended in tragedy. We had created life, but it had landed in the wrong place—had missed by just a few inches an environment that would have helped ensure survival. It was impossible not to think of the what ifs.

Shortly after learning about our loss, my unsupportive brother Anthony said something I will never be able to forgive him for: "It's a good thing that happened. Who knows what kind of monster it would have been."

❖ ❖ ❖ ❖ ❖

Nancy and I were determined to have a baby, and we waited eight weeks before trying to conceive again. This time, we decided to do the insemination ourselves. The first time around, in a doctor's office, had been a stream of errors. We trusted that we could go through the process in the comfort of our own home. I again started testing my hormone levels with my fertility monitor, waiting for it to indicate my brief window of ovulation. By then I knew my cycle pretty well, so we got ready to order another two vials of our donor sperm. I tested "high" on the day I guessed I would, and immediately sent for the sperm. The next morning, the fertility-monitor test strip displayed a tiny little egg—a symbol of peak fertility.

Later that day, our donor sperm arrived at our warehouse via Federal Express. The FedEx lady was all smiles as we signed for the package. She could tell it was from a cryobank, and I suspect she thought she knew what was going on: that Nancy was the one getting inseminated. We loaded the tank in the back seat and, once again, carefully secured it with a seat belt for the drive home. Was our baby in there this time? Nancy and I were nervous and excited.

We lugged the big canister to our master bathroom, and I went into our bedroom to get ready. All I had to do was use the $25 speculum kit I had found online to pinpoint just where my cervix was. Easier said than done. The kit consisted of a tiny blue flashlight, a white plastic mirror, and a translucent speculum that felt so rickety, I was afraid it would collapse inside me. Even after everything was in place, I had no luck finding my cervix. I realized I had no idea what a cervix looks like.

In the bathroom, Nancy had a far tougher task. She was in charge of the delicate, timely procedure that would give us a chance at getting pregnant. We knew that if we botched this insemination, we'd have to wait five weeks to try again, and that put a mountain of pressure on us. Every day we waited seemed like an eternity to us. We wanted to get it right this time; we were extremely focused and serious.

Nancy had gone to several stores in search of a syringe to inseminate me with, and to her dismay hadn't found anything suitable. Finally, she went to a pet store and bought a cheap little plastic syringe used to give medicine to birds. All of this science and technology, and we were dependent on a $2 bird syringe. Nancy cut the cylinder's seal and carefully pulled out the metal cup containing one vial for ICI insemination. I noticed that she was shaking. She put the vial in a cup containing water heated to the recommended temperature, and checked the clock to see when ten minutes was up. Suddenly she heard the vial pop, and she feared that maybe the water had been too hot. But at ten minutes she withdrew it, and it was just fine.

Now she had thirty seconds to get the donor sperm into the syringe and inseminate me. Nancy put her finger over the pointy end of the syringe to seal it, then carefully poured the donor sperm into the back. When she was done, she put the plunger on the back of the syringe and came into the bedroom. We were somewhere around the twenty-second mark. Nancy got into position and searched for my elusive cervix, but, like me, she couldn't find it. Twenty-five seconds.

Nancy's hand was shaking even harder now; she took a deep breath and inserted the syringe inside me. She was flying blind. "I think I squirted it off to the side of your cervix," she finally said. I hadn't felt a thing. Now that the pressure was off, we both broke down laughing. It was surely the least romantic ten minutes and thirty seconds of our lives. I was supposed to stay in bed for half an hour to make sure the donor sperm had a chance to get where it was going. I lay there for two hours, taking nothing for granted. Within minutes of the insemination, I had started to feel queasy. I remember a doctor telling us that some women can be allergic to seminal plasma and not even know it; perhaps that was the case with me. I lay there and had the same thought I had had four months earlier: *This can't* possibly *have worked.* It felt so imprecise, so willy-nilly—was this really how it was supposed to happen?

Later that day, I returned to work and promptly vomited. The date was October 11, 2007. I knew right then, as I bent over to throw up, that the insemination had worked.

❖ ❖ ❖ ❖ ❖

Two weeks passed. On a crisp fall morning I unwrapped a home pregnancy test and went into the upstairs bathroom. I sat on the edge of our Roman tub and breathed in deep to calm my nerves. I peed on the strip and waited for something to happen. You're supposed to wait three minutes, but after just seconds I noticed something forming on the strip. A single pink line—negative. But then, right before my eyes, a second line appeared, clear and bright and strong. Two pink lines. I was pregnant.

Chapter 14

SECRET JOY

The surgery that cost me a fallopian tube left a four-inch scar on my left lower abdomen. The scar is roughly the shape of a question mark, or the letter Z, though Nancy observed that it resembles a seahorse. I looked in the mirror and saw that she was right. Suddenly, I got chills. Seahorses, I knew, are part of the only family of animals in the world in which the males are the ones that get pregnant. The female seahorse shoots thousands of eggs into the male seahorse's pouch, and the male can give birth to as many as two thousand babies. Was there a better symbol for me than a little seahorse? Nancy gently traced her finger along my scar as we both studied it in the mirror. When I did a little more research, I found out that seahorses mate for life.

❖ ❖ ❖ ❖ ❖

When I was a girl, I never yearned to be pregnant. I never fantasized about what it would be like to carry a child. I suppose part of me thought that I'd just have a baby someday, but the pregnancy part never really factored into that, somehow.

But as soon as I found out I was pregnant, I felt as if a lifelong dream was coming true. I sat on the edge of my Roman tub and wept when those two pink lines showed up. I called for Nancy, and when she looked at the stick, she started crying too. Everything about this test was different from the last one. This was it. This time it was going to work out. There was a sureness about it, with none of the dread and anxiety we'd experienced two months earlier. I felt thrilled and excited and giddy and all that, but I also felt, deep inside, a sense of calm. I felt real pride in my little unborn baby. The odds against it were astronomical, but I felt that this baby was undaunted by its task. It would not be denied. I knew we had to get an ultrasound to confirm the results of the home test, but I was already sure. I was bringing a life into this world.

Along with the joy, there was a certain inevitable sadness for us that came from our feeling like we couldn't tell anyone, other than Amber and Jen, about it. Not my father, who I knew would make things worse; and certainly not Anthony, who'd had the nerve to tell me that my baby would be a monster. Not Nancy's mother, who had stopped speaking to her right after Nancy pressed her about her real father. Not Aunt Tyler, who had already made her feelings about our decision quite clear. And not Jim, Nancy's real dad, whom we felt we needed to give more time. We wanted to announce to the world that I was pregnant, but the truth was, we didn't have a soul to tell.

We scheduled an ultrasound for the six-week mark. Meanwhile, I was doing everything I'd ever heard you're supposed to do when you're pregnant. Even before my inseminations, I'd changed my diet and started taking a slew of prenatal vitamins. And once I knew I was pregnant, I felt more conscious about being in touch with my body than ever. I have been an athlete most of my life, and I know what to eat and how to exercise to keep my body in top shape. This was probably my primary reason for not wanting to go with a surrogate. I can't imagine any surrogate ever being as attentive to the physical demands of being pregnant as I would want her to be—as I knew I would be.

As soon as I decided to get pregnant, I cut out alcohol and coffee completely, saying goodbye to my cherished caramel macchiatos. I stopped drinking my favorite energy drink because it was loaded with caffeine and other stimulants. No sushi, no deli meats, no hot dogs, no unpasteurized cheeses, no seafoods high in mercury. I cut out sugar, too, which meant no desserts, unless they were sugar-free.

I also postponed a visit to the dentist. I knew I'd have to get an X-ray of my teeth, and they would never have asked if I was pregnant—and it would have been awkward to bring it up. My daily ritual of prenatal vitamins included a multivitamin with folic acid, extra vitamins C, E, and B, and calcium. I also took lecithin, choline, and DHA in the form of omega-3 fatty acids from algae, because these things help enhance eye and brain development in the fetus. I took nine pills during the day, six at night. I took them religiously, never once missing a turn; had I forgotten, Nancy would have made sure I remembered.

I was nearly obsessive about wanting to provide the best foundation for our baby. I suppose lots of expectant parents feel this way. I went online and researched, making exhaustive lists of things we would need and taking note of things I should avoid during pregnancy.

I went out and bought a bunch of pregnancy books: *In the Womb, Heading Home with Your Newborn, Your Baby's First Year, The Official Lamaze Guide.* I trolled websites like I-am-pregnant .com. I wanted to know precisely when I should start feeling the baby kick, what major tests were in store, which sensations were normal and which weren't. I bought a pregnancy journal and marveled at the enormously pregnant woman on the cover. I felt my own flat stomach and wondered if I would get that big. Keeping the journal was thrilling for me, but it also made me sad. It made me realize just how much I missed having my mother around. All of the stories and tips and insights she would have shared with me, and all of the joy she would have taken in my being pregnant, were lost to me.

Nancy and I drove to see Dr. J. for our six-week doctor's visit. After she performed the surgery for my ectopic pregnancy, we both agreed we liked her. She was smart and kind and professional and, if not exceptionally warm toward us, at least as accepting as any doctor we had encountered. After I took the home pregnancy test, we decided we wanted her to be our doctor, but we weren't at all sure she would want to help us. So we called her office and made an appointment to see her. We could tell she was a little surprised to see us. Perhaps she thought it was presumptuous for us to act as if she had already signed on as our ob-gyn. When I sensed her reluctance, that familiar feeling of rejection crept in. But I was wrong about her. She agreed to be our doctor. Nancy was beaming. Having an ob-gyn we liked and trusted made everything more official—more real.

So now here we were, back in Dr. J.'s office for our first official appointment. We watched as the cone-shaped image on the screen jumped and fizzed. Somewhere in there was evidence of my pregnancy—I was sure of it. But try as I might, I couldn't detect anything that even suggested a fetus. All I saw was a microscopic dot, and a strangely blinking light. For a few moments, I felt a wave of panic wash over me. What if I wasn't pregnant? What if that little blinking light signified something bad?

"What is that?" I finally asked, pointing to the flashing dot.

"That," the attendant told me, "is your baby's heart."

❖ ❖ ❖ ❖ ❖

Morning sickness knocked me for a loop. In the early days, I was sick 24/7. Just the mention of food would make me want to vomit; it felt like a combination of sleep deprivation, jet lag, and a hangover all at once. About the only thing I could keep down was edamame—my very first craving. Nancy dutifully made me a bowl every night, until I couldn't stand those anymore, either.

But no matter how sick I felt or how big I got, I found myself in situations where I had to pretend I wasn't pregnant. Bumping into neighbors was one thing; as long as I wore baggy shirts, I was pretty sure none of them would suspect a thing. But what about having to spend four days with a group of people intent on getting to know me, scrutinizing my every quirk? That's exactly what happened to me in November 2007, when Nancy and I attended her family reunion in Phoenix, Arizona.

This was, of course, no ordinary reunion. Nancy had only recently discovered the identity of her biological father, and now she was going to meet all of his children—her new siblings and their families—for the first time. Nancy was understandably nervous, especially because she was going to be meeting her four brothers. All they knew about me was that I was Nancy's husband; maybe Jim had mentioned that I was a black belt. But no one knew that I used to be a woman—not even Jim. So the one thing I knew for sure was that no one was expecting to meet me and find out that I was nine weeks pregnant.

For days before the reunion, I worried myself sick. Would Nancy's brothers be able to detect some kind of pregnancy glow? Would I have to come up with some made-up excuse to get out of playing golf with them in the hot Phoenix sun? Even though I wasn't showing all that much, I *felt* very pregnant, and the idea that people wouldn't notice seemed far-fetched to me. But then I would think, *Of course they won't notice. You are a man, and men don't get pregnant.* Still, what if someone at the reunion got suspicious? I couldn't think of a worse way for Nancy's father to find out about me than at a big family reunion. I needed to keep my secret for at least another four days.

I never purposefully act manly. I don't feel pressure to prove my masculinity to anyone. I just try to act naturally, and that is more than enough for people to perceive me as male. But suddenly, faced with meeting Nancy's new family for the first time, I felt like I might have to put on a bit of a show. I was off testosterone, I felt more emotional and vulnerable than ever, and I had a nine-week-old fetus growing in my belly. And despite all that, I had to come across as a regular guy. This was Nancy's big moment, and I wasn't about to do anything to ruin it. So I packed my clothes and sucked in my gut and I told myself, *You are a man, damnit, so be manly!*

Nancy and I flew to Phoenix and met up with Amber and Jen, who had flown in from California and Kentucky, respectively. They hadn't seen us since we'd told them about my pregnancy, so this was their first chance to touch my belly. They both did, marveling at my tiny baby bump. It was a sweet and tender moment, and I felt so proud and happy, yet we all knew we'd have to start pretending as if I were just another dude with a slight beer gut. We met up with the family at a local Italian restaurant for the first night of the reunion, marching right into a boisterous gathering of happy relatives. Watching Nancy meet her six new siblings, and get along with them so effortlessly, was emotional for both of us.

Jim's family was extremely gracious to me, and I felt very comfortable around them. Even so, I was on guard right from the start. I couldn't afford to slip up in any way. When I was handed a bottle of beer, I'd politely shrug it off and say, "I'm watching my carbs." When I felt a wave of morning sickness, I'd simply slip away for a few moments to catch my breath. So far, so good.

But then the whole family decided to take a three-hour hike up Camelback Mountain—*in the rain!* I couldn't beg out of it—what would Nancy's brothers think of me then? Yet I hardly relished the idea of trudging uphill and downhill through mud for three hours in my, um, condition. Still, I knew what I had to do, and somehow I mustered the strength to do it—I hiked up the mountain along with everyone else, making sure no one noticed how out of breath I was.

This was the way I made it through four days of continuous activities—one night we had Mexican cuisine at Nancy's oldest brother's house; the next day we went bowling; on the last night we had a barbecue at Nancy's younger brother's house. It was enormously satisfying to see Nancy have so much fun and be surrounded by family. For me, too, being accepted into a warm and happy clan was beyond wonderful. On the last night of the reunion, Nancy and I took Jim and his wife, Brenda, out to dinner at Benihana. It was a belated celebration of Jim's seventy-second birthday. This was the moment Nancy and I chose to spring our surprise on him.

"Dad," Nancy said, "we're having a baby."

The look on Jim's face as he took in the news is one I will never forget. His eyes watered, his lips sprang into a smile, his whole face beamed. He knew, of course, that Nancy couldn't get pregnant, so we opted to tell him we were using a surrogate. This wasn't exactly a lie—it just wasn't the whole truth, since the surrogate we were using was me. There would come another time when we would share our secret with Jim—but this was not that time. Jim was so happy, so excited, so proud. Even though we hadn't told him the whole story, the fact that he reacted to our pregnancy the way he did was a gift to both of us. I could only hope that when the time came to tell him the truth about me and my pregnancy, he would continue to feel the same way.

"I will be a grandfather for the fourteenth time," Jim declared. "It can't get any better than this."

❖ ❖ ❖ ❖ ❖

Week twelve was a special week for me—I was aware that the most likely time to miscarry is during the first trimester, and I was anxious to get beyond that point so I could relax a little. Week twelve was our second ultrasound, a milestone moment. Nancy and I drove to Dr. J.'s office; I lay down on the examining table and tried to hide my apprehension. What I saw on the screen this time absolutely floored me. I was no longer looking at a dot that someone had to tell me was a fetus. This time I was looking at a little human being. I could see a face, eyes, and a mouth—my distinctly human baby. It was pushing its head down, wiggling its shoulders, moving its fingers. "Oh my, you guys are going to have your hands full," Dr. J. told us. "This baby is bouncing all over the place already."

I burst into spontaneous laughter, and it took me a while to realize that I was crying at the same time. Our quest wasn't just a wish or a hope anymore—it was real. The proof was right there on the screen: a busy, bustling, beautiful little life.

A few weeks later, I put on the biggest pair of jeans I owned and found I couldn't button them anymore. My waist had long been a 28 or a 30—these "fat" jeans were a 32, and even they were too small. Every day I checked myself in the mirror, looking for more of a baby bump. Nancy went shopping for pants for me, but naturally there weren't any maternity clothes designed for men. We joked that we should start a line of "manternity" clothes.

Two weeks later, once we felt comfortable that we were past the first trimester and in a safety zone, Nancy and I drove to Portland to look at baby furniture. We didn't buy any, but we came back with a stroller. I logged everything in my journal. "I notice that my hips are expanding," I wrote in week seventeen. "My hips are starting to ache, and I'm happy to see my bulge is even bigger." I jokingly started to ask Nancy, "Do I look fat?" so many times that even Einstein, our African Grey Parrot, started to repeat the question. Indeed, I was starting to feel fuller everywhere: the backs of my legs, around my arms, you name it. It felt as if every cell in my body were expanding with fluid.

The physical changes were extraordinary, but that, of course, was only part of it. Incredibly, some sensation returned to my nipples, which started to grow and swell. I no longer have mammary glands, yet my brain was sending signals there to get ready for a baby. Something similar happened to Nancy, too. She noticed that in the early stages of my pregnancy, she began to feel as if it were she who was pregnant. When I got morning sickness, she, too, felt nauseated. And as my body began to ache, her back acted up as well. We knew that men sometimes experience empathetic pregnancies while their wives are expecting; now we know that it works the other way, too.

Being pregnant changed not only my body but also my way of thinking. I felt more in touch with my emotions than I ever had, either as a woman or as a man. I felt more vulnerable and sensitive about things, and as a result I took fewer risks. I had always been in control of my body, shaping it at will, but now I had no idea where my body was taking me, and that made me more philosophical about everything. I felt like I was on a journey—a journey that made me think about the meaning of life. I felt an awesome sense of responsibility, and it was a good feeling. This swirl of emotions, whether caused by hormones or by the idea of having a child, made me feel mature and human and connected to the world—in ways I could never have fathomed.

And each week the child inside me grew and grew. "I can really feel you moving for the first time," I wrote in my journal. "It feels like a rolling and fluttering. You kicked twenty or thirty times today. That was incredible." Because of my ectopic pregnancy, I was hypersensitive to anything I felt in my stomach. I couldn't always be sure it was the fetus; it might be indigestion, or maybe I was getting sick. "Do you think the baby's okay?" I'd ask Nancy. "Yes, the baby's fine," she'd always say. She was my rock—always there to make me feel calm, assured, safe.

Our lives were so consumed by the pregnancy that it became impossible for us to keep it a secret, the way we could in the beginning. We were starting to bring strollers and other baby items into the house; neighbors were sure to catch on pretty soon. Still, we didn't want to tell anyone the truth just yet. No one in Bend even knew that I used to be a woman. I was just Thomas, the guy down the block, to them. And that was precisely how I wanted to keep it—simple and uncomplicated. After all, that was one of the big reasons I moved to Bend in the first place—to start over and be accepted as a man. True, being accepted as a man and getting pregnant are pretty contradictory goals, but I wasn't ready to have to explain myself to the public just yet.

Nancy and I decided, instead, to tell neighbors the truth— sort of. "We're pregnant," we would say, and everyone would automatically assume it was Nancy who was expecting. At work, Nancy had our baby's ultrasound as her desktop image. Everyone there congratulated her, too. It didn't feel like we were lying; we just weren't sharing the whole story. I learned to live vicariously through Nancy as customers congratulated her and asked how she felt physically. I had a few passing moments when I wanted to say, "Touch my belly" or, "Ask me how I feel." There was no such thing as pregnant-man blogs to share my feelings. Instead, I let Nancy speak for me.

Of course, having people think she was pregnant put Nancy in a pretty weird position. Once they found out, people would tell her that she looked pregnant, or that she was positively glowing. When we went shopping for baby things, the salesgirls asked Nancy when she was due. Trooper that she is, she took it all in stride. The only thing Nancy minded was when people would reach out and try to touch her belly. She would subtly pull back or change the subject or do something else to avoid being pawed. Nancy did not look pregnant, of course, but the power of suggestion is an amazing thing. We told our hairdresser, Morgan, that we were expecting, and she began asking Nancy a bunch of questions about being pregnant. Nancy cheerfully answered them all as I stifled a laugh. Finally, Morgan turned to me and said, "Thomas, you're not going to be one of those dumb husbands who asks a lot of dumb questions during the delivery, are you?" As I felt the baby kicking inside me, I said, "Um, no, I don't think so."

Withholding the full truth proved tricky in lots of other ways as time went on. Since I was pregnant, I had to avoid some of the strenuous chores I was used to doing—shoveling snow, lugging heavy stuff, lots of things around the warehouse. The doctor told me not to lift anything over twenty pounds. I felt a bit disabled at times. Fortunately, Nancy is as strong as they come, and she picked up the slack. But when people began to believe she was pregnant, we had problems. Once, a neighbor spotted her digging through two feet of snow in our driveway. He ran over and said, "What are you doing, you're pregnant! Where's your lazy-ass husband?" After that, Nancy would sneak out in the middle of the night to shovel the snow. As I got bigger, Nancy also had to go into the post office by herself to ship off boxes of shirts, each weighing over fifty pounds, to our customers. She'd push three or four at a time on a dolly and heave box by box up onto the counter. Because they knew us there, she received looks of concern and an occasional "Where's Thomas?" Another time, we had to return two patio heaters to Costco. Each one weighed about two hundred pounds, and Nancy was the one who had to heave them out of the truck. I was the lookout, making sure no one we knew saw my "pregnant" wife wrestling a giant heater while her husband paced around nearby with his hands in his pockets.

Nor could Nancy ever let anyone we knew see her enjoying a simple glass of wine. Early on, it was easy for both of us to forget our little ruse. We'd be in a restaurant and Nancy would take a sip of her wine, and suddenly we'd notice someone we knew looking at us in horror. Nancy would sheepishly push the glass toward me.

I felt bad that Nancy had to jump through hoops to keep our situation secret, and she in turn was sympathetic toward me, her pregnant husband. To a degree, that is. You see, Nancy had been a fiery teenager when she got pregnant. She climbed Yosemite Falls when she was in her eighth month, and she shied away from very few physical chores. Now she was on the other side of a pregnancy, and sometimes it was hard for her to muster all that much sympathy for me. Part of her wanted to tell me, "Get off your butt and go mow the lawn. Man up, already." In truth, I missed doing all of the things

I had chosen to take on as my duties as the traditional head of the household. I had always been the one to hammer things in, take out the trash, install new blinds, all of that. But now my instinct was to put the baby above all else; to be extra cautious and take no chances.

Late one night, when I was upstairs sleeping and Nancy was downstairs watching TV, she heard a noise in the back yard. Seconds later, someone banged on one of our windows. Freaked out, Nancy ran up the stairs just as I came running down. I grabbed a baseball bat that we kept handy and whipped open the patio door that led to our back yard. But in the very instant that I rushed into the darkness, ready to take on the intruder and defend my wife and home, a thought flashed in my head—*No, you are pregnant. You must protect the child first.* So I quickly turned around and came back inside, put down the bat, and locked the patio door. All of my male instincts—to fight, to challenge, to confront— had been overtaken by a stronger instinct to protect my child. I was frustrated, but I understood that the second instinct was the right one. So did Nancy; she has shoveled mountains of snow and mowed acres of lawn and carried tons of equipment without complaining. Her instinct, too, was to protect the child, and to protect me.

❖ ❖ ❖ ❖ ❖

January 31, 2008—week eighteen. Time for another ultrasound, to see if everything is going along as expected.

I lay on the examining table and watch the technician spread gel on my stomach. I now have a real, honest-to-goodness baby bump. The ultrasound image lights up, frizzy as always. There is our child, even more distinctly human than six weeks ago. The technician writes down the baby's measurements—each and every one of them normal. Our child does not have spina bifida, or Down syndrome, or trisomy 18. "You don't have a cleft palate, and your arms and legs are long and beautiful," I later wrote in my journal. "All four chambers of your heart are there, and your blood is flowing in all the right directions. Your umbilical cord has all three paths for blood supply. Your heart is beating at 153 beats per minute—just perfect."

This is also the ultrasound that will let us know what gender the child will be. Weeks earlier, we sent away for an online gender test: I pricked my finger and sent in a small blood sample in a secure envelope, and a lab tested for the presence of a Y chromosome. The process seemed scientific to me; the lab, for instance, permitted only women to work there, lest a male worker somehow taint a sample. Still, the test was not 100 percent reliable. A week later, our results came back. I knew that Nancy was hoping for a boy because she had lost her son, Shawn, to crib death, and would have loved to raise a boy. I told myself that I had no preference, though deep down I thought I might rather have a girl. I look back now and realize that I had a specific reason for wanting a girl: I felt I could equip a daughter with enough integrity and independence and confidence to smash through society's limiting expectations of her. Having a girl would be redemptive; as my daughter, she would not have to face the same trials I had.

The test results told us we were having a girl.

At our next appointment, we met with Dr. J. to discuss our ultrasound results. She weighed me and said I had put on less weight than normal. A pregnant woman at week eighteen should be heavier than I was.

"But Dr. J., he has no breast weight," Nancy reminded her.

"Oh, right," Dr. J. said, seemingly surprised at herself for overlooking that fact. In addition to losing muscle mass, I was probably at my target weight. There were no other pregnant men to compare me with.

When Dr. J. asked us if we wanted to know the sex of the baby, we told her we already knew. Though the home gender test wasn't 100 percent reliable, we also just knew it was right. It was the same feeling we had about knowing we had found the right donor and that had made us believe the second insemination had gone well.

"So, you know it's a girl," Dr. J. said. "You're having a baby girl."

Later that day—truly one of the most memorable and moving days of my life—Nancy and I sat on our sofa and discussed what we would name our daughter. We decided that her middle name would be Juliette, which had been both Nancy's and Nancy's mother's middle name.

And for her first name, she would have my mother's name. We would call her Susan.

Chapter 15

MANTERNITY

When I was in my early twenties, I was thrown out of a public women's restroom by a security guard who thought I was a man. "Okay, pervert, let's go," he said as he dragged me away. Apparently, someone had seen me go in and complained. I'd been thrown out of several other restrooms in my life; plenty of other times I'd left in a hurry because women were giving me accusing looks. And even though I looked like a man, I wouldn't dare go into a men's restroom. Something most people take for granted—using a public restroom—was, for me, a potential nightmare.

Things got a little easier when I started taking testosterone, grew a beard, and legally became a man. Then I abandoned women's bathrooms altogether, of course. I didn't get funny looks, since people assumed I was a man. I still use only stalls in men's restrooms, though, and I prefer to avoid public restrooms if I can.

Once I got pregnant, the funny looks and uncomfortable situations started all over again. Once, when I went to a doctor's office for a routine blood test, one of the nurses laughed openly at me when she saw that I was being tested for pregnancy hormones. Another time, shockingly enough, Dr. B., the transgender doctor we'd seen in the Portland area, later emailed us that we ought to prepare ourselves for the scorn of the world. "People are going to think of your baby as an abomination," she said.

My point is, I know I am different, and I am used to people giving me strange looks. It has been the story of my life. One of the big reasons I transitioned and moved to Oregon was to get a fresh start, to escape from all the funny looks and awkward moments—in essence, to fit in. Genderwise, our society is dimorphic—it insists on two, and only two, categories. There are men and there are women, and that's all there is. If you are a woman who prefers to live as a man, you simply don't fit into this unvarying gender paradigm. You aren't allowed to be on the fence about your gender—it is strictly an either/or proposition. Thus, society forces you to choose one or the other, even if you don't feel the need to do so. I could have easily lived my life as a man without legally changing my gender; I always felt that I was simply me, in all my uniqueness. I didn't have to define my gender one way or the other for myself, because that definition wouldn't have affected the way I was living my life. After all, if I were stranded on a deserted island, my legal documentation wouldn't make any difference to me. But I realized the world I live in doesn't tolerate fence sitters when it comes to gender. It doesn't invite grayness—it insists on black or white. The spectrum of gender and sexuality is constantly broadening, and far from fixed, yet the poles on either end—male and female—are, in our society, absolute. That is part of the reason I legally became a man. I wanted the world to see me as I already saw myself, and for that to happen, I had to come down squarely in one camp or the other. When I officially switched from an "F" to an "M," my life became immeasurably easier.

So why, then, did I choose to sacrifice that security by getting pregnant?

It's simple, really: I am not the type of person to shy away from something just because it might get messy. A lifetime of insults and strange looks and prejudices small and large has toughened my skin. I will never run away and hide from who I am, nor will I change just to please someone else. I am stubborn, always have been—my mom used to tell me that. I have always been able to will myself to become the person I wanted to be—a straight-A student, a black belt in karate, a legally recognized male. I am also a risk taker; I've never been afraid to take chances. I started my own business, bought a home online sight unseen, and made some pretty good money as a day trader. I am a peaceful person, but I'll fight if I have to; I know how to strike back and defend myself. On top of all that, both Nancy and I are politically active people; we have strong opinions about issues, and we stand up for those beliefs. Once we decided I was the best person to carry my own child, we didn't let the inevitable complications that lay ahead shake us from our convictions. I didn't let the fact that I was inviting a whole new round of funny looks and disapproving stares influence my decision. I'm not saying that I wanted to pick a fight—all I wanted to do was have a family. But if accomplishing that goal meant having to fight for my rights as a human being then I was more than ready to do that.

And make no mistake about it—both Nancy and I knew from the start that we were in for a long and difficult struggle. After all, I was now becoming someone the world had never seen before—a pregnant man. I was about to challenge the most immutable gender truism of them all—that it is a woman who gives birth to a child and brings life into this world. I knew that I would not be embraced by society, that I would be shunned and ridiculed and insulted. I knew most people would be confused by me, and I knew that when people feel confused, they tend to get angry and lash out. I knew what I was doing would be controversial, and even though I could not fathom just how vast a minefield I was walking into, I tried to prepare myself for the very worst. We expected that the Christian Right would have its say, and that media pundits like Bill O'Reilly would also tee off on us. I did not expect that Nancy and I would be able to change people's minds about us, nor did we go into this wanting to force our beliefs on anyone. Nancy and I hope the world will catch up with us soon enough. But the one thing we both insist on is that we be treated fairly and equally—that people respect us and our cherished American right to have a family.

That was the battle line we drew: respect, fairness, equality. I had played by the rules to become a man; I had jumped through every legal, psychological, and physical hoop required of me by the state and federal government. I was not breaking any laws by becoming pregnant—I was doing only what my body was naturally designed to do. I felt sure that, at least legally, I was on solid ground. But I would soon learn that that was not the case.

Before I was inseminated, Nancy and I sat down and designed a strategy for how we might handle certain scenarios, particularly if I were to start to get any kind of public attention. We started calling everyone we could to get professional opinions on what sorts of obstacles we might be facing. We didn't want to leave anything to chance; we wanted to be ready for all the twists and turns that lay ahead. We called several legal groups, a bunch of private attorneys, and a few gay and lesbian organizations. We called the ACLU, the venerable civil rights organization. We called Lambda Legal, which bills itself as the oldest national organization pursuing litigation and advocacy on behalf of gays, lesbians, and transgender men and women. We called the National Center for Transgender Equality in Washington, D.C. We told them all what we were planning to do, and we asked them what we could expect.

What we heard back was shocking. Several attorneys told us that my getting pregnant could lead to our marriage being deemed invalid. Their thinking was this: Only women have babies; therefore, I was a woman; therefore, Nancy and I were a same-sex couple—and same-sex couples can't get married in Hawaii. Broadcasting to the world that I still had my reproductive organs could force some legislator to overrule my transition to male; by getting pregnant I was, in effect, disproving that I was male. Never mind that removing your reproductive organs is not required for you to become a legal male. And never mind that our marriage is fully recognized by every state in the nation, and that we receive all of the more than 1,100 federal benefits earmarked for married couples.

More than one lawyer suggested that Nancy and I apply for a domestic partnership as insurance. Again, this was shocking to us. How could top legal minds be advising us to do something *we aren't legally allowed to do*? I am legally male, and Nancy is legally female; thus, as a couple, we are ineligible to apply for a domestic, same-sex partnership. In order to do so, Nancy and I would have had to get a divorce, and one of us would have needed to get a sex change. The lawyers warned that if I were to die during the delivery, Nancy would have no legal claim to the baby. She would not be the mother, they said, because she played no part in the birth and had no blood relation to the child. It seemed unthinkable to us that Nancy, my legal wife, would not be considered the rightful mother of our baby, but the lawyers insisted we were on shaky ground. One lawyer even told us that Nancy should immediately adopt the child once it was born. His thinking was that the birth certificate would list me as the mother, leaving no place for her. To protect her rights, she should adopt the baby—even though, according to law, a spouse automatically becomes a coparent.

Everyone we talked to was worried about the birth certificate. Who would be the father, and who would be the mother? We knew what we wanted—I wanted to be listed as the father, even though I was giving birth. I did not at all feel like what I was doing was maternal. I was not going back to being female in any way—I was not toggling between genders. Throughout the pregnancy I would still be a man, not least because that's what it says on my driver's license, social security card, birth certificate, and passport. How could I, a legal male, be listed as the mother? And what would that make Nancy—the father? I had fought too hard to become a fully documented male to start listing myself as a female or a mother on any documents. It seemed more than reasonable to me to be listed as the father on the birth certificate. I was a man before the pregnancy, and I would be a man after the birth, which made me the baby's father.

As I started doing more research, I found out that a birth certificate is a record of live birth, a record of legitimacy. When

Nancy was born, Marvin was recorded as her father, even though he was not biologically related to her. If Nancy were able to carry our child, I would have been automatically listed as the father and she as the mother, even if it had been my egg, and even if the baby were not her biological child. Therefore, in more instances than one that I could think of offhand, the biology or biological relationship of the mother to child was often irrelevant. Still, the lawyers seemed convinced we'd have to list me as the mother. Nancy and I decided to circumvent the massive bureaucracy behind issuing birth certificates and go directly to the nurse at the hospital who would be in charge of listing the parents on the certificate. We told her about our situation, and about our desire to list me as the father. Fortunately, she was sympathetic. She told us that the parents are the ones who fill out the birth certificate. "You can write down anything you want," she told us.

Some people may ask why I didn't just agree to list myself as the mother, or as a female, on the dozens of forms I had to fill out. For me, listing myself as a female would have been a flat-out lie. I am not a female by any legal definition, and checking "F" on medical or insurance forms would amount to fraud. Transgender people exist and should have the right to have their medical bills covered by insurance. I wasn't doing anything wrong or illegal; why should I have to lie or fudge the facts? Checking an "M" on forms is not merely a symbolic gesture for me. My masculinity is the very essence of who I am, and I was not willing to subvert it in this or any other moment of my life.

The insurance companies, unfortunately, saw things differently. I constantly had to cross out "Fs" that had been pre-checked for me on insurance application forms. Even before I got pregnant, it was difficult to get insurance. I was open and up-front about my history, transgender status, and legal standing as a male, but the medical insurance companies didn't have policies in place for transgender people. I refused to classify myself as a female just to get insurance; I felt it would be fraudulent and open me up to a host of problems down the road. Fortunately, we finally found an insurer in Oregon who agreed to help us, and who worked out a special insurance policy for me. They agreed to handle it internally, though they balked at the idea of covering my pregnancy when it ultimately came to that.

The biggest disappointment by far, however, was the reaction of gay and lesbian groups and the transgender community. Officials we spoke to at GLBT organizations did not embrace us with open arms, as we'd expected they would. On the contrary, they expressed fear that my pregnancy could have a negative impact on the upcoming vote by the California Supreme Court on whether to continue the state's ban on same-sex marriages—this despite the fact that we are not a same-sex couple and were already legally married. By getting pregnant I would be rocking the boat, with no greater purpose, in their eyes, than my own narrow self-interest. Politically, I was a hot potato.

I also contacted three very high-ranking officials in transgender organizations, including a well-known transgender attorney who has handled important litigation involving men and women who have transitioned. We had questions that needed to be answered, after all. Our whole future was at stake. Again, I fully expected to be embraced by these transgender organizations. I naively anticipated that they'd welcome the challenge of shepherding us through my unique pregnancy. Just like all the other organizations and legal groups we had contacted, though, they let us down. The people I talked to suggested that I hide my pregnancy and not make a big deal out of it. They said society just wasn't ready for a pregnant man, and that my pregnancy posed a threat to the welfare and security of all transgender people. "A case like yours is a hundred steps ahead of where the trans community needs to be," one official told me. They feared that I would be seen as a freak, thus tarring the image of everyone in the community. Their goal was to see transgender people blend seamlessly into society so that their gender identity became a complete nonissue. My pregnancy, they said, would do the opposite—it would put the matter of my gender identity front and center. More than a few people felt I was selfishly switching between genders to suit my personal needs at the expense of any progress transgender people had made in integrating into mainstream society. This was coming from a community that was supposed to be ultra-aware of and sensitive to the vast spectrum of gender and identity, and that was supposedly able to champion the diversity of self-expression. All of the most high-profile people in the community refused to budge: They didn't want me to talk publicly about my pregnancy, and if I did, they wanted to coach me on what to say. They had all kinds of advice—"talking points," even.

I was beyond shocked by how cold and hard they were in their position. I would be lying if I said this was an easy thing for us to swallow. They did not see me as an individual who desperately needed their help; they saw me only as a threat to the broader goals of their organizations. One would think this goal would be to include me, not ostracize me. They tried to scare us with legal hypotheticals: For instance, we were told that the state could sue us and nullify our marriage; that I'd get a court order in the mail stating that I was now female; that the IRS would audit us for all those years we filed jointly; that if I were to die, not only would my life insurance policy not pay out to my wife, but others might try to take our child away from her. They accused me of being selfish and immature. They suggested I might not be sound of mind, and that my motives for doing what I was doing were based on doing something that was "potentially lucrative." We were prepared for the general populace and the medical community to shun us. Having our gay and lesbian colleagues turn their backs on us was devastating, but that, too, was something we could handle. However, we figured we still had the tiny, close-knit transgender community on our side. I was one of them, and they would be there for me when I needed them. Ironically, the transgender officials proved to be some of the staunchest critics of what we were doing. To this day, it is a betrayal that hurts my heart.

After making hundreds of phone calls and winding up with what we believed was bad, misguided advice, Nancy and I realized that we were on our own. Our support group had dwindled to basically two—she and I. We had found no precedent for what we were doing—no articles, no court cases, nothing. We couldn't find a single lawyer to stand up and fight for us. Whatever happened to us from here on out, we would have to figure out how to handle it by ourselves. The truth is, we were scared. It was starting to dawn on us that nothing about this pregnancy would be normal or easy. Any faint hope we might have had that the world would somehow champion us as brave trailblazers disappeared the day the transgender community shut its door on us. If they wouldn't support us, who on earth would?

❖ ❖ ❖ ❖ ❖

Our little baby doesn't like it when I lie on my back. That's when I feel her start to kick, and boy, can she kick. She's like a little soccer player in there. Sometimes she'll kick me so hard it's shocking. She likes it when I lie on my side; that seems to make her all peaceful and sleepy. Sometimes I have to sprawl out on my living room floor to get comfortable, and just when I find the right position—wham!—she kicks me good.

Susan Juliette and I started this little game: When she kicks, I tap. I wait for the kick, then tap my belly—and sure enough, she kicks again. After a while I started tapping twice. Before long, she responded by kicking twice. I was convinced right then and there our daughter would be a genius.

I talk to her all day long, and sometimes I'll even sing a little. I read her books and play classical music just for her. Nancy's fond of putting her mouth to my belly button and pretending it's a microphone. "Hello, baby!" she'll say. "Whatcha doin'? Come out and play, already!" Nancy loves putting her hand on my belly and feeling the baby kick; I like resting my head in Nancy's lap as she gently strokes my hair.

What a thing it is to have a life growing inside of you. What an incredible, awesome experience. I have never felt more alive and aware of my body than during my pregnancy. I believe that being pregnant will make me a better father; I'm not quite sure in what ways yet, but I know it will. I feel such an incredible bond forming between us—in a way, it's the ultimate father-daughter bond. I wonder, if all men had the option to carry a baby, how many of them would do it? And if men carried babies, would they be more sensitive, more emotional, more compassionate? Would the world be a different place? A better place?

It makes me wonder, too—what makes a man? What is the definition of a male? Some will say it is having a penis. But what about a man who loses his penis in an accident—is he suddenly not a man anymore? Or how about a transgender man who has lower surgery to construct a penis from the flesh of his forearm—is he suddenly more of a man than a transgender man who opts out of lower surgery? Some people say that a male is defined by chromosomes—if you have a Y chromosome, you're a man. It's reported that 1.7 percent of the population is intersex,[1] and has ambiguous genitalia at birth; that means that in a darkened movie theater of one hundred people, two people's sex chromosomes, may not match their outward appearance. Traditionally, males have been identified as having XY sex chromosomes, and females as XX. But there are numerous conditions under which the sex chromosomes are either paired or not paired in such ways that all kinds of variations occur: androgen insensitivity syndrome can produce babies with female-looking genitalia, despite their having XY chromosomes; congenital adrenal hyperplasia can cause XX babies to have male-appearing genitalia; some babies are born with just one X chromosome, some with XXY, and some with both XX and XY. Are chromosomes what really define a man or a woman?

Hormonally, people think that men have testosterone and women have estrogen. But it's not that simple. Both men and women have degrees of both hormones. Taking exogenous testosterone

---

1 http://en.wikipedia.org/wiki/Intersex

or estrogen makes a human body undergo physiological changes that reflect that dominant hormone. It causes certain secondary sex characteristics to develop. But hormones alone are not the determinant of sex.

Reproductive organs aren't the final judge, either. In the Dominican Republic, there's a high incidence of people with a condition referred to as *huevos a doce* or "eggs at twelve."[2] Children who were raised as female suddenly develop male genitalia at around age twelve. Some people even have both sets of reproductive organs, or none at all. Is a sterile person either or neither sex? Are we judged by whether or not we use our reproductive organs to reproduce? What about people who are unable to conceive or choose not to procreate?

So perhaps it's the government that has the final say on what makes a man or a woman. Still, there are those who insist on calling me female, despite my legal male credentials. So it seems that the government doesn't have more pull than biology over this question of what makes a man.

What, then, is it? People tell me all the time, "You're not really a man" or, "You're not really married." These same people would be the ones to call security on me if I were to walk into a women's restroom. For me, the answer to the question "What makes a man a man?" is this: There is no scientific answer. It is a personal conviction—it is how you feel inside when you wake up in the morning. The traits of masculinity and femininity are blurred; plenty of little girls like to play with Tonka trucks, and lots of boys play with dolls. There are men who are frail and vulnerable and indecisive, and women who are tough and strong

---

2 http://en.wikipedia.org/wiki/5-alpha-reductase_deficiency

and have bigger muscles than most guys. Even our preferences for color are irrelevant. Pink and blue are just wavelengths on a gender-neutral color spectrum. To place emphasis on archaic and changing definitions doesn't make much sense at all. Your likes and dislikes don't define you as a male or a female, nor does a penis or an ovary—or a lack thereof. Perhaps the very terms "man" and "woman" are archaic. Why can't we simply be whoever we are? Why can't we be respected as who we want to be and for how we want to live our lives?

Yet I know better. I know the world does not work this way. In this world there are nurses who point and laugh at you, and who go home and tell their boyfriend about the "pregnant man," and that boyfriend tells all his buddies, and then people in grocery stores and Blockbusters are soon pointing and staring, too. Nancy and I were not living our lives with our heads in the sand; we knew that sooner or later, our secret would come out. Hiding a pregnant man is like hiding an eight-hundred-pound gorilla. By week nineteen, I was really starting to show, and I had to wear at least two layers of baggy shirts. We believed most people would assume I had a big beer belly, but with more and more doctors and nurses learning about us, how much longer would it be before everyone in our neighborhood knew about the pregnant man? It was already getting back to us. A neighbor said that his mother-in-law had been at the hospital and a nurse had told her about the pregnant man— and, worse yet, exactly who I was. I was tired of hunching over and hiding my belly, and walking around beneath mounds of clothing. Nancy was getting fed up with everyone telling her she was really growing. Part of us wanted to keep our secret forever, but another part no longer wanted to act as if it were something shameful. The better course of action, we knew, was to come clean about my pregnancy—tell our friends, tell our neighbors, tell everyone. It was becoming increasingly clear to us that the most straightforward course of action would be to do something we'd actually dreaded: go public with our story. Our days of blending in were over.

And so, right around the midway point of my pregnancy, we decided to tell the GLBT community about our struggle. Who knew, maybe someone could help us with all of our unanswered questions. Not in our wildest dreams did we anticipate what might happen when, with a single article in a national gay magazine, the world learned about us and beat a thunderous path straight to our door.

Chapter 16

OVERNIGHT SENSATION

Once Nancy and I made the difficult decision to go public with our story—to, in essence, tell it before my secret got out in other ways—we decided we wanted an outlet that would allow us to stand up for what we believed in.

On February 4, 2008, I sent an email to *The Advocate*, a well-known, gay-themed magazine with a circulation of about ninety thousand readers—a pretty small figure by most standards—describing our unique situation and essentially reaching out for help. Going public with our story did not stem from a narcissistic desire to be famous, which many people have since accused us of. In the beginning, I believed my pregnancy would be a private affair, but by this point, Dr. M. was violating his Hippocratic oath and people were starting to talk about us within our small Oregon community. National legal and transgender organizations had dismissed us, despite our unprecedented legal crossroads. The discrimination and seemingly insurmountable obstacles were bringing out the fighter in me.

The Advocate agreed to run my story, and simply requested that I write a small first-person article and submit a current photo of myself. Believing that someone out there might come to our aid, I proceeded to describe our struggle to what I hoped would be an empathetic GLBT audience. After all, the discrimination we'd faced was coming from officials with political agendas—not from this community that has always united to ensure civil liberties for all, especially its own members.

It all started with 729 words. "To our neighbors, my wife, Nancy, and I don't appear in the least unusual," the article reads. "To those in the quiet Oregon community where we live, we are viewed just as we are—a happy couple deeply in love. Our desire to work hard, buy our first home, and start a family was nothing out of the ordinary. That is, until we decided that I would carry our child."

Nancy and I submitted the essay and held our breath. What if *The Advocate* didn't like it and decided not to publish it? Deciding to go public was at once a frightening step and an enormous relief. Both Nancy and I were tired of sneaking around, and standing up for our beliefs was much more in keeping with the type of people we'd always been.

Within days, we heard back from *The Advocate*—they were going to publish my essay. However, they slotted us for publication nearly two months later, for the April 8, 2008, issue. I was in touch with the magazine staff a couple of times, and they informed me that the title would read: "Labor of Love: Is Society Ready for This Pregnant Husband?" The subtitle I'd submitted read: "Is Society

Ready for the First Pregnant Husband?" Apparently, the magazine wasn't willing to characterize me as the first pregnant husband, even though those are the facts. Indeed, there have been people who have gotten pregnant before transitioning to a male gender, and one person that I know of who, back in 1999, identified as male yet was legally female and unmarried. My situation was entirely uncharted, yet my story wasn't going to be a cover story; it was short compared with other articles *The Advocate* tends to run; it seemed they were handling it as a quirky aside, rather than as breaking news.

Nevertheless, we decided to move forward with our original strategy just in case. That meant coming clean with our friends and neighbors, and telling Nancy's father, Jim. We didn't want certain people we cared about finding out about us from an outside source; we wanted to be the ones to break the news ourselves. Nancy was understandably nervous about telling her father, and so was I. He'd become so important to both of us, and the idea that we might lose him just after having found him was horrifying. Still, we began steeling ourselves for the inevitable moment when we would have to tell him the truth—that I not only used to be a female, but was also now pregnant.

And then—on March 13, 2008, twenty-six days before its scheduled publication date, *The Advocate* ran our story on its website. It appeared alongside a striking photo that Nancy had taken of me, with my full beard, shirt off, and baby bump in full view. That photo remains, to this day, the single most iconic image of me. I read aloud the words I'd written: "Our situation sparks legal, political, and social unknowns. We have only begun experiencing opposition from people who are upset by our situation. Doctors have discriminated against us, turning us away due to their religious beliefs. Health care professionals have refused to call me by a male pronoun or recognize Nancy as my wife. Receptionists have laughed at us. Friends and family have been unsupportive; most of Nancy's family doesn't even know I'm transgender."

Reaction to my essay was swift. *The Advocate* immediately regretted not making a bigger issue of my story, and promptly began giving interviews on my behalf to boost its visibility. Within a day, the story had been picked up by more than one hundred other websites; within a week, a Google search of my name yielded more than one hundred thousand pages. Dozens of media outlets somehow got my personal cell phone number and were calling me for interviews. We heard from every major United States network, as well as from newspapers, radio stations, talk shows, documentary filmmakers, and networks across Europe. We also heard from all of the tabloids in the U.S. and many more around the globe. Webpages in foreign languages prominently displayed that pregnant picture of me. Our story was being talked about in over fifty different countries, from China to South Africa, Malta to Brazil. The *National Enquirer* and a handful of U.K. tabloids all desperately wanted to write a major story about us, and they offered us outlandish sums of money for our cooperation. We turned down every single request.

As I started to read through the numerous articles and posts about us, I was dismayed by the degree of misunderstanding and negativity about us. I was a cardboard figure, an "it," a "shim," a "(s)he." Even transgender people—people who've historically been rejected and beaten down—were hurling insults at me and calling me a "freak." Apparently, I was not a human with a heart and feelings. Some people were even advocating for my and my unborn baby's deaths.

Nancy and I, once private citizens, now turned accidental public figures, had to do something. We wanted to tell our story so people would understand our motives. We turned to *People* magazine, which arranged an exclusive joint venture with a well-known talk show. These two sources were large and reputable and would surely help to right the wrong. It was obvious that interest in our story was global and voracious, and we felt it was smart to provide fuller coverage—as long as we could continue to control the story as much as possible. Looking back, Nancy and I were pretty naive about how much control we'd be able to maintain; once your story hits a nerve with the public, it ceases to be your story—instead it belongs to the world, to do with it as it wishes. Nancy and I handled the dissemination of our story with integrity and restraint, but we quickly got used to the idea that there would always be speculation and misinformation, no matter what we did.

One of the biggest misconceptions about us is that we sold our story for vast sums of money—that we exploited our daughter for financial gain. Nothing could be further from the truth. Nancy and I did not make any money at all from the media during my pregnancy—*not one single dime*. On the other hand, *People* magazine and the prominent talk show we were interviewed on did benefit from telling our story. We actually lost money during my pregnancy; we took weeks off from work to accommodate the interview and shooting schedules. Our income dwindled to next to nothing during that time. At the same time, extravagant offers from tabloids and major U.S. networks kept pouring in. We were offered hundreds of thousands of dollars to tell our story to the tabloids, and one American network said it would give us a million dollars if we agreed to cooperate with them. We turned down every one of those offers, instead opting for *People* and a single daytime show to tell our story, neither or which paid us to do so.

There were rumors that *People* struck a financial deal with us, but that is untrue. *People* approached us as just another news subject; as journalists, they cannot pay the subjects of news stories for their cooperation. A senior writer from the magazine came to Bend and spent three days with us, interviewing us about our childhoods, our marriage, and the pregnancy. There were absolutely no limitations on what he could ask about, or any opportunity for us to influence how he perceived us as story subjects. It felt good to be able to talk about our story at length, but scary to realize that we were at the mercy of how other people might interpret our situation.

In many ways, going with *People* was riskier for us than selling our story to an outlet like the *National Enquirer,* because the latter is a publication that would have allowed us more control over how the story was presented. Yet, we felt that *People* was the right spot for us; it has massive weekly readership of more than forty million people, and it balances its coverage of celebrities with real, human stories about ordinary people. It is, in many ways, the voice of America, and to Nancy and me our story is a quintessentially American one. In fact, *People* sent the famous photographer Mary Ellen Mark—known for her portraits of Americana—to take our pictures for the story. "The man of the house is sprawled on his sofa, sneakers off, with his hands—as men's hands tend to be— resting on his belly," the *People* story reads. "But just as he's getting comfortable, the kicking starts. 'The baby hates it when I lie on my back,' says Thomas Beatie, 34. 'She'll wake me up at night with some pretty good kicks. Like now—wow, she's really being feisty. She's like, "Get me out of here already.""" The piece ends with something else I told the writer: "Our daughter is beating these incredible odds to get here—physical obstacles, social obstacles, everything. And in my dreams I dream the world will see her just the way we do. As this amazing gift to us. As a miracle."

I would guess that we passed up anywhere from $1 million to $2 million. But money was not the reason we were doing this—it never has been. Even down to this manuscript. Writing this book has been a pursuit of mine since the age of seventeen. After everything is said and done here, it's actually cost me thousands of dollars to achieve this goal. Believe me, there are easier ways to make money than to become a controversial and potentially despised and threatened public figure. I'm aware that certain people will always be skeptical about our motives, and I am sure there is nothing I can say to convince them otherwise, but I still feel it's important to be clear that Nancy and I went public not to make a profit, but to make a stand.

Within days of the online article's release, we began noticing strange cars and vans passing slowly in front of our home. People would ring our doorbell posing as deliverymen, hiding cameras, and hoping to get a shot of the pregnant man. We knew that neighbors were noticing all the commotion around our home, and we knew that we had some explaining to do. Things were happening quickly; we were fielding dozens of phone calls a day while peering out our windows to see if the coast was clear for us to go to work. *People* scheduled its own publication of our story in its April 14, 2008, issue, which would hit newsstands on April 5. We were scheduled to appear on the talk show a day before that, on April 4. About a week before those dates, our neighbors George and Victoria—who lived across the street and were our friends in the development—asked us about all the cars they had seen parking in front of our home. It was time to tell them the truth.

❖ ❖ ❖ ❖ ❖

We invited George and Victoria to brunch at a nearby restaurant. Pretty much as soon as they sat down, Nancy gave me a little shrug of her shoulders, as if to say, *Okay, here we go.* And then she smiled her warm and nourishing smile, and I knew that everything was going to be okay. I took a deep breath and looked at George and Victoria, who believed we were any old husband and a wife, just like them. They were right, of course, but that was only part of the story.

"Did you ever find anything different about us?" I asked them.

"No, not really," said George, a big bear of a man. I could tell neither he nor his pretty blond wife had any idea what we were about to tell them. I asked them to guess what our secret might be. Again, they couldn't even fathom it. And then I just handed them a copy of the *Advocate* article, and we waited as they both read it.

And with that, our secret was out. George and Victoria sat there, stunned, trying to digest what they'd just read. This was a familiar response by now. Our new home state, Oregon, is a logging and fishing kind of state, with deep conservative roots and a lot of small, insulated, old-fashioned towns. But Portland is a very liberal city, and the state in general is known to be progressive and tolerant. We knew that some Oregonians, and indeed people in our little development in Bend, were going to think of us as freaks. We knew that others were going to embrace us. We just didn't know who was who. We didn't even know what George and Victoria, who genuinely liked us and enjoyed our company, would say once they found out.

We didn't have to wait long. George broke the ice by saying that he actually thought all the commotion in front of our house was a Mafia thing. After the initial shock, they both said they were happy for us and delighted that we were having a child. George later told me that hearing the truth made him want to protect us, and to make sure that the rest of our neighbors treated us with respect and dignity. "You are a very compassionate, sensitive couple," he told us. "We can tell you are good and loving people. And we can tell your baby is going to get all the love and attention she needs." If anything, their knowing the truth about us deepened our friendship. Nancy and I looked at each other and shared a giant figurative exhale. We had made it through our first big moment of revelation. Maybe, we allowed ourselves to think, we would be similarly embraced by the world. We knew better, of course. But over brunch with our friends George and Victoria, it didn't seem all that harmful to indulge in that sweet little dream for a while.

❖ ❖ ❖ ❖ ❖

Nancy and I had to fly out of state to appear on the talk show, and when we got back to our hotel room after the recording, we were exhausted. But we knew there was one more thing we had to do. We knew that before the show aired, we had to call Jim and tell him the truth. It was the phone call we dreaded the most; Nancy had barely been able to sleep for days, because she was so worried that he might react negatively. She had dreamed about having a father who loved her, and out of the blue she had found him after more than four decades. And he had loved me, too, right from the start; he called me his hero and he became a wonderful friend. Both of us found in him the father we had never had. It was a special, amazing, intimate bond, so rare and precious for us both, but it was also relatively new and possibly fragile. We would now have to tell Nancy's father that I was our surrogate.

Right there in our hotel room, Nancy dialed Jim's number on her cell. I could tell she was dying inside, and so was I. When he answered, Nancy slipped right into small talk, and that went on for a while. But then, abruptly, she said, "Dad, I hope you're sitting down. I don't know what Mom told you about us, but there's something we have to tell you. So here goes: Thomas used to be a woman. He transitioned to a man, and he has all his legal documents. And, yes, we are expecting a baby. But there's no surrogate. Thomas is having the baby."

I could not hear what Jim was saying; I suspected he wasn't saying anything at all. I watched Nancy's face; her reaction would tell me everything I needed to know. Would her face scrunch up in a frown, and then tears? Would I have to watch my wife be shattered right in front of me? Nancy was silent, her face a mask; I waited and watched, waited and watched. What was going on?

And then—one of the greatest things I have ever seen in my life: Nancy smiled. They talked some more, in normal tones, almost as if no bombshell had been dropped. Perhaps it had not been a bombshell for Jim; he loved us—that we knew—and hearing this about us seemed to make no difference at all. Nancy later told me that, aside from a brief pause right after she told him, Jim had been exceptionally calm. He didn't seem bitter or angry or confused or anything. Was acting as if everything was normal just a way for Jim to buy time to process what he had heard? Was he in some kind of shock? Possibly. But he could just as easily have hung up on Nancy, or told her he needed time to think things through. Instead, he was loving and accepting, just the way we knew him to be.

"I will tell the whole family," he said to Nancy. "I will take care of that. Don't you worry about anything."

Nancy handed her cell to me so I could speak with Jim. "I'm sorry we didn't tell you sooner," I said. "It's just kind of difficult to come out with this kind of news." Jim was gracious to me; he told me his feelings for us would never change, no matter what. His reaction was almost too good to be true. We had spent so many hours worrying that we might lose him, but here he was, embracing us all over again. Jim made me feel that everything was going to work out just fine. He and Nancy still talk almost every day, and Jim couldn't be prouder of having another grandkid. He loves being surrounded by his children and their children, and now that was going to include our little Susan Juliette.

❖ ❖ ❖ ❖ ❖

Our long, exhausting, emotional day was almost over. But one weird twist remained. By sheer coincidence, I got a call from my own father right after Nancy hung up with Jim. He had no idea where we were, but he had heard about me on the radio, and he knew that my story was going public. He was calling me out for commenting on how unsupportive my family had been. I am guessing the article in *The Advocate* had hit hard in Hawaii, prompting some local reporters to track down my family for their reaction. I tried to explain to him that my article said that "family was unsupportive," which included Nancy's mother's side of the family and my aunt. We rarely spoke on the phone, and I hadn't seen him in nearly three years. I knew through my brothers that he was embarrassed by me, and the pregnancy had only worsened those feelings. But my father would not want anyone outside the family to *think* he was unsupportive; that would be a huge blow to his self-image.

My father chewed me out good in that conversation. This time, Nancy watched my face, and watched as I went ashen. I didn't realize it, but I was shaking. "You had better not bring the family into this," he warned, his voice rising. "You had better not mention me at all." He said that a military attorney friend of his had said that our marriage was a fraud. It was a silent threat. "You better get yourself a good attorney," he said before hanging up the phone.

I wanted to say, *What, are you going to hit me now?* but I didn't. I wanted to tell him that he couldn't harm me any longer, that I wasn't that scared, cowering little girl anymore. The irony, of course, is that was just how I felt listening to my father—I felt like a scared, vulnerable kid all over again. I do not like arguing with my father, even over the phone; when he raises his voice it feels like he is going to jump right through the phone, rabid and furious. My father was so pissed off during that brief conversation that his eyes were probably bleeding. At the end of it, he said, "Okay, Tracy, take care," but he said it in a sarcastic, sort of singsong way. He said it as a warning. We were opponents now, squaring off, past yelling and screaming, coolly preparing for battle. His message was clear: *Go ahead, do what you have to do, and I will do what I have to do as well.* We were not father and child. We were enemies.

I quickly hung up the phone. That was the last conversation I ever had with him.

❖ ❖ ❖ ❖ ❖

When I was about seven months pregnant, someone rang our doorbell. Nancy peered out the window and saw six teenage boys bunched together at our front door. She opened it a crack and asked what they wanted.

"Can we come in and meet your husband?" one of them said.

They were neighborhood kids, and they had heard the pregnant man lived among them. Naturally, they were curious—and fearless, as teens can be. Nancy is fiercely protective of me, and she never lets anyone into our home just to gawk at me. But these boys had been polite and respectful—they didn't even ask to see the pregnant man. They asked if they could meet her *husband.* Nancy let them in.

I was sitting on our living room sofa as they filed in. Sheepishly, they lined up side by side in front of me and stood there with their hands in their pockets, looking down at their feet. I felt just as shy and curious about them as they seemed about me. They were skinny, handsome, suntanned boys, in jeans and shorts and T-shirts and Pro-Keds sneakers, like teenagers everywhere. They didn't say anything; they just stole nervous glances at me. Nancy asked where they lived, how school was going, things like that. Then she said, "Do you want to see his stomach?"

"Yeah," said the most assertive one.

I stood up. They stared at my swollen belly. A few minutes later, they thanked us and said goodbye and shuffled out. I imagine they ran off and told their friends they had just seen the pregnant man. I hope they saw that I am a regular person. The next day, two of them returned and rang our doorbell again. This time they ran off before Nancy could answer it. But on our doorstep they left a package. Inside was a gift: a music box designed to hold baby wipes. When you open it, it plays "Rockabye Baby." It is one of the sweetest gifts we've ever received.

By that point, a little less than a month since *The Advocate* article had run, I'd been featured on more than a million websites. I was no longer Thomas Beatie.

I was now the Pregnant Man.

Chapter 17

WHAT PEOPLE SAY

On April 1, I was the subject of David Letterman's Top Ten List. "These are the top ten messages left on the Pregnant Man's answering machine," Letterman told his *Late Show* audience. I listened as he counted them down:

Number 10: I thought you said you were using protection.

Number 9: It's Angelina Jolie. I'd like to adopt the baby.

Number 8: This is your wife. Can I borrow your Gillette Mach 3 razor?

Number 7: It's Maury. I'd love to test to see if you're the mother and/or the father.

And so it went, on down to the final message:

Number 1:   Michael Jackson here. Just wanted to reach out to another androgynous freak show.

This pretty much sums up my experience being famous, or infamous, or whatever you want to call me. After living most of my life as an ordinary, anonymous citizen—whose closest brush with fame was being crowned a distant runner-up in a teen beauty contest—I suddenly found myself going from complete obscurity to becoming the most controversial pregnant person on the planet. There are few sensations as surreal and startling as turning on your television, hearing your name, and seeing yourself, but that happened to me routinely in the days and weeks after my story broke.

So what does that feel like? Weird, nerve-racking, exhilarating, exhausting, scary—you name it. It was never just one sensation, it was always two or three at the same time. Like with David Letterman's list. Part of me was tickled and flattered that I was being featured on one of America's favorite programs. But then I had the distinct displeasure of hearing Letterman refer to me as an "androgynous freak show." To be a controversial public figure, I would soon learn, is to be subject to a wild roller coaster of emotions.

Within a month of going public, I was everywhere. Andy Samberg stuffed a pillow under his shirt to impersonate me on *Saturday Night Live.* The guys behind *South Park* wrote me into an episode. Jay Leno cracked a couple of jokes on Mother's Day at my expense. Whoopi Goldberg defended me on *The View.* One of the stranger sensations I experienced was hearing real celebrities talk about *me*. I remember watching Kevin Bacon being asked about me during a BBC interview, and appearing sort of shocked; I recall *American Idol*'s acerbic judge Simon Cowell being asked about me, too, and surprising me with his support. Friends would call me every day and say, "Did you know you were on *Inside Edition* last night?" or, "I saw your photo on *Good Morning America!*" There were long segments on many mainstream shows, even though I wasn't giving any interviews. I had no idea I was on any of these shows. A guy in Britain even posted a video on YouTube, wearing a prosthetic stomach and pretending to be me for a day.

When we returned home to Bend after our talk show appearance, we had a police vehicle escort us off the tarmac to avoid a commotion. Paparazzi from the U.K. got shots of me tending to my front yard, and I made front pages all across Europe. Even though I was barely leaving my own house, the world would just not stop talking about me. Me! Thomas from Bend, Oregon! It was a dizzying and often disturbing scenario, and one that I had no clue how to handle. Not one source, aside from us, had our story completely accurate. I was hoping that by going public, we would touch people with our story, but I was not prepared for how quickly and thoroughly the media machine sucked me in and chewed me up and turned me into, for better or worse, a household name.

Early on, it became apparent that the issue of my pregnancy was extremely divisive. People had strong opinions about it, both pro and con. We got one message on our phone from an angry man saying, "God made you a woman, Mr. Beatie," followed immediately by another caller saying, "I have so much respect for your bravery in being true to yourself and telling your story."

I could have turned off my TV and shut down my computer and insulated myself against the torrent of opinion that followed the announcement of my pregnancy, but Nancy and I decided that we would not shield ourselves from what people were saying. We wanted to be aware of the good stuff and the bad stuff—we wanted to know just what the country thought of us. Along the way, we received hate email and angry phone calls and several death threats. We fortified our home and installed a video-surveillance system to protect ourselves against these threats, which we took very seriously. The *National Enquirer* wouldn't leave us alone and trolled our neighborhood, chasing down neighbors and bribing people with money to say anything about us. They even stole the iconic picture that Nancy took of me and ran it on the cover of their trashy magazine five times (that I know about). Those articles about me were ridiculous, to say the least.

We also received countless messages of support from people all over the world, and these bolstered and strengthened us in ways we can hardly express. Whenever we allowed a really hateful message to get us down, a positive one would inevitably follow, picking us right back up. The roller coaster drops to the gutter before swooping toward the sky.

Opinions about me were expressed in a number of ways: in panel discussions on talk shows, on thousands of Internet blogs, in countless newspaper and magazine articles, and in the letters we received. Believe it or not, out of those hundreds of letters, not one of them was negative. The letters included those from people we had never met offering us friendship and sending pictures of their families; pastors supporting our decisions and welcoming us into their congregations; a pediatrician apologizing for her profession's behavior of turning us away; professors who said they'd be offering discussions about me in their syllabi; couples struggling with fertility issues congratulating us on our success; midwives offering to assist us gratis; high schoolers who'd written a song for us; and even transgender men saying that they, too, would get pregnant.

My response to this outpouring of support was one of gratitude and disbelief. I couldn't believe that strangers had so much compassion for our family. I was inspired by their inspiration, and it fueled me to want to be generous and reach out to other people in need. Compared with the negativity, the positive outpouring gave me hope for the human race.

Most of the online articles presented themselves as neutral news reporting, but there were quite a few negative pieces. Following are excerpts from some of the more positive articles.

From "Transphobia runs deep: What's so weird about a pregnant man? Maybe you guys should get out more," by Jesse Thiessen at Dailyvanguard.com:

> "Would you ask a non-transperson about the size and shape of their genitals, even if you had reason to be curious? Of course not. Yet transpeople encounter that question all the time, among other more invasive inquiries. And that goes back to the whole heart of the controversy surrounding Thomas Beatie and his wife: It's not anybody's business but theirs. It's not anybody's body but his. And it's not anybody's child but theirs. His lifestyle is not anybody's to condemn."

From "How to wrap your head around the pregnant man," by Steven Petrow at Indyweek.com:

> "Here's the kicker: The Beaties are a mind-bender. No, they're not 'just a husband and wife who are having a baby,' as Nancy Beatie has claimed. They've pushed our buttons and our boundaries about sexuality and gender identity because we're so used to thinking in binary terms: man/woman, masculine/feminine and gay/straight. The world's more complicated than that, as Thomas Beatie is certainly showing us."

From "Guest View: Sex distinct from gender," by Patrick Finnessy on Windycitymediagroup.com:

> "I also believe wholeheartedly that each life is an experiment, and Thomas Beatie is creating a life. Whether he self-identifies as a man (he does) or not, he gets to be who he claims to be, not what society imposes upon him to be. And he gets to create life and raise a child in a loving environment whereby that child might learn a little bit more about self rather than about society's expectations of self based on that ounce of flesh. Sure, we currently live in a gendered and bigoted world. And with the Cro-Magnon mentality I've heard recently, even in evolving times, we're likely going to stay this way for an unfortunate while."

On July 4, 2008, *Good Morning America* ran a segment about our story and called in Helen Fisher, world-renowned biological anthropologist, as an expert on the subject matter. "What's astonishing about this particular pair is that they actually behave like a man and a woman in a very traditional marriage and will probably bring those roles to the family, and the little girl will grow up like all little girls grow up—with a daddy and a mommy," she said.

Some of the most mainstream negative reactions were the most shocking to me, because they came from TV news anchors who are ostensibly impartial journalists. The anchors on MSNBC's *Morning Joe* show, for instance, talked about me with complete revulsion. "I'm going to be sick," one of them said when my story was brought up. "It's disgusting. This kind of news makes our business terrible." Not to be outdone, Greg Gutfeld, host of Fox News's *Red Eye Show,* seethed with contempt and refused to call me a "he" while reporting on my story, preferring "she" or "it." "Twenty years ago this person would be traveling in a carnival," the host said. "What is there for her child out there? To go to events with this creature who is her parent?" A female panelist on his show chimed in: "I hope the pregnancy is the worst experience of his life. I hope the blood vessels burst in his eyes." Another male panelist quipped, "We don't know what this thing [my baby] is going to look like. It might even have a third eye." Saying the "n-word" in the media gets you fired, but reporters can talk about my child as if she were a monster and experience no repercussions whatsoever. Amazingly, GLAAD, the organization created to protect against GLBT defamation in the media, didn't step up to the plate to support me during this slamfest.

Most of the real venom, though, appeared in the blogosphere. I want to give you a sample of these opinions to give you a sense of the depth of the emotions my pregnancy provoked. It was interesting to see that I triggered such a vast national debate, even if I wasn't happy to come across harsh and devastating opinions about me. You never really get used to hearing yourself referred to as a freak, or worse. "So if this 'guy' has both male and female equipment, I guess he could actually comply with someone's angry instruction and 'Go fuck yourself!'" read one blog entry I came across, followed closely by this one on the same site: "As long as the child is born to parents who love her, it should not be anyone else's business. That's one of the HUGE problems we have in America—intolerance."

This pattern was actually quite common, regardless of the website—angry, hateful opinions were mixed in with encouraging sentiments. I could easily imagine that across the country, next-door neighbors—and even close friends—had starkly contrasting opinions about me. The hatred and casual cruelty of some was disturbing, I must admit. But I had already decided not to bury my head in the sand, and I vowed to turn the animosity of others into motivation for myself. Besides, I came to realize that most people were not angry with me, Thomas Beatie. They didn't know me or understand my situation, so how could they genuinely hate or even dislike me? Instead, they were reacting to what I represented. They hated Thomas Beatie the symbol, not Thomas Beatie the man. This became an important distinction for me, and it allowed me to read the blogs with thick skin, so that I could keep track of what people were saying about me. Here, then, are some samples of readers' comments, both positive and negative, posted on a variety of blogs since my story came out:

- It took balls to do what he did.

- Tracy is just a bearded woman who should be thrown in a crazy bin, sterilized, and lobotomized! We need to have laws for basket cases like this.

- Is Thomas male or female? Here's the answer:
  Chromosomally: Probably Female
  Hormonally: Female or Male
  Secondary Sex Characteristics: Male
  Emotionally: Female and Male
  Reproductive Organs: Female
  Socially: Male
  Genitalia: Female and Male
  Legally: Male
  Physiologically: Mostly Male
  Psychologically: Male
  What matters most is what Thomas and his wife and child think.

- Men who donate their sperm are so selfish. Can you imagine tossing your seeds and finding out your the real father of the pregnant man's spawn?

- I'm terribly concerned for the safety of that family. I would not be surprised to hear that they had become the victims of hate crimes.

- all i have to say is you should die & go to hell because your one of these people ruining what god made. HOPE TOMORROW MY AGENT KILLS YOU & YOUR BABY. GOODBYE MY FRIEND.

- AWESOME. just plain AWESOME. that kid will be the most creative, open-minded kid ever.

- I would like to say that this is not a miracle but a hoax. It is the end of the world manifesting just like it says in the bible.

- Have you ever seen the image of a pregnant man in history? This is a great social feat. That's why this is a big deal.

- This is a kind of criminal child abuse that laws could not foresee. The kid should be taken by social services and given a proper family. Short of actual physical abuse, I never thought I'd consider Britney Spears a better parent than someone else. Britney meet Beatie.

- His story was worth telling, and if the media attention he's getting is any indication, it obviously is.

- A true trans f-to-m would not want to produce a child. this is so damaging to the gay community, as we are entangled in the trans movement. WTF! Should we really include this "confused" man's/woman's in our movement. This is so damaging!!!!!!!!!!!!!!

- Just because he was born a woman, doesn't mean that he has to stay a woman. It takes a real man to do this for his wife. CONGRATS THOMAS AND NANCY!!! Xoxoxox

- Now THAT's family values! Congratulations to the happy couple! They will obviously take wonderful care of their new daughter, and quite frankly, I don't care how she got here.

- My greatest pity goes out to the Beatie's poor baby, and the miserable life of confusion and mixed messages that poor kid will have to grow up with. If he or she manages to be even half normal, that will be the true miracle.

- Mr. Beatie sounds like one of the least confused people on the planet. He and his wife wanted to have a baby, and they used the body parts available to them as a couple to create a new life—nothing "confused" about that! I'll reserve "confusion" for those little minds that can't keep up with modern times.

- We as woman so often curse and say, "If only a guy could give birth for a change, so he can tell other guys exactly what we go through and the hardships that come with making a beautiful child"—[and now we're] complaining that finally one can do just that.

- One is not born a man, one becomes one.

- Thomas, your bravery to go public with your story is very inspiring to me, as I have always been transgendered but just started therapy and transitioning this year. I figure to myself, if this man can be so brave, what do I have to be scared of?

- The people of Oregon are proud of Thomas and Nancy. They have done nothing but create another beautiful, happy, and loving family on earth. To me, it's pretty simple: love knows no boundaries and does not judge.

❖ ❖ ❖ ❖ ❖

In addition to sharing their opinions about us, people also sent us lots of baby gifts. Altogether, we've received dozens of gifts from around the world. I cannot tell you how moving it has been to open up presents from friends, family, and complete strangers who spent their hard-earned money on clothes or toys for our daughter. Nancy and I received a cute black-and-white sailor outfit from RoseAnn, my mother's childhood friend; a framed, stitched record of birth with a footprint kit from Nancy's younger brother, Tom, and his wife; a playpen and an entire box full of clothing from Christine's mother; and classic nursery-rhyme books from Nancy's father. We were sent a virtual baby shower of onesies and bibs and blankets and toys from the Indianapolis Women's Chorus; hangers, bottle, spoons, and rattles from the Gay Student Alliance of Waterford Kettering High School in Michigan; and a dozen individually handcrafted clothing items from a knitting group in Emeryville, California. We were given a "Dad, you're my hero" trophy and an antique picture frame from an Alex in New York; a stream of gifts, including a photo album, baby bouncer, and gift card from Jackee in Ohio; and a locket and stuffed animals from Kristian in Melbourne, Australia. One of Nancy's childhood friends, Lisa, and her mother gave us an incredible line of high-end cachcach baby clothes. My godmother, Sam, sent us an unforgettable and symbolic gift: a handful of the original outfits and dresses I wore as a baby.

Considering that I have never received anything for Susan Juliette from my own father and brothers, it was all the more emotional for me to get beautiful gifts and letters from people who didn't even know me. It has been a heartening and inspirational experience, and it has made me feel good about the world we live in. I want to thank all of you who sent us these lovely presents, and everyone who posted positive and encouraging comments about us. From the bottom of our hearts, Nancy and I thank you. You have made a difference in our lives.

Chapter 18

A DREAM COME TRUE

W eek thirty-four: I'm as big as a house.

Before I got pregnant, I weighed about 156 pounds and I could bench-press 260. Now, in week thirty-four, I'm up to 174 pounds, and the heaviest thing I've lifted in months is one of Nancy's BLTs. Besides my massive belly, though, the rest of my body looks the same as it did before I got pregnant. I can't believe how big my stomach is; my skin feels like it's stretched to the breaking point. With just six weeks to go before my July 3 due date, I can actually feel the baby dropping lower and lower, getting into position, sensing her moment is near. Nancy and I both have a feeling that little Susan Juliette is going to make an early appearance—my guess is June 28, my mother's birthday.

Nancy has started to kick into overdrive. She has been han- dling all the preparations—making hospital arrangements, packing our bags, figuring out how our parrots are going to make due without us for a few days. She is remarkable, and I can breathe easy knowing she will not leave a single detail untended to.

Her efforts are even more amazing considering something else she is doing to prepare for our daughter's arrival. Together, we decided that Nancy should breastfeed the baby. We felt that if she could breastfeed, she should—it would be an invaluable bonding experience and further solidify us as a family. It would also be better for the baby, as it helps build immunity. Still, doctors told us they weren't sure if she'd be able to. Nancy had three things working against her: She's forty-six, which is older than most breastfeeding mothers; she no longer has her uterus; and when she was younger, she had breast-augmentation surgery, though the implants were later removed. The odds were against her, but we both wanted to give it a try anyway.

We ordered a breast pump, and Nancy began taking fortifying hormones—a process called induced lactation. She would run around all day, handling different chores, then sink into a chair and get her breast pump going for fifteen minutes every two or three hours. Within weeks her breasts had grown three sizes. But even before she started inducing, she felt strange sensations in her breasts. "It's like my brain is telling my body to get ready to breastfeed," she said. All along, Nancy had experiences that made her feel like she, too, was pregnant, and here was yet another example of that. In many ways, we were going through this experience together. It was truly a shared pregnancy.

We'd agreed that we'd have a midwife, rather than a doctor, help us through the birth. (We felt that a midwife would be better suited to provide constant emotional support during the entire birthing process, whereas a doctor would be rushing in and out.) There would be doctors available at the St. Charles Medical Center should anything go wrong, but our midwife would otherwise be in charge. When she called to check in on us a couple weeks before the birth, she expressed a concern that shocked both Nancy and me.

"We're worried that the baby might be undersize," the midwife said. "We're worried that all the testosterone you took might be having a negative effect on her weight and size."

Up to that point, our baby's weight and measurements had always been right in the target ranges, so this was a stunning bit of news. But beyond that, our midwife's concern about my use of testosterone rankled me—I knew that there were no studies that showed that testosterone use prior to conception could adversely affect a pregnancy. In fact, I had a feeling that Susan would be a big baby. Why this sudden concern? Had someone gotten in the midwife's ear? I asked what had brought this up.

"I consulted with a doctor who consulted with a doctor, and we discussed some studies they've done on animals that show testosterone use could harm a baby," she said.

I was sure I would have come across those studies, considering all the research I'd done. No one could possibly have been more diligent in researching the issue of testosterone use than I had been. There was simply no evidence of any kind to suggest that it would be a problem. Dr. J., our ob-gyn, had told us she considered our pregnancy absolutely normal, no riskier than any other pregnancy. I pressed the midwife for more information about the studies, and asked her whether she had seen them herself.

"We're just trying to cover all our bases," she said. "We want you to come in for an ultrasound so we can make sure everything is okay."

I saw no reason to accommodate her request, and yet I was also determined to prove her wrong. When someone challenges me, I tend to challenge them right back. I am also aware that people's prejudices can seep into their professional decisions. Had our midwife perhaps spoken with Dr. M., the doctor who initially turned us away and who made monthly visits to the same clinic the midwife worked at? I agreed to the ultrasound, but I pushed the midwife to show me the studies and tell me the name of the doctor she'd consulted.

On May 22, Nancy drove us to the ultrasound appointment. I was nervous, despite my feelings that this was all for nothing, and that the studies weren't legitimate. A technician named Brian escorted us into an exam room and started prepping the ultrasound. The room was dim, with a paper-butterfly mobile dangling overhead. Brian, thankfully, turned out to be a nice guy. A lean and fit surfer type with blond hair and a gentle demeanor, he had been performing ultrasounds for twenty years, and he had two children of his own. When he pushed down hard with the wand to get a good scan, he apologized. No sooner did Susan's image appear on the screen than Brian declared, "Our baby looks healthy."

The baby was exactly thirty-four weeks old, and should have weighed somewhere around four and three-quarters pounds. Brian took us through all the signposts—Susan was swallowing her amniotic-fluid, which was good; her bladder had a dark spot, indicating fluid, which was good; her amniotic fluid index was 15.6, and anything between 5 and 20 is normal; her brain and kidneys and lungs were all perfectly fine. As Brian took our baby's measurements, he told us he fully supported what we were doing.

"If you guys are gonna be loving this baby, that's all that matters," he said. "Being a parent is all about being a parent."

We looked at our daughter on the monitor. Her lips and nose looked a little smushed, pressed against the wall of my uterus. She was very active—Brian told us this was a fetal respiratory motion, which meant the baby was instinctively simulating the motion of breathing. "Not all babies do it," he said, "but it's a sign of a happy baby." We noticed something wispy right above Susan's head. "That's her hair," Brian said.

Now we just had to find out what our daughter weighed. Had the midwife been right? Should we be worried? As the amplified *whap-whap* of Susan's heartbeats—153 of them per minute—filled the room, Nancy and I held hands, waiting for Brian's verdict. He measured Susan's limbs, punched numbers into a keyboard, wrote things down. I knew she was okay—but at the same time, I *didn't* know. Finally, Brian finished measuring and turned to face us.

"Your daughter weighs six pounds," he said. "She's ahead of the average pace by far."

Our midwife ultimately admitted that she'd never seen those studies—in fact, they'd never existed. There was one thing we were sure of, though: We had a tough little fighter on our hands.

❖ ❖ ❖ ❖ ❖

I wake up at five on the morning of June 28—what would have been my mother's sixty-fourth birthday—feeling contractions. Nancy gets our stopwatch and we start timing them. We call the midwife to give her updates. The contractions are one minute long and coming every five minutes. Nancy knows just what to do. She says we should go through as much of the labor as we can at home before driving to the hospital.

The contractions get quicker and more intense throughout the day. The pain rolls in and out from somewhere deep inside me. I sit in my comfortable recliner and try to relax. "Remember to breathe during the contractions," Nancy keeps telling me. "You look like you're holding your breath until they're over." I still have the feeling that this is the day, and as afternoon turns to evening I ask Nancy if we should go to St. Charles. Nancy is calm and knowing, which helps me stay calm, too. "Let's ride it out here for a while," she says. "It's not time yet."

She's right. I am in labor, but there is no point in rushing to the hospital just yet. I should have known that little Susan Juliette would not adhere to anyone else's timetable—not the midwife's, not mine. She will arrive when she is good and ready. I had hoped that she would show up on my mother's birthday, but as the day passes I realize it's better that she have her own day. When I go to bed that night, I manage a few minutes of sleep here and there and dream about Hawaii.

Early the next morning, it's time. Nancy is already up, doing some last-minute repacking. It is a hot June day, so she brings along a onesie with short sleeves and a tiny pair of duck booties for Susan. As we've practiced, Nancy gets everything into our truck as I slide into the back seat. The windows are newly tinted so we can hide from any paparazzi who might try to snatch images of us going to or from the hospital. My contractions are fierce now; they come around every three minutes and last a good, solid minute and a half from start to finish. Nancy, who likes driving fast, eases us slowly toward St. Charles. When we get there, she finds a spot near the front, in an area reserved for patients.

EXPECTING MOTHERS PARKING ONLY, the sign says. Nothing about expecting fathers.

We check into our private room at 8:00 AM. I am six centimeters dilated, and the nurse backdates the official start time of my labor to 5:00 AM, though in truth it started the day before. The walls of the room are pale green, and when the overhead lights are shut off it doesn't look like a hospital room—it feels more like a bedroom. An attendant has strapped a band around my wrist. It says, THOMAS BEATIE, MALE. Hospital staffers have been great to us; they've taken steps to keep the paparazzi out, and whenever someone from the media calls to ask if I am there, they follow standard privacy protocol and decline to give out any information whatsoever. A security guard is also posted right outside our door to keep any unwelcome visitors away.

Overall, about a dozen nurses come in and out of the room to help us throughout the day. They are all respectful, and only once or twice does someone slip and refer to me as a female. "All mothers metabolize at different rates," one of them says. "And all fathers," Nancy quickly corrects.

My contractions are intensifying. It is easily the worst pain I have ever felt in my life—deep, seizing, radiating pain. I know I am approaching a physical experience that I cannot back out off. Nobody can do this for me, and nobody is going to say, "Let's call it a day and try again tomorrow." Nancy had warned me that I might want to scream and cry out, and I am wondering if it will come to that. "There's nothing like this, Thomas," she had told me. "You'll see what I mean. But you'll also see that it's worth all the pain."

I ate a banana earlier this morning, and I instantly regret it. It's giving me heartburn, and the last thing I need is another source of discomfort. Nancy puts a cold cloth on my forehead and kisses me gently. She feels my stomach and says, "She'll be out soon." A couple of things help lower my anxiety. I've been given a blue foam ball to squeeze, and while it doesn't alleviate the pain, it does help me relax. I also have straps hooked around my belly to monitor the baby's heart rate and the intensity of my contractions. Watching those numbers shoot up and then slowly lower on the monitor gives me a comforting sense of control over what is happening.

The baby had been in the wrong position, her back facing my back, but now she is turning, getting into her proper place. "When the baby isn't aligned right, it hurts a little more and takes longer for her to come out," a nurse tells us. Around noon, our midwife takes a long rod with a small hook at the end and uses it to break my water. I feel a little tugging and then I hear a pop, and warm fluid pours out of me. There is a new urgency to everything now; my baby no longer has any amniotic fluid to protect her. I want to bring her into the world as quickly as I can.

But, still—nothing. Nancy eats a few M&M's; I stick to ice chips. Nancy remembered to bring white chocolate, my favorite, so I unwrap a piece and let it dissolve in my mouth. I get up and walk around, sit down for a while on an inflated Swedish ball. "Gravity is your best friend," the midwife reminds me. I sense the time is almost here, but something is wrong—I just don't feel the urge to push. We shut off all the lights in the room, except for three sconces. Around 3:00 PM, the midwife suggests that I lie in a deep tub with jets that's in the room. She pads the edge of it with towels for my back and head, and Nancy helps me lower myself in. The midwife pours warm water over my belly, and the trickling sound is soothing. I focus on finding a calm place inside me from which I can summon this child.

By late afternoon, my dilation reaches the full ten centimeters. This is supposed to be the final leg of my journey, but my uterus, I am told, is fatigued from all the contractions. I feel a ton of pressure in my belly, but I still don't feel the crucial urge to push. A nurse sets up a bar at the foot of my bed and wraps a towel around it. When the time comes, I'll be able to hold on to each end of the towel and pull myself up as I push my baby out. The midwife is concerned that our baby is being stressed by her prolonged elevated heart rate. I can hear the urgency in her voice when she says, "We need to get busy and push. Come on, Thomas, do it for Susan." I know that if we're not successful in the next few minutes, she will likely turn her duties over to an attending physician. My pregnancy is about to become a medical intervention. I feel scared and desperate—I am pushing, but the baby isn't coming out. Our midwife tells us she can see the baby's dark head of hair, but then she disappears back in. Push after push, and Susan is simply rocking inside me.

A doctor is summoned. "Thomas, because your uterus is tired, we're going to use this suction device to help Susan out," the midwife tells me. "We're going to place it at the top of her head, and the doctor is going to pull when you push. We'll try this first before we resort to an emergency C-section." I start to push like I've never pushed before. All I want is to bring my daughter to safety. I can hear myself groaning from the intensity. I am sweating profusely, and Nancy is right there, trying to take my pain away. She looks like she wants to crawl right into bed with me and trade places. Nurses bustle back and forth as the doctor gently pulls on Susan.

And then, at 8:55 PM, thirteen hours after we checked in, I hear Nancy cry out.

"Her head," she says. "Her head is out."

The mind does a funny thing with pain, especially when we try to remember it. It was certainly there and it was beyond intense. But at the peak of my labor, all I remember is the joy of knowing Susan is nearly out. On the second push, I am able to see her shoulders and torso slip into the doctor's arms. She is motionless, and for that moment my heart stops beating. If I could have, I would have jumped out of bed that very second to try to get her to breathe. And just then, her leg moves and she opens her mouth and lets out a soft cry. It is the most beautiful sound I have ever heard.

A nurse puts a pair of scissors in Nancy's hand, and with one swift clamp of metal on her umbilical cord, my baby becomes a separate human being, capable of living and breathing on her own. For thirty long minutes, I am not able to hold my baby. I can barely see her behind a blur of activity. A nurse gently places her on an elevated neonatal station, where her elevated heart and respiratory rates are monitored. She receives a vitamin K shot to help blood clotting, and ointment is swabbed into her eyes to protect them from infection. I can see the doctor's face open up with surprise when our baby is weighed. "Nine pounds, five ounces," he says with a smile. At 21.75 inches long, she is over an inch longer than I was at birth—and two pounds heavier. I knew she was going to be a big baby.

At last, they bring Susan over to me. She is wrapped in a white and pastel-colored receiving blanket. The weight of her body is finally in my arms and not in my belly. I can hardly believe it. Here she is, Susan, our daughter. Nancy immediately comes to my side and lies next to us. We are no longer just two people—we are three. Susan is quiet and staring straight up at me. I feel like she is reaching for me with her eyes—and I am reaching back. This is it, the moment I've been waiting for. It is everything I had hoped it would be, and more. *This* is the meaning of life.

"I love you, Thomas," my wife tells me.

"I love you, too," I say.

It occurs to me then that I am no longer the Pregnant Man. I am a father now, and this is my family.

Chapter 19

FOR THE RECORD

Not long ago, I got an email from a Japanese television network asking if I wanted to be on a TV show in Japan. "We are planning to produce a two-hour TV special titled *Sanma Answers,* where a Japanese comedian/talk show host named Sanma Akashiya receives any kind of questions from celebrities in a wide variety of genres and answers them," the email read. "The producers would like to make a TV segment about you as the Pregnant Man and your life story with your wife and child. The producers also would like you to ask Mr. Akashiya any kinds of questions you would like."

I can't imagine what kind of question I would want to ask Sanma, other than maybe "Is there anything you'd like to ask *me?*" Since I became a public figure, I've been asked the same questions over and over and over, both face to face and in letters, blogs, and articles. There is an undeniably high level of curiosity about me, and no matter how much information becomes public, it seems that people have a hard time figuring out just who I am. I get it—there simply has never been a pregnant man or pregnant husband before. Certainly, nobody has seen the image of one. I am new and different, and as such, people have stuff they want to ask me. I don't mind answering questions at all. When people ask questions, at least I know they are taking me seriously. It's when people don't ask questions, and reach quick, unyielding conclusions, that I know I'm not going to get a fair shake.

And so, for the record, I would like to answer the ten questions I am asked most frequently. Here goes:

1. WHY DID YOU WANT TO HAVE A BABY?

This one's easy—why does anyone want to have a baby? It's more than just the American dream. It is a fundamental imperative of families everywhere to procreate and bring children into this world. Nancy and I reached a point where we felt we were ready to become parents: We were financially secure, we were in a safe and healthy environment, and we loved each other madly. We believed we could provide a strong, stable home for a child, and that we could raise our baby to be a good, loving, intelligent, and compassionate person. The fact that I switched genders and became a legal male does not have anything to do with my desire to have a child. The simple answer is: My wife and I are in love and we wanted to start a family together. Anyone out there who is in love, or who has had a child, can certainly understand this.

2. WHY DIDN'T YOU JUST USE A SURROGATE? OR ADOPT?

How many parents would use a surrogate if they could get pregnant themselves? I'm guessing none. Nancy and I discussed the idea, but doing so would have created even more complications than if I were to carry a baby myself. People who ask this question assume that by using a surrogate, we'd be avoiding the inevitable controversy my pregnancy would create. This is untrue. Namely, we'd need more than just a doctor's signature to get access to a sperm bank; we'd also need a fertility specialist to give me fertility drugs, harvest my eggs, perform an in vitro fertilization procedure, then transfer embryos to a surrogate. Being able to find a fertility specialist who would not discriminate against us was a challenge, and doctors were part of the reason our story went public in the first place. Ultimately, using a surrogate came at too steep a price for me; it meant turning over the responsibility for carrying my child to someone else, a stranger—and hoping this person would be as diligent about taking prenatal vitamins and protecting the baby as I knew I would be. Instead, I chose to be my own surrogate—to use my own body to go through this process, and not someone else's. I don't think anyone anywhere can begrudge me the right to carry my own child.

And as for adopting? People who ask me, "Why didn't you adopt?" aren't likely to ask this of the next happy, married couple. In truth, most parents who can have children of their own aren't likely to turn to adoption. People who ask this question most likely mean to say, "You shouldn't have had your own biological baby." Well, I had a very real desire to pass on my own genes and to be biologically related to my child. I realize that a lot of people wish we had adopted, or even used a surrogate, but I cannot live my life based on other people's wishes. If neither Nancy nor I could have gotten pregnant, we would have considered surrogacy or adoption, but not just to make other people happy or comfortable. That's not how we operate.

3. WHY DIDN'T YOU JUST KEEP YOUR PREGNANCY PRIVATE?

Aside from the medical discrimination we were facing, I have a two-part answer for this one. First, it would have been nearly impossible for me to conceal my pregnancy from friends and neighbors. Even without my beard, I look like a man, and everyone in my hometown of Bend knew me to be a man. Early on, I could pass off my baby bump as a beer belly, but what about when I was seven or eight months pregnant? What about all the nurses and doctors who knew that I was a man and pregnant—and what about all of their husbands and wives and friends whom they told about us? The chances were really good that someone was going to discover that I was a pregnant man, and not far-fetched that they might take the story to the media. Word about my pregnancy was already getting back to us, and Nancy and I didn't want certain people dear to us finding out about us through the *National Enquirer* or some other tabloid. We wanted to tell them ourselves, and we wanted to be able to control how our story was made public. That's why I wrote an essay for *The Advocate.* Aside from telling people about the challenges we were facing, my goal has always been to help people understand what I'm doing. The second part of my answer is: Why *should* I have kept it private? Why should I have hidden my pregnancy beneath baggy clothing? Why should I have walked around in a permanent stoop so people didn't notice my belly? Having a child should be one of the best and proudest moments of your life, and I wanted my pregnancy to be that kind of moment for

Nancy and me. I have as much right to be pregnant as anyone else. And I also have the right to be happy and proud about it.

4. DIDN'T YOU JUST GO PUBLIC TO BECOME FAMOUS AND MAKE MONEY OFF YOUR STORY? AND AREN'T YOU JUST EXPLOITING YOUR DAUGHTER FOR PROFIT?

Nancy and I have never, ever been motivated by money. Believe me, there are a lot of easier ways to make money than to become a controversial, unpopular, and even despised public figure. We moved to Oregon to start a new life and be recognized and respected as a hardworking husband-and-wife team. Nancy and I actually lost money during my pregnancy because the presence of paparazzi and media made it impossible for us to be open to the public and work at our custom-T-shirt warehouse. And, contrary to rumors, *People* magazine did not pay for the stories it ran. Nor did any TV show pay us to appear or run our story. Once little Susan was born, we did accept a modest amount of money for the sale of pregnancy and baby pictures to a photo agency, but it was less than our regular income from work, and far, far less than the amount that others have speculated we received. Basically, it is enough to start a college fund for Susan, which is exactly what we did. As far as this book goes, there's indeed a possibility that we might make some money if we sell a lot of copies, but I've already invested thousands of dollars in this project, and the advance was relatively modest. Any money we do make will, again, go into Susan's college fund. After Susan was born, Nancy and I also accepted payment to be part of a documentary about the pregnancy and birth. Yet we refused other documentary offers for double the money. We chose the company we chose because we felt it would offer us the ability to tell our story with dignity and respect. Again, the idea that we made a fortune off of Susan's birth is ridiculous. We turned down nearly $2 million in offers because we did not want to sensationalize the story. We accepted the money we did—from small, reputable companies—because it will help us raise and educate Susan. But our primary motive for doing a book and documentary is telling our story—and helping those who come after us, and giving voice to those who choose different paths in life.

5. AREN'T YOU JUST SWITCHING BACK AND FORTH BETWEEN GENDERS TO SUIT YOURSELF?

Not at all. My gender is constant—I am a male. Even when I was a female, I identified with the male gender—and once I transitioned to a male, and was granted legal status as a male and husband, there was no turning back. Had Nancy been physically able to carry a child, she would have been the one who was pregnant. But because she can't, and because I had retained my reproductive organs—as most transgender people do—I chose to become pregnant. People say that you have to be a woman in order to give birth, but I am proving that this is not so—I am a fully legal male, and I gave birth. My pregnancy challenged the socially accepted definitions of "woman," "wife," and "mother"; in other words, it's a social issue, not a biological one. I was a man before I gave birth, I was a man during my pregnancy, and I am a man now. Those are the facts. I understand that people will interpret those facts differently, but they are irrefutable. I did not switch back to being a female in order to give birth. I am a male who was capable of carrying a child, and I did just that.

6. DID YOU HAVE A BABY SHOWER?

Indeed, a couple of neighbor friends generously threw one for Nancy and me. I had never attended a baby shower before. It came as a complete surprise, as I had underestimated the compassion and understanding of the people around us. I got dressed up in expandable-waist cargo pants and a blue silk dress shirt and tie. Over forty friends and neighbors turned out for the baby shower, many with their own young children in tow. We played silly games (Guess the Baby's Weight!), passed out door prizes, and cut into a big white cake. The support from our community was overwhelming. We're all the closer because of it.

7. ARE YOU REALLY THE FIRST PREGNANT MAN? HAVEN'T OTHER TRANSGENDER MEN BEEN PREGNANT?

Believe me, we looked—and there was no one else on record. People have tried to tell me I'm not the first, mostly because it seemed unlikely that there weren't any others before me. Due to the biological, social, and legal constraints a situation like this poses, it takes a concerted effort for a person in my standing to get pregnant. It doesn't happen by accident—there are way too many obstacles. That being said, I am the first legal male and husband in the world to give birth to a child. It would have been great for us if someone else had blazed this trail. But the fact is that no one had, so there was no precedent for us, or anyone who had to deal with this, to fall back on. There has been at least one instance in which a woman who was in the process of transitioning got pregnant, but she was legally female and unmarried. And there have been women who gave birth who later transitioned to men. This brings up an interesting question about *why* I am the first, but our research, and months of our story being public, have not produced a single case of another legal male and husband giving birth.

8. ARE YOU THE BABY'S MOTHER OR FATHER? OR BOTH?

I am our baby's father, and Nancy is her mother. It's that simple. Yes, I was the one who gave birth to our child, and existing definitions equate "birth parent" with "mother"—but that is only because no one like me has ever come around before. By those same definitions, all mothers are female—and I am legally and unequivocally a male; therefore, I can't be a mother. I have assumed a traditional male role in my family, and I will likewise assume the traditional role of a father. I understand that people just want to classify me as a mother to avoid this debate, but that's not fair to me or to society. There will surely be other transgender men who get pregnant down the road, and eventually they will be accepted as fathers, not mothers. I am neither a woman nor a mother—I am both our child's father and the person who gave birth to her.

9. ARE YOU AFRAID YOUR MARRIAGE MIGHT BE NULLIFIED? AND AREN'T YOU JUST A COUPLE OF LESBIANS, ANYWAY?

It saddens me that anyone would want to undo my legal marriage to Nancy. She and I are, in every way, a married couple recognized in every state in the country. We meet the first criterion, which is that I am legally a man and she is legally a woman. We had a justice of the peace marry us, and we have a marriage certificate. We own several properties together as husband and wife, we file taxes together, and we make medical decisions based on our status as legal spouses. We are afforded more than a thousand state and federal rights that accrue to married couples. Were we to lose all that, it would be an enormous blow to us. What's more, I don't see what grounds our marriage could be dissolved on. Yes, I gave birth to a child, but I remained legally a male throughout the process. Nothing happened to change my status as a male or a husband. To be honest, Nancy and I are worried that someone may want to try to come after our marriage, and right from the start we talked to lawyers about how we could protect ourselves. Whatever happens, Nancy and I will fight as hard as we can for our rights, and we will never allow anyone to casually overturn what we worked so hard and so long to make happen. The battle to overturn our marriage would be huge and far-reaching, indeed.

It's strange to me when people ask me if Nancy and I aren't just two lesbians. By definition, a lesbian is a woman who is sexually attracted exclusively to other women. Therefore, because I am legally male and identify as male, I'm not a lesbian. Years ago, before I decided to transition, I lived my life as a woman, and I was attracted to other women. But even then I knew that inside I was a man. I dressed and looked like a man, and often women were attracted to me because they thought I was a man. Certainly, when I transitioned and became a legal male, the term "lesbian" ceased to apply to me. When you boil it all down, Nancy and I are just two human beings in love.

10. HOW—AND WHEN—WILL YOU TELL YOUR DAUGHTER, SUSAN, WHERE SHE CAME FROM?

This question comes up more than any other. Even doctors and psychologists we met seemed preoccupied with what our daughter would think of me. As Susan grows and matures, we will be open with her every step of the way. We will tell her how much her parents love her, and how hard we fought to bring her into this world. I'll explain to her that she exists because I loved her enough to carry her myself, and because her mother couldn't conceive anymore. Babies aren't born with biases or preconceived notions—they are taught them. If other children tease Susan because of what their parents teach them, we'll tell her that not everyone understands our unique family. We'll raise her with tolerance, dignity, and respect. We'll teach her that no family is exactly alike or better than any other, and that love is all that matters. The only way to combat prejudice is through education and compassion. And that is the best thing we can do for our child: raise her to be nonjudgmental, to be compassionate, to look past labels and love people for who and what they are.

Recently, I found a book called *Mr. Seahorse,* by Eric Carle. It's a delightful and colorful children's book that explains how a pregnant male seahorse travels around the ocean, meeting other male fish who carry their own babies: the stickleback, tilapia, nurseryfish, pipefish, and bullhead catfish. I've already begun reading this book to Susan. Page by page, I point to the growing male seahorse and explain to her that I, her father, did just that with her. On the final page, I show her all of the babies Mr. Seahorse gave birth to, but let her know that all I had was one special baby—and I point to her. Susan will always know the truth about where she came from.

Chapter 20

A NEW BEGINNING

They let us leave the hospital with our bundled-up new baby on July 2, three days after she was born. Both Susan and I had to fight off fevers before getting clean bills of health. Bringing our little daughter across the threshold of our home—*her* home—was a powerful moment. The predominant emotion I felt was awe: I simply couldn't stop looking at Susan and marveling at her presence. I couldn't be in the same room with her without staring at her precious little face; at night I couldn't return from the bathroom without pausing at her bassinet to watch her sleep. I just kept thinking, *Wow*. When you dream about something for so long, and fight so hard to make it happen, the reality of it can be overwhelming. Babies truly are a miracle.

I am biased, to be sure, but Susan is beautiful. She has long legs and arms, big bright eyes, a shock of dark brown hair, and puffy

313

little lips. Nancy and I discovered right away that our baby is a happy baby. We tickle her cheek and she forms a tiny smile; early on she was smiling *and* giggling when we kissed her. She rarely cries and never wails; when she wants something she'll grumble a bit, but she never has any long screaming jags. She is a strong, healthy, excitable baby, and whenever we look at her we know how lucky we are.

I have recovered amazingly well. Stepping on the scale right after giving birth, I was two pounds lighter than I'd been before I got pregnant, and had no stretch marks. My midwife told me that I healed up so well that it didn't even look like I had just given birth. Nancy jokes with me that it must be a perk of being a pregnant man. I don't know what to make of it, other than the fact that I did lose a lot of hard-earned muscle.

❖ ❖ ❖ ❖ ❖

Susan's birth made news in countries around the world. Hundreds of thousands of websites in dozens of languages announced her arrival—and so did nearly every major network, newspaper, and news magazine in the United States. Paparazzi flocked to Bend to try to get the first photo of the Pregnant Man's baby. Susan's birth was the most popular story on *People* magazine's website for three days in a row, even beating out the cover story about presidential hopeful Barack Obama.

Oblivious to her global stardom, Susan Juliette sleeps and sleeps. Her favorite place to doze off is right on Nancy's chest; in fact, she now insists on it. Nancy and I will put her in a Moses bassinet, or in her crib, or someplace else, and she'll make little fussing sounds. We know just what she wants. Once she's comfortably on Nancy's chest, she drifts right off to sleep.

Right after Susan was born, Nancy called her father, Jim, to tell him the good news. When he finally saw a photo of Susan, he completely choked up. "Not every baby's perfect, but she looks perfect," he exclaimed. Nancy calls him every day and tells him his granddaughter wants to talk to him; if Susan feels like it, she'll giggle into the phone for her old granddad. Soon, Jim will visit from Arizona and meet Susan face to face. I'm wondering who is going to cry more—Jim, Nancy, or me.

No one from my side of the family has called me since Susan was born—not my aunt, my two brothers, or my father. My father was aware of her due date, and I'm sure that he's heard about her birth in the news, but I have yet to hear from him. It makes me sad, of course; despite all the negative feelings I have about him, part of me wants him to know how well I am doing. Part of me wants him to come to my home in Bend and meet my sweet daughter; part of me wants to tell him, "Look, Dad—look what I've done. Look at how beautiful she is. Look at my lovely family." Part of me wishes that he would fall in love with Susan, just as everyone else has. But I know deep down that this will never happen. My father has no interest in meeting my daughter. He flies often from Hawaii to Las Vegas, but he will not swing by Bend on his way. He does not accept how I live my life; in fact, he is embarrassed by me. The saddest truth of all, and one that I grapple with, is that I do not want Susan to ever know my father. I don't want to expose her to his harshness and hatred. My instinct is to protect her from him, to never, ever allow him to harm her the way he harmed me. She will be safe from him—this much I can promise—and she will never know what it feels like to love him and have him not return that love.

I don't know what will happen between my father and me—it's possible that we will never speak or see each other again. I suspect, though, that we will have more run-ins at some point, that we are not yet done with our battle. But I am not just fighting to protect myself anymore. I have a daughter now, and she means everything to me. I am stronger because of her, and my mission is to keep her safe and happy. In a way, Susan is protecting *me* from my father; her being here means my father cannot hurt me the way he used to. I have my own family now; I am a father, just like him—only not like him. In fact, I'm grateful to him for showing me what sort of father I *don't* want to be. He is part of my past, and my life is about what lies ahead, not behind. I still have dreams about my father, about him trying to drag me back to Hawaii, to pin me down and hurt me. But the dreams are coming farther and farther apart, and soon, I hope, they will stop coming altogether. I hope that my father, too, will be able to find some sort of peace in his life.

Not long ago, I had a vivid and telling dream about my father. It was an impossible scenario, as most dreams are, but I dreamed that he came to visit me in Bend. He went on a snowy mountain-climbing expedition with a group of people, despite his bad knee, and I got word that he'd gone missing. In my dream, I remember being taken over by such strong emotions—panic, grief, and sorrow—so much so that I woke myself up sobbing. When I realized I'd been dreaming, my first feeling was relief. However, I wasn't relieved that it was just a nightmare, or that my father was actually still alive; I was relieved because I could cry for him. I was so worried that when it came time to grieve for my father, I wouldn't be able to shed a tear. And here was my answer, my closure. I have permission to move on without him, even though I'll always love him.

Since giving birth, I have also been thinking a lot about my mother, Susan, for whom my daughter is named. I do recognize a bit of my mother in Susan; my daughter is adventurous and happy, just as my mother was for much of her life. Little Susan is headstrong, literally; I have seen her prop her head up and support it for nearly a minute, something that's rare to see in a baby less than one week old. She is gentle and peaceful, and in this way she reminds me of my mother, too. I feel that there is a very definite connection there, between the woman who gave birth to me and the girl that I gave birth to. I cannot fully define it, but it's real and nourishing to me. Susan Juliette is not only passing on my mother's name—she will also be keeping the very best part of my mother alive in the world today. My mother would have been so proud and happy to see the beautiful child I named after her.

Two weeks after Susan came home, I looked at the calendar and realized it was the two-year anniversary of Christine's death. I had been thinking about her a lot in the days since Susan was born, and it broke my heart to think of what she was missing—the chance not only to meet our daughter, but also to have a child and a family of her own. I can only imagine how happy Christine would have been to hold little Susan in her arms, to bounce her on her lap and buy her little outfits and give her silly nicknames and try to make her laugh. Christine would have been *wonderful* with the baby. She is one of the big reasons why I got pregnant in the first place, and she will always be an inspiration to me. When Susan is old enough, I will tell her about her aunt Christine.

When Susan was almost one month old, Nancy's daughters, Amber and Jen, came to Bend to meet her. They each held her for hours and looked as if they wanted to pack her up and take her home with them. Watching them play and cuddle with Susan made Nancy and me feel warm with a sense of family. What can be better in this world than having your daughter meet her sisters for the first time, and seeing their hearts melt as they fall in love with her?

❖ ❖ ❖ ❖ ❖

What does the future hold for the three of us? I cannot say. I know only that Nancy and I will do our best to give our daughter all the love and support she could possibly want. Sometimes I think about our daughter throwing her first tea party and inviting all her little friends over; sometimes I picture her playing softball, tough as nails, like I was. But the primary vision I have of Susan Juliette is of a loving, wise, and tolerant person, raised to see the goodness in people, and to judge them on their merits. Nancy and I know more than most people about prejudice and intolerance in this world. And because of that, we are determined to raise our daughter to think for herself and not rush to judgments. We will always be proud of her, no matter what, but we want her to be someone the world can be proud of, too.

When I first transitioned from Tracy to Thomas, it took people a while to get the hang of calling me by my new name. People would slip all the time and refer to me as "she," or Tracy. Even Nancy slipped a couple of times, calling me Trace instead of Thomas. It was understandable, and I never got too upset about it. People who first knew me as a female had a little trouble fully accepting me as a male, while people who have known me only as a male never call me "she."

However, there was one notable exception: my very intelligent African Grey Parrot, Einstein. He would always call out "Trace! Trace!" when I walked into the birds' upstairs room. For years he called me Trace, delighting in calling the name whenever I came into view. But then I transitioned, and Nancy started calling me Thomas. Einstein heard her do this—and almost immediately switched to calling me by my new name. "Tommy! Tommy!" he would call out, excited to see me, as always. He never once reverted and called me Trace. I was forever Thomas to him now, just like that.

I think of Einstein sometimes when the subject of my gender comes up. There is something very lovely and touching about how quickly Einstein adapted to my new name. To him, my name and gender do not really matter. I am the same *me*, after all, and as long as I come up to see him, Einstein is happy. Labels and definitions are unimportant; love and understanding are everything. Einstein's apparent generosity and compassion are heartening to me. And even if he doesn't realize he's doing it, at least in terms of my name he is steps ahead of some people. It's nice to dream of what the world could be like without prejudice and with unending tolerance.

This is the kind of world we want Susan Juliette to live in. It is not a realistic wish, but it is something well worth fighting for.

Nancy and I know that there are people who will always hate us because of who we are, who will discriminate against us and call us names and try to put us down. We can handle people discriminating against us, but how can anyone be prejudiced against the innocent little baby we brought into the world? It is nearly inconceivable to me that someone could hold their dislike for us against her, and I like to think that that will never happen—that Susan will thrive and prosper in this world, free of stigmas, free of abuse. But part of me knows better, and in my darkest moments I am afraid to show her the truth about how mean this world can be. All Nancy and I can do is raise her to be strong and resilient, so that she can face whatever challenges await her in this life.

But for now, we will cherish every tiny, fleeting moment we spend with her. One month after she was born, Nancy and I sang "Happy Monthday" to her. I held her and got on the scale to weigh her. She clocked in at a strapping eleven pounds, two ounces. She is a big girl, that's for sure. Her body is lean and tight and long. She quickly outgrew her infant clothes, and was wearing three-month-old outfits by her third week. The other day I put her on her stomach, and I swear she crawled a couple of inches. Crawling at four weeks old! That was when I dubbed her Super Baby.

Susan Juliette loves to take baths; she *loves* water. She is also starting to focus on things; her eyes are open all the time, wide as saucers, taking everything in. Another amazing thing is how quickly I got used to holding her. I had never felt comfortable holding someone else's baby; I guess I was afraid I might somehow break it. The first time I held Susan, in the hospital, I had a little bit of that fear, too. But when we got her home, and when I could pick her up without anyone watching and just feel her against my body, I instantly felt like she was a part of me. Now I pick her up, swing her from hip to hip, instinctively support her head, walk around with her wherever I go. It just feels natural to me, and so wonderful.

Susan Juliette is a little miracle to us, an angel on this earth. Years of struggle and hardship and pain and prejudice and dashed hopes and small victories, and now here she is, making it all worthwhile. The debate about my pregnancy, and what it means to society, will go on for a long time—this I know. Even some of you who have read this book might not agree with what we did. But if the world could know one thing about us and accept it as truth, it would be this: All Nancy and I ever wanted was to have a family, just like couples in love everywhere. Our dreams were not male or female dreams, and our hopes knew no gender. We are just people—blood and bones and beating hearts, unique and special and yet no different from anyone else, all at once. Our story is about so much more than just a man giving birth. This is a story of being true to oneself, following one's dreams despite the challenges, and overcoming adversity. It's about reconciling the past, defining and embracing family, and finding one's place in this world. Moreover, this is a love story. I'm sure everyone can see a little bit of themselves in us. Our journey has been uncommon, our path unfamiliar—but then, all of our adventures are distinctly our own, original and entirely new. In the end, we are a family, no less and no more. That is all we ever wanted to be.

At night, Nancy and I lie in bed with Sweetpea—that's what we call her—lying in between us. Sometimes we don't say a word, and we just listen to her shallow, sleepy breathing. Sometimes we talk, about funny things that happened during the day, or about how amazing it is to have this little baby in our lives. I love Nancy dearly, and we never get tired of each other; we even miss each other when I am upstairs and she is in the kitchen. We love doing things together—whether it's skipping rocks on Devil's Lake, or kayaking on the crystal-clear waters of the Cascade Mountains, or giving our daughter a bath. Nancy made me feel safe and secure enough to bring a baby into this world. Quite fittingly, hers was the hand that helped create Susan—through conception—and hers was the hand that brought her into this world—by cutting the umbilical cord. Watching her with Susan makes me realize how much I love my wife—now more than ever. Nancy truly is the loving mother of my child. Together we have created something magical, and together we're creating something we missed out on when we were children. I am so thankful for everything I am, so grateful to have Nancy and Susan in my life.

The other night, we whispered a delicate wish we both have—that Susan not be an only child. Nancy and I would like to have another baby. We want our little family to grow.

Chapter 21

LETTERS TO SUSAN

My precious Susan,

The first time I ever saw you, you were just a twinkling star on an ultrasound screen. But even then I knew you were going to be beautiful. And now here you are, with your daddy and me, and you are even more beautiful than I ever dreamed—your brown hair that tumbles past your shoulders; your pretty blue eyes; your perfect lips and cute ears and tall, strong body.

I can't wait for us to play dress-up, to race Hot Wheels cars, to dig in the dirt, and to bake goodies. I've imagined brushing your hair and reading to you, teaching you how to tie your shoes, showing you off to family and friends, kissing you, hugging you, loving you. But nothing I ever imagined compares with the wonder of having you here. There's not one moment when your daddy and I aren't right by your side. We even miss you when you're sleeping. There aren't enough minutes in the day now that you're here.

Your daddy and I find ourselves staring at you all the time. We study your face, your nose, your fingers and toes. Susan, thank you for letting us be your parents. We will do our very best to raise you and take care of you. When you get your first ouchie, we will be there for you. On your first day of school, we'll be there. Your sweet sixteen, your first crush, the day you get married, if you decide to, the day you have your first child—in all those times and on every day in between, we will be there for you, always and forever.

Please know, sweet Susan, that you are very loved. You are part of a family, and you have two big sisters who will always be in your life. You are my father's grandchild, and he, too, loves you very much. I hope you get to know him like we do.

Know, also, that you are here because of our deep and endless love for you. You have filled our hearts with warmth and affection. I am a mommy again, and because of you I feel like the luckiest person alive. You are just six weeks old, but already you have given us a lifetime of joy.

Sweetpea, I love you so, so much. And I always will.

Love, Mommy

❖ ❖ ❖ ❖ ❖

Dearest Susan,

Dreams are a wonderful thing. Sometimes when you dream long and hard enough for something to happen, it becomes a reality. This is how you started out—as a childhood dream of mine. And as I grew up, still you were there, subconsciously sleeping within me. When I met your mother, she was able to see every part of me, inside and out, including my dreams of you. In this way, you became *our* dream.

There have been so many nights we've imagined what it would be like with you here. There have been so many days we've fought to try to make those imaginings real. And now here you are—our dream come true.

You smiled the very day you were born. I read somewhere that newborns don't smile so soon. But you did. I was holding you when you were one week old, and you managed to chuckle. I don't know what you were thinking; perhaps you thought my scraggly beard was silly, like your mother does.

The day we brought you home, we set you belly-down on a blanket and you rolled over by yourself. I offer you my pointer finger and you grip it like there's no tomorrow. You are strong, a fighter.

When I hold you in my arms, I can't take my eyes off you. I am transfixed with a mix of feelings: curiosity, vulnerability, profound love. Also, there is a new emotion I have never felt before, a protecting and benevolent emotion that is strong, pure, and good. I know I will always be here for you—to support you and to listen to you.

You are going to grow so quickly in front of our eyes. It's happening already, and we feel anxious as time slips past us. You will be three months, six months, two years, then twenty years.

There are so many things I want to show you in life, the little joys: picking blueberries as big as grapes, waking up to freshly fallen snow, skipping rocks on a tranquil lake. I can't wait to speak French with you, watch your first piano recital, walk you down the aisle. I will savor every moment. And, of course, your mother and I will leave your decisions up to you.

We have a special bond, you and I—you were inside me. You are my daughter, separate and unique, though I see myself in you. Ask me anything you like—I will be open and honest. My greatest hope is that I can be the best father to you.

Sometimes when you look at me, it seems like you're not a baby anymore; it's as if your mind is wise and mature and you are looking at me with all the wisdom of my past and future. Look as deep and as far as you can see. You are the center of my universe. I will give you everything you need and want. You can have all of me, for you will always be my baby. I will scoop you up and hold you to my heart forever.

I love you more than words can say.

Daddy

ACKNOWLEDGMENTS

I can't imagine where I'd be in life without my wife, Nancy. She is my best friend, my conscience, my stability, and my love. She is my everything. With Nancy I have realized all that I can be. Her endless, selfless, and tender support has enabled me to reach a new level of happiness and human potential. Over the last seventeen years, I have witnessed the depth and richness of her maternal instinct, and I would have chosen no other woman to be the mother of my child. This book and everything redemptive within it would have been only a dream without her. Thank you, Nancy. I love you dearly.

I also wouldn't be where I am today if it weren't for my gentle and kind mother, Susan. She is the reason I started writing this book. She was a teacher, and she taught me how to be not only a good parent but also a good person. She gave me the power to look within myself, and she encouraged me to choose my own path in life. Through the example of her patience and goodness and generosity, she let me see what it means to be a loving and nurturing parent. These are the very lessons and values I hope to pass down to my children. Mom, I think about you every day, and I wish you were here with us now.

I would also like to thank Christine, who changed my life by believing in me from the very beginning. She encouraged me as I embarked upon this amazing journey to parenthood, and she inspired me to celebrate life. I have never stopped loving her, and I never will.

Thanks, also, to Amber and Jen, who welcomed me into their home and their hearts and always saw me as a part of the family. They have been there with Nancy and me through all the highs and lows, and they have championed me without judgment and with unqualified love. Today, I am so proud of them, of their maturity and independence, and I know they are going to be incredible big sisters.

I also have to thank all the people in the world who came across our story and extended their hearts to us. I can't tell you how much their kindness meant to me. So many people have told me that I am an inspiration to them, but the truth is that their goodness has been a beacon of hope for us. These people have inspired me to be a better person. The unexpected support of everyone who sent us letters, baby gifts, and crucial words of encouragement has changed my view of the world. The goodness of these people has far outweighed any negative reaction to our story.

This book really came to life because of Alex Tresniowski, my compassionate and talented cowriter. Thank you, Alex, for listening to my words not only with your ears, but also with your heart. You believed in us from the start and stayed by our side through the storm. Nancy and I consider you a dear friend.

Thank you, also, to my wonderful and patient literary agent, Andrea Barzvi at ICM. She believed in our story and worked tirelessly to make this book happen. She always shared my passion for this project, and when things were the most difficult, that's when Andy fought the hardest to make this a reality. Thanks, also, to Seal Press, for its courage and enthusiasm, and for being such a positive force in this process. The folks at Seal, particularly the amazing Brooke Warner, recognized the humanity in our story from the very beginning, and we wouldn't want to have been involved with any other publisher.

I would also like to acknowledge my father. All of my drive, all of my success, is rooted in my lifelong wish to make him proud of me. If it weren't for him, I simply wouldn't have all the things that I cherish today. He gave me life, and I am half of him. And, in a strange way, I learned from his mistakes what it means to be a good father.

Finally, I want to thank, with all my heart, my beautiful daughter, Susan. Precious Susan, you are my purpose, my passion, and because of you my life has new meaning. Everything in my world has already changed because of you, and when I think of the future, you are my guiding star. You are a survivor, strong and good, and in you I see all the love that I have—for my mother, for Nancy, for life. Lovely child, you are my heart.

ABOUT THE AUTHOR

Thomas Beatie was born and raised in Hawaii—as a girl, Tracy. Thomas transitioned in the late 1990s. He is a custom screenprinter and owner of Define Normal Clothing Company. Thomas lives in Bend, Oregon, with his wife, Nancy, and their daughter, Susan, who was born to Thomas on June 29, 2008.